Also by Clare Hanson
KATHERINE MANSFIELD,
with Andrew Gurr (St. Martin's Press, 1981)

Short Stories and Short Fictions, 1880–1980

Clare Hanson

St. Martin's Press   New York

All rights reserved. For information, write:
St. Martin's Press, Inc., 175 Fifth Avenue, New York, NY 10010
Printed in Hong Kong
Published in the United Kingdom by The Macmillan Press Ltd
First published in the United States of America in 1985

ISBN 0–312–72220–6

Library of Congress Cataloging in Publication Data

Hanson, Clare.
  Short stories and short fictions, 1880–1980.

  Bibliography: p.
  Includes index.
    1. Short stories, English – History and criticism.
  2. Short stories, American – History and criticism.
  3. Short story.
  I. Title.
  PR829.H34 1985   823'.01'09   84–11652
  ISBN 0–312–72220–6

For Antonia

Contents

Acknowledgements

I should like to thank Andrew Gurr for his encouragement and for the time he has given to discussion and helpful criticism of the manuscript. I am grateful to Patrick Parrinder for his comments on the Introduction, and to John Pilling for his comments on the last chapter of the book. My thanks must also go to many friends and colleagues who have made helpful suggestions. Finally, I am grateful to Lilian Argrave for her expert typing.

The author and publishers wish to thank the following who have kindly given permission for the use of copyright material:

Jonathan Cape Ltd, on behalf of the Estate of Elizabeth Bowen, and Alfred A. Knopf Inc., for the extracts from *The Collected Stories of Elizabeth Bowen*.

Chatto & Windus Ltd and Random House Inc., for the extracts from *Collected Stories* by V. S. Pritchett.

A. D. Peters & Co. Ltd, on behalf of the Estate of Frank O'Connor, and Alfred A. Knopf Inc., for the extracts from *The Stories of Frank O'Connor*.

Introduction

Lawrence's famous dictum 'Never trust the artist. Trust the tale'[1] is apposite for a consideration of the development of the short story over the last hundred years. The period 1880–1920 was marked by changes in the short story which profoundly affected the relation of the artist-as-narrator to the tale. The authority of the teller, usually a first-person 'framing' narrator who guaranteed the authenticity of the tale, was questioned by many modernist writers. Conrad, for example, multiplied narrators in such texts as 'Youth' and *Heart of Darkness* so that the status of each narrator was undercut. Subsequently writers such as Joyce and Katherine Mansfield adopted the 'indirect free'[2] style of narration, in which a third-person narrator's voice blended with that of a dramatised character so that the narrator appeared to merge into the text and to relinquish responsibility for it.

Those short story writers who dispensed with an authoritative teller-figure were also those who had begun to review the concept of the story or tale. 'Teller' and 'tale' were inextricably linked: the teller made the tale and his assumptions of knowledge and understanding were reflected in the consistency and coherence of the finished product. But as Gertrude Stein was to write in 1934, 'Inevitably one has to know how a story ends, even if it does not.'[3] She suggested that the obligation to provide a finished story might prevent the writer's giving sufficient weight to the inconclusive and indeterminate nature of experience. To capture these qualities of experience, one might have to 'abandon' story, or, at least, reshape it.

The short story underwent decisive change in the modernist period, 'in or about December, 1910' in Virginia Woolf's evocative phrase.[4] She was referring to the opening of the first Post-Impressionist exhibition in which the paintings of Cézanne, Van Gogh and Matisse were first publicly shown together in England. Very broadly, one might argue that the movements from 'teller' to indirect free narration, and from 'tale' to 'text' in the short story were part of a wider movement from 'discourse' to 'image' in the art and literature of the period.[5] Discourse, or narrative, was abandoned in painting first in

1

favour of Impressionism, the registering of 'fleeting impressions'. This in turn gave way to the more stable art of Post-Impressionism, explained in the following terms by Matisse:

> Underlying this succession of moments which constitutes the superficial existence of beings and things, and which is continually modifying and transforming them, one can search for a truer, more essential character, which the artist will seize so that he may give to reality a more lasting interpretation.[6]

Matisse evokes an ideal not unrelated to that which Pound proposed for poetry. According to Pound, the poet should reject the discursive in favour of the 'Image' – 'that which presents an intellectual and emotional complex in an instant of time'.[7] The image was Symbolist to the extent that it acted as an 'equation' for an emotion. A concern for the expressive image also underlies Virginia Woolf's writings on the novel. She rejected conventionally coherent narrative discourse and wanted instead to 'trace the pattern, *however disconnected and incoherent in appearance*, which each sight or incident scores upon the consciousness' (my italics).[8]

It would make for over-simplification if we were to tie these analogous developments in the arts too tightly together. Yet, for the purpose of placing the short story in the picture, it is worth looking back to the one unifying figure who can be cited as a source for the preference for 'image' over 'discourse'. This is Edgar Allan Poe, who in a celebrated essay entitled 'The Poetic Principle' stated firmly that 'a long poem does not exist. I maintain that the phrase "a long poem" is simply a flat contradiction in terms.'[9] Poe separated the poetic moment, characterised by excitement and intensity, from what he felt was the anti-climax of narrative. According to him, even in *Paradise Lost*: 'After a passage of what we feel to be true poetry, there follows, inevitably, a passage of platitude which no critical pre-judgement can force us to admire.'[10] We may quarrel with Poe's use of the word 'inevitably' but we can still feel the force of his argument for the primacy of the short lyric over the longer narrative poem. In his own terms it remains true that the lyric can preserve intensity and unity of impression – coherence of tone might be a better phrase – in a way not possible in a longer poem. And the distinction he made between lyric and narrative effects fell on ripe ground. His ideas were eagerly taken up by the French Symbolists, who adduced his theories as support for their ideal of non-discursive expressiveness in literature.

Poe's ideas are more interesting when viewed in relation to the development of the short story. His poetic theory reads like an oblique commentary on the assumptions underlying his short fiction, assumptions which were more boldly stated in his 1842 review of Hawthorne's *Twice-Told Tales*. This is widely known as one of the earliest specimens of serious short story criticism, in which Poe staked out ground which the short story has not lost since. In the review Poe made three crucial points about the short story. First, he elevated it firmly above all other prose fiction forms: 'The tale proper affords the fairest field which can be afforded by the wide domains of mere prose, for the exercise of the highest genius.'[11] The short story stood in the same relation to the novel as did the lyric to the narrative poem. It was above all a concentrated form, wrought out of an intensification of thought and feeling and demanding an equivalent stylistic intensity.

Secondly, and again by analogy with the lyric, Poe held that the short story could produce 'unity of impression'. Because it could be read at one sitting it could avail itself of 'the immense benefit of *totality* . . . the author is enabled to carry out his full design without interruption.'[12] By using the term 'design' Poe hints at the way in which the tight structure of the short story is perceived in almost spatial terms by the reader. The pictorial analogy for the short story is picked up again when Poe makes his third point: because the story can be read without interruption, the writer can involve the reader in it to an unusual degree. Anticipating some perspectives of recent criticism, Poe suggests that the story is in a sense jointly created by reader and writer, as 'a picture is at length painted which leaves in the mind of him who contemplates it *with a kindred art*, a sense of the fullest satisfaction' (my italics).[13]

Poe anticipates much Symbolist aesthetic theory, and in consequence we would expect his short stories themselves to display Symbolist preoccupations. 'The Fall of the House of Usher' is probably the best-known example of a Symbolist story. In some respects more like a prose poem than a story, its static, enclosed quality is uncannily prefigured in an opening description of a motionless pool which, like Poe's art itself, reflects yet simultaneously distorts:

> I reined my horse to the precipitous brink of a black and lurid tarn that lay in unruffled lustre by the dwelling, and gazed down – but with a shudder even more thrilling than before – upon the remodelled and inverted image of the gray sedge, and the ghastly tree stems, and the vacant and eye-like windows.[14]

This image or 'picture' is at the centre of the story because the disintegrating House of Usher is simply the material embodiment or correlative for a disintegrating mind. Its precarious stability mirrors Roderick Usher's frail hold on his sanity. As the narrator remarks, looking at the façade of the house:

> In this [the appearance of the house] there was much that reminded me of the specious totality of old wood-work which has rotted for long years in some neglected vault, with no disturbance from the breath of the external air.[15]

The seemingly casual reference to a lack of 'external air' and to a 'vault' point forward to our discovery of the incestuous relationship between Usher and his sister and to her premature burial in a 'temporary vault' towards the close of the story. 'The Fall of the House of Usher' is textured in this way throughout: each descriptive and narrative detail also has a symbolic dimension. The symbolic suggestions accumulate in such a way that the literal narrative values of the story tend ultimately to fade, leaving us with a kind of negative impression of a story, which approximates to Poe's *abstract* subject – a 'terror of the soul'.

Stories such as 'The Fall of the House of Usher', 'Ligeia', 'The Oval Portrait' and 'Eleonora' are essentially static works in which images and stylised dramatic scenes act as 'objective correlatives' for states of mind or feeling. Yet these stories represent only one side of Poe's talent. He was not only a Symbolist and master of mood and atmosphere: he was also a master of the tale with an intricate plot. From Poe's tales we can trace the growth of the modern detective or mystery story. 'The Murders in the Rue Morgue' is an excellent example of this type of tale. It is replete with violent, indeed with Gothically horrid action. None the less the tale is reduced to manageable proportions by an amateur detective within the story and by a framing narrator 'outside' it. Much is made of the parallel between the detective solving the mystery and the artist/narrator imposing order on the chaos of impressions. Yet the parallel is not exact: the order created by the detective is illusory, while that of the artist exists on a different plane and remains valid. Poe has often been called the master of ratiocinative processes, of narrative which progresses through deduction and induction. Yet when we look closely at his stories we do not find true logical consistency but only a carefully contrived 'air of consequence and causality', in Poe's own words. The appearance of logic was important to Poe only in so far as it enabled him to create pleasure for the reader through a perception of design. The concept of 'design' will emerge repeatedly in connection with the role of plot in the short story. Poe discussed this issue in terms which defy any easy notions about the 'pleasures of plot'. In his view, 'To look upwards from any existence, material or immaterial, to its *design*, is, perhaps, the most direct, and the most unerring method of attaining a just notion of the nature of the existence itself.'[16] The term 'design' has of course both metaphysical and artistic implications, and in practice it is impossible to separate Poe's belief in absolute form from his transcendentalist beliefs. By extension, it is tempting to link, for example, Kipling and T. F. Powys's love of symmetry in the short story with a similar belief in a universal purpose or design.

Poe's Symbolist stories seem to work towards a validation of experience through the self, while his 'plotted' tales look outwards to a design or form beyond the individual. This dichotomy in his work foreshadows a division and conflict which we will find running through the history of the short story in the period 1880–1980. Throughout this period, despite the development of Symbolist and Modernist short story forms, the 'traditional' tale continued to appear. Indeed, the major point which I wish to make about this period is that it is possible to distinguish in it two quite separate lines of development in the short story. An analogy might be made with an early bifurcation in the development of the novel. Ian Watt, in *The Rise of the Novel*, distinguished between two early narrative types. First is the novel informed by concern with the 'intricate mechanism . . . of human society' which we associate with Fielding and second is the novel of 'individual consciousness' associated with Richardson. In the short story the primary distinction which can be made is between those works in which the major emphasis is on plot and those in which plot is subordinate to psychology and mood. This distinction is a simple but fundamental one which immediately clarifies our picture of the development of the short story in English, offering at least a starting point from which we can begin to analyse, rather than merely describe, the evolution of the form.

The binary development of the short story will be explored in detail in the following chapters, but the potentialities of an analysis based on this division may become apparent from a brief sketch, at this point, of the attributes of the two 'forms'. The first type of story, with a primary emphasis on plot, is that most closely linked to the traditional oral tale. In written form it dates from the work of Boccaccio and Chaucer, whose stories were however highly sophisticated and removed from folk art to the extent that they were 'literary'. The flowering of the tale in the late nineteenth century was in the spirit of a fairly conscious revival of traditional written forms. In the tale, significance tends to inhere more in a particular configuration of events than in an individual human nature or response. The subject *is* the situation – extraordinary, bizarre, extreme in some way – which is usually referred back to the response of an ordinary, 'typical' human being. The stories are essentially communal in intention and effect,[17] depending on a fundamental agreement between reader and writer (or teller and listener) as to what constitute 'the great and the little things of life': such a consensus must exist if events are to act as a communicative code. The characters in such stories tend to be viewed externally and are not highly differentiated – often they have only a generic name such as the child, the prince and so on. An exotic background is frequently deployed and may be combined with elements of the marvellous and fantastic. This points to a recurrent difference between stories with a strong plot and 'plotless' short fiction. The emphasis in the former is on an extension of the reader's sense of human potentialities. Such stories tend to deal with what is felt to be the strange and the new in human personality, something which is partly revealed in response to, and partly imaged through, the 'unheard of event'[18] which is at the heart of the story. The forms of such stories (for example the joke, mystery and fantasy) tend to be relatively stylised. This stylisation has two aspects. First, it means that the story depends for much of its effect on the reader's familiarity with the code employed, and on his ability to recognise departures from it. The stories are not exactly formulaic in the medieval sense, but work within certain assumptions of shared formal knowledge. Secondly, stylisation suggests a strong feeling for 'design' in the sense in which we have encountered the term in connection with Poe. Yet an attraction towards narrative symmetry is frequently seen in conflict with a pull towards disorder and formlessness, and it is in exploring exactly this undertow that many writers have extended the boundaries of the short story in formal terms. In a related fashion, but in terms of content, it is remarkable how many 'traditional' stories have been concerned with the idea of limit, and with its corollary, a sense of the un-limited, the unknown, towards which language may only gesture.

By contrast the plotless fiction is concerned with the realm of human probabilities. It does not deal with the avowedly strange or marvellous but tends to reveal that quality of the marvellous which is hidden within the mundane, obscured by habit or by dullness of perception. Joyce expressed something of this in his well-known definition of the epiphany:

> This triviality made him think of collecting many such moments together in a book of epiphanies. By an epiphany he meant a sudden spiritual manifestation, whether in the vulgarity of speech or of gesture or in a memorable phase of the mind itself.[19]

Each of the stories of Joyce's *Dubliners* (1914) is structured around an epiphany (literally, a showing-forth), and in many 'plotless' fictions a moment of heightened awareness acts as a focus, a structural equivalent for conventional resolution of plot. Katherine Mansfield has described this development:

> If we are not to look for facts and events . . . we must be sure of finding these central points of significance transferred to the endeavours and emotions of the characters portrayed.[20]

'Plot' and 'design' become interiorised and also dislocated in the 'plotless' fiction, for we are entering a world which properly speaking has no plot, where there are no absolutes. As Nadine Gordimer has written, in this type of fiction, 'A discrete moment of truth is aimed at – not *the* moment of truth.'[21] The plotless fiction operates more closely under the constraints of realism than the story with a plot, but it is usually a realism which is subjectively conceived. The plotless fiction originally owed a good deal to the strategies of Symbolist poetry. In order to convey those 'impressions of the individual mind' to which, according to Pater, 'for each one of us experience dwindles down', short fiction writers of the 1890s had to move away from conventional narrative prose towards the more suggestive language of image and symbol. Their stories and sketches were structured around mood rather than event, and details of setting or scene were consciously devised to act as 'objective correlatives' for abstract states of mind or feeling.

In view of this primary distinction, I would argue that the term 'short story' is insufficiently flexible to cover all the fiction written in the short form over the last hundred years. Thus the term 'short story' might best be applied to short *narrative* writing, while the term 'short prose fiction' might be introduced to denote the range of short fiction not primarily biased towards narrative. 'Range' is indeed a vital concept, for there is enormous variety and vitality in the writing of the period under consideration. The fundamental distinction between short story and short prose fiction merely offers a way into this variety, providing a theoretical framework which can shed light on diverse material without unduly distorting it.

The year 1880 has been chosen as a convenient opening date for this study because it marks a point when the short story began to flower in England. In Chapter 1 the diverse nature of this flowering is examined. The origin of short prose fiction is located in the prose poem and psychological sketch, forms favoured by writers of *The Yellow Book* and *The Savoy* magazines. It is suggested that the Symbolists' concern for the minutiae of prose expression, and their attention to rhythm, cadence and 'sound-sense', fostered a new rigour in prose writing, especially in the short form. The development of the exotic or adventure tale is also discussed in this chapter, with special reference to the work of Stevenson and Kipling; a renewal of interest in the Gothic story is also considered. Chapter 2 deals with the period between 1900 and 1930 when the short story as such can be virtually defined through the achievements of Kipling, Saki and Maugham. Chapter 3 is concerned with the development of modernist short fiction in the same period. The short form in general terms was especially prominent in this period, and it is suggested that there was a particularly important connnection between modernist short fiction and the structure of the modernist novel. The work of Joyce, Virginia Woolf and Katherine Mansfield is considered here; also that of Gertrude Stein and Hemingway. Stein's short pieces are particularly radical and are included for that reason. They opened up new possibilities for short prose fiction and link with the work of postmodernist 'experimental' writers. Chapter 4 deals with the short story in the period between 1930 and 1960, and looks specifically at the association between the short story form and regional or rural subject matter. The 'Irish' stories of Frank O'Connor, and the rural stories of T. F. Powys are examples. In Chapter 5 the 'free story' is considered: this was an impressionistic form which succeeded the modernist fiction, but has not previously been distinguished from it. As its name suggests, it is an ambivalent form which does not fall easily into the category of either 'story' or 'fiction'. The free form differs from the modernist story most strikingly in its response to contemporary social pressures. The work of Elizabeth Bowen (who coined the term),

William Sansom and V. S. Pritchett is representative. In Chapter 6, post-1960, postmodernist short fiction is considered. In these brooding, minimalist pieces there is an emphasis on textuality and atmosphere which takes us back to the qualities of the Symbolist prose poem. Beckett is the major figure to concentrate on short prose fiction in this period. He also provides a link with the early modernists, for his prose pieces *More Pricks than Kicks* were published in 1934 very much under the shadow of Joyce.

The short story is a form which mediates between the lyric poem and the novel: within this 'space' it exhibits a protean variety. There is a great gap, to take an obvious example, between a short piece by Beckett and a short story by Kipling. Yet a fairly coherent pattern of development emerges if we follow the progress of the short story as a *soi-disant* literary form, separable from the short prose piece as a 'novelist's by-product'.[22] Over the last hundred years the short story has steadily gained in stature, not only in terms of the number of writers who have turned to the form, but also in terms of the seriousness with which the form is regarded. Thus Borges can now reverse the conventional relationship between story and novel, not out of bravado, like Poe, but with decision:

> The feeling that great novels like *Don Quixote* and *Huckleberry Finn* are virtually shapeless served to reinforce my taste for the short story form, whose indispensable elements are economy and a clearly stated beginning, middle and end. As a writer, however, I thought for years that the short story was beyond my powers.[23]

It is for this reason that I have chosen to concentrate on those authors whose work has been primarily in the short form. The omission of such figures as Hardy and Lawrence may seem wilful, but the more precise focus is I think justified by the clearer picture which emerges of the special characteristics of the short form. The decision to concentrate on the English short story was made for similar reasons, though reference is made to American fiction, in particular, at times of marked cross-cultural influence.

1 The 1880s and 1890s: Impressionists and Imperialists

The short story did not come to flower in England until the 1880s, later than in America, France and Russia. Many commentators have stressed the causal link between the rise of the short story and the development of a popular periodical press. Somerset Maugham, for example, has written that:

> Many hard things have been said of the annual and the lady's book, and harder things still of the magazine which succeeded them in public favour; but it can scarcely be denied that the rich abundance of short stories during the nineteenth century was directly occasioned by the opportunity which the periodicals afforded.[1]

The rise of the magazine was less sure and swift in England than in America and Europe. In *Fiction and the Reading Public* Q. D. Leavis has documented closely the development of a mass reading public in England in the second half of the nineteenth century. This changed, in her view, the relationship of author to publisher and adversely affected the scope and nature of periodicals. She laments the loss of the 'polite code' which dictated the tone and preoccupations of the eighteenth-century *Rambler* and *Spectator*. Like other critics, she also sees the demise of the triple-decker circulating library novel as crucial in the formation of a proto-modern novel form. This change would also seem to relate to experiment and development in short fiction towards the close of the century, although no definite link can be established.

In her study of women's magazines Cynthia White focuses more precisely on the boom in the periodical market of the 1880s, a development which she views rather more positively than Q. D. Leavis. She writes that:

> The publishing industry as a whole was entering a phase of rapid

expansion consequent upon social, economic and technological change. The main social development responsible for the publishing boom was the spread of state education which created a vast new potential market for cheap literature.

As a result, and she quotes from *The Young Woman* of 1892:

> There is no more startling phenomenon in the life of today than the enormous increase of journals and newspapers. We have now reached the point where the full effect of national education is being felt. Everyone can read. Books have become cheaper and cheaper. The entire intellectual life of the nation has received an enormous quickening. Hence journals play a part in national life wholly undreamed of in the days when the realm of letters was governed by *The Edinburgh Review and Quarterly*.[2]

The 1880s saw a proliferation of magazines chiefly at the cheaper end of the market. Malcolm Elwin joins Q. D. Leavis in seeing this as militating against the higher development of literature – he writes of the 'last organised stand of the literary periodical against the invasion of its province by the popular magazines' in the 1860s and hints at decline in the 1880s.[3] In the long run, however, it could be argued that the expansion of the 1880s had a beneficial effect on the 'literary' periodical, for it forced it to become more specialised, and to take greater risks in terms of content. Editors began to cultivate specific reading publics and in this we can see the beginnings of the association between literary innovation and specialised coterie magazines which has persisted to this day.

In the last two decades of the nineteenth century the first coterie magazines fell into two distinct groups. On the one hand *The National Observer* and *The New Review*, edited by W. E. Henley, were associated with nationalism and imperialism; on the other hand *The Yellow Book* and *The Savoy*, edited by Henry Harland and Arthur Symons respectively, were associated with Symbolism and decadence, using the second term in the sense suggested by Symons: 'the term is in its place only when applied to style; to that ingenious deformation of the language, in Mallarmé for instance, which can be compared with what we are accustomed to call the Greek and Latin of the Decadence.'[4] A look at the doubling relationship between imperialism and decadence takes us some way further into the history of the development of the short form.

Frank O'Connor suggests in his study of the genre, *The Lonely Voice*, that the short story flourishes best in an incompletely developed culture, for example in a regional settlement still lacking total social cohesion. It is demonstrably true that the short story has flourished in the last hundred years in Ireland, and in the Deep South (one thinks of O'Connor's namesake Flannery O'Connor); also in colonial societies (with writers such as Janet Frame and Frank Sargeson in New Zealand, George Lamming and V. S. Naipaul in the West Indies). The short story seems to be the mode preferred by those writers who are not writing from within a fixed and stable cultural framework. It has also been favoured by writers who find themselves to be personally opposed to the society in which they live and for whom the idea of society and shared values is problematic.

It is in this light that we should regard the stories of *The National Observer* writers Stevenson and Kipling, as well as those writers clustered around John Lane's *Yellow Book*. From this point of view imperialism can be linked with decadence, for both phenomena can be viewed as symptoms of loss of simple social faith.

Disaffection is indeed a key term in reviewing the climate of those closing years of the century in which the short story flowered. In the 1880s and 1890s Darwin had already made his impact; Nietzsche was in the process of being translated. In Marxist terms one might argue that at this juncture bourgeois ideology was becoming increasingly vulnerable and that it was for this reason that the quintessentially bourgeois art form, the novel, came under pressure. Whether or not one accepts the premises of Marxist analysis it is clear that the novel form did go through a crisis in this period. In England this was made manifest in unprecedented debate over moral and formal issues: in James's 'The Art of Fiction' (1884), Stevenson's reply 'A Humble Remonstrance' (1884), Meredith's 'Essay on Comedy' (1887); later in exchanges between Wells and James, and Wells and Bennett. It will be argued both here and in subsequent chapters that the rise of the short story is related to the nature of this crisis in the novel.

FIRST IMPRESSIONS

As religious belief and faith in the stable forms of art and society were shaken, value for the artist became increasingly only that which he himself could create. A retreat into subjectivity is already clearly signalled by Pater in his 1873 *Renaissance*:

The whole scope of observation is dwarfed into the narrow chamber of the individual mind. . . . To such a tremulous wisp constantly re-forming itself on the stream, to a single sharp impression, with a sense in it, a relic more or less fleeting, of such moments gone by, what is real in our life fines itself down.[5]

The years which followed publication of Pater's programmatic work saw a movement towards subjective impressionism in literature and the visual arts and a hedonistic emphasis on the value of the passing moment. Impressionism, moreover, provided new forms in literature: in particular, the prose poem and the psychological sketch.

The prose poem originated with Baudelaire, but was appropriated and 'translated' by Wilde and other writers associated with *The Yellow Book*. Hubert Crackanthorpe's *Vignettes* (1896) and Richard Le Gallienne's *Prose Fancies* (1894, with a second series in 1896) are well known and representative collections. A brief quotation from Le Gallienne's second series of *Prose Fancies* conveys much of the self-consciously atmospheric flavour of such pieces:

It was a March afternoon, bitter and gloomy; lamps were already popping alight in a desolate way, and the east wind whistled mournfully through the ribs of the passers-by. A very unflowerlike man was dejectedly calling out 'daffadowndillies' close by. The sound of the pretty old word, thus quaintly spoken, brightened the air better than the electric lights which suddenly shot rows of wintry moonlight along the streets.[6]

The writing is not in itself distinguished, but what is of importance is the writer's aim. He is clearly striving after a kind of concentration of effect in prose analogous to that found in poetry: consequently he is not afraid to cram a sentence with metaphor and fill it with alliteration and assonance.

The vogue for the prose poem, and enthusiasm for the extracted 'purple patch' in longer writings (a celebrated example would be Pater's description of the *Mona Lisa* in his essay on Leonardo da Vinci in *The Renaissance*), was symptomatic. To 'express everything to the last extremity', to 'fix the last fine shade' of mood and feeling was the aim of a whole school of writers in the 1880s and 1890s: the titles of their collections of prose poems and sketches are indicative of this – *Keynotes*, *Discords*, *Monochromes*, *In the Key of Blue*. An important point emerges: that these writers were interested in prose in preference to poetry. Prose was privileged as the more inclusive, promiscuous medium which was by definition better suited to the *discrimination* of feeling, to the creation of nuance by reflection, comparison and shading in language. The prose poem retained this privileged status until the emergence of free verse. In France in particular a link can be established, perhaps paradoxically, between horizons opened by experiments in prose and the development of *vers libre.*

Such an interest in prose prepared the way for Pound, Hemingway and Katherine Mansfield's concern for the prose medium. These three writers shared the belief that good prose was harder to write than good poetry (prose was a medium which imposed far fewer automatic, external controls on writing). The prose poem, together with the psychological sketch, created the formal base from which modernist short fiction was to develop.

A prose poem is usually structured around a trivial visit or encounter, and is narrated in the first person, the author's commentary being of far greater importance than any one incident. If we return for a moment to Le Gallienne's 'A Poet in the City', quoted above, we find that the prose poem is 'about' the poet's visit to the city to draw a somewhat undignified small pension. Le Gallienne uses the incident as a starting-point for a reverie on 'modern life'. The technique comes near to a clumsy form of stream-of-consciousness:

> Once more in the street, I lingered a while to take a last look at the Falls. What a masterful alien life it all seemed to me! No single personality could hope to stand alone amid all that stress of ponderous, bullying forces. . . . The more people buffeted against me the more I felt the crushing sense of almost cosmic forces. Everybody was so plainly an atom in a public company, a drop of water in a tyrannous stream of human energy.[7]

The piece is given some sort of overall structure by a parallel/contrast which is drawn between the 'daffadowndillies' for sale in the midst of the busy city and a book which the author-figure also finds hidden away unexpectedly in the metropolis: 'I held it up. How tiny it seemed, how frail amid all this stone and iron! A mere flower – a flower from the seventeenth century – long-lived for a flower! Yes, an *immortelle.*'[8]

This seemingly unstructured prose with a strong underlying aesthetic design offered one starting point for the modernist story writers, but a more important model was provided by the psychological sketch. The psychological sketch was a type of story particularly associated with the writers of *The Yellow Book*. Its form was 'plotless' and to this extent the stories closely resemble those of Chekhov. However, the psychological sketch was a native growth, albeit one coming out of Impressionism, and we cannot locate the influence of Chekhov with any certainty – he was not after all widely translated until nearly a quarter of a century later. The psychological sketches are like prose poems, with the introduction of a more directed and mediated sensibility. They tend to deal with an apparently trivial incident which has significance for what it reveals of a character's inner mood or state of mind. Often the subject of the story is a major change of feeling, but this will be conveyed obliquely, through symbol and repeated imagery, and will not be directly stated. The psychological sketch was the particular province of women writers of the period who were eager to explore what seemed to them uncharted areas of women's subjective experience. A writer like Evelyn Sharp is fairly typical of this generation. She wrote highly personal and emotive sketches about women for *The Yellow Book*, but her writing changed when she became involved with the suffragette movement. Her new-found political commitment was reflected in the directly polemical nature of the sketches and plays she produced in the early years of the twentieth century.

One of the best-known women writers associated with *The Yellow Book* was 'George Egerton' (the pseudonym of Mary Chavelita Bright, née Dunne). A story which she contributed to the first number of *The Yellow Book* is paradigmatic, revealing the ideals and also exposing some of the limitations of writers of her type and era. The story turns on a writer's disillusionment. On returning to the city from a country jaunt he finds growing within himself a 'precious little pearl of a thought . . . this offspring of my fancy, this rare little creation, perhaps embryo of genius' – only to have his reverie shattered and his 'thought' lost for ever because of the sudden, distracting appearance of 'a woman, a little woman . . . hurrying along in a most remarkable way. It annoyed me, for I could not help wondering why she was in such a desperate hurry.'[9] The piece ends on a declamatory note: 'Blame her, woman of the great feet and dominating gait, and waving umbrella handle! – blame her! I can only regret it – regret it!'[10] At first sight this sketch seems to anticipate in a curious way Virginia Woolf's little sketch about 'Mrs Brown', the incarnation of that unwieldy material 'life' which is the subject of fiction. It is possible to view the presentation of the narrator as parodic in Egerton's sketch and to see the disruption caused by the Mrs Brown figure as a necessary corrective for an effete young man whose inner speech can be read as a deliberate satire on the 'fine writing' of the period:

> At Chelsea I boarded a river steamer bound for London Bridge. The river was wrapped in a delicate grey haze with a golden sub-tone, like a beautiful bright thought struggling for utterance through a mist of obscure words. It glowed through the turbid water under the arches, so that I feared to see a face or a hand wave through its dull amber – for I always think of drowned creatures wasting wearily in its murky depths.[11]

Yet there are the unremittingly unpleasant terms in which the Mrs Brown figure is described:

> She had square shoulders and a high bust, and a white gauze tie, like a snowy feather in the breast of a pouter pigeon.
> We stop – I look again – aye, there she is! Her black eyes stare boldly through her kohl-tinted lids, her face has a violet tint. She grips her gloves in one hand, her white-handled umbrella in the other, handle up, like a knobkerrie.
> She has great feet, too, in pointed shoes, and the heels are under her insteps; and as we outdistance her I fancy I can hear their decisive tap-tap above the thousand sounds of the street.[12]

Towards the close of the story she is presented quite straightforwardly as the image of ugly reality (in time) intruding upon the fragile (and timeless) dreams of the artist: 'What is she hurrying for? We can't escape her – always we stop and let her overtake us with her clumsy gait, and tight skirt shortened to show her great splay feet – ugh!'[13] Not an elegant conclusion. The piece is indeed characteristic of its period in that it strikes an attitude which is by definition exaggerated and capable of being read as satire but which is in essence endorsed by the implied author. The precious yet artificial pearl of art is consciously opposed to the ugliness of contingent reality. And the descriptions of the narrator's artistic ideals have much to tell us about the dynamics of the psychological sketch. The narrator insists on an art emphatically of the inner, rather than the outer, life: the artistic process is at one point described in these terms: 'delicate inner threads were being spun into a fanciful web that had nothing to do with my outer self'.[14] The importance of mood is stressed: the artist is an Impressionist caught 'recording fleeting impressions with delicate sure brushwork for future use'. Moreover, while he muses, as this English river scene flashes by, lines of association form angles in my brain; and the point of each is a dot of light that expands into a background for forgotten canal scenes, with green–grey water.[15]

This is virtually an analogy for the means by which the sketch is constructed, through metaphoric association of ideas on the grounds of similarity. The stress on the small scale of the 'lost masterpiece' is also significant – it is 'an unique little gem', 'a little masterpiece', a 'lovely illusive little being'.

The psychological sketch fanned out from the John Lane–*Yellow Book* nexus in collections of stories such as *Keynotes* and *Discords* by George Egerton (1893, 1894), or *Monochromes* (1895) by Ella D'Arcy. The pioneering use of the technique of interior monologue in these stories, associated with women writers in particular, marks an important stage in the formal development of the English short story. Again, what is important is not the quality of the writing but the aim of the author. A writer such as 'Frances E. Huntley' (Ethel Colburn Mayne) tries in her sketches to come close to her characters through language. A clear effort is made to fuse author and character through the adoption of a freer, fresher idiom for inner speech. Such an effort should be seen against the background of the 'heavily latinate, abstract prose style' of the Victorian era, which H. E. Bates has suggested was antipathetic to the development of the short story in England. Here is an example of Frances Huntley writing in *The Yellow Book* in 1895 about the feelings of a young girl who has just been jilted:

> Everything was going on just the same – and he was married. But then she had always known it must end so – every one had known it. There were two sorts of knowing, though, she thought, drearily.
>
> It all seemed quite natural; even having no letter to expect when the post came seemed so natural. . . . Did everything happen so? It was odd. Browning's poignant question came into her head: 'Does truth sound bitter as one at first believes?' She used to imagine he had been wrong for once ('that omniscient Browning of yours'), but now that she knew . . .
>
> How *was* it? She could laugh quite naturally, read and be interested in her book.[16]

Despite the author's lack of skill, the effect is technically very different from that created by novelists such as Hardy and Meredith who were exploring similar areas of women's subjective experience in this period. The more direct and colloquial style offers a starting point for the development of 'indirect free' narration in the modernist period.

An attempt to bring the freshness of colloquial speech into the short story was made by a further group of writers, the 'new realists' of the 1890s. Professed admirers of Maupassant, these writers were important in making Maupassant's work more widely known and ultimately more influential in England. Their own productions, however, were uneven. The cultivated realism of such figures as Henry Harland (the editor of *The Yellow Book*) and Hubert Crackanthorpe tended to degenerate into a narrow cynicism which defeated their original large purposes. This is true of a story like Crackanthorpe's 'The Haseltons', published in *The Yellow Book*. An uneasily mannered style mars this study of marital infidelity:

> He was *vaguely* uncomfortable; yet his heart was full of a sincere repentance, because of the lowering of the strain of his anxiety; because of the smarting sense of humiliation, when he recollected Swann's words; because he had caused her to suffer in a *queer*, *inarticulate* way, which he did not altogether understand, of which he was *vaguely* afraid. [my italics][17]

Very different is the narrative voice of Arthur Morrison's *Tales of Mean Streets* (1894):

> It was with a shamed face that Neddy confessed; for among those in peril of hunger it is disgraceful to be hungry. Sam unpocketed a greasy paper, enveloping a pallid sausage-roll. ' 'Ave 'alf o' this,' he said. It was a heavy and clammy thing, but Ned took it, furtively swallowed a large piece, and returned the rest with sheepish thanks. He did not turn again towards the others, but went through to the room where the ring was pitched.[18]

Morrison was one of the first to see that a newspaper idiom could be used effectively in dealing with 'sordid' subject matter. He put the technique of the reporter to good use, employing factual, non-emotional language in order to throw into greater relief the misery and pain he depicted. The technique was one which George Orwell was later to use very successfully in essays and sketches (for example in *The Road to Wigan Pier*): it was also employed by Kipling and Hemingway in dealing with similar subject matter.

LIMITS AND RENEWALS

The various types of story considered in the first part of this chapter have their interest chiefly as proto-modern forms which must be acknowledged in any account of the genesis of the modern short story. They cannot be said to make heavy demands on us in terms of their intrinsic literary merit. Ironically, it is those writers who were the overt experimentalists and who appeared most dedicated to the genre who now seem to us minor figures. The finest story writers of the period, Stevenson and Kipling, were interested in 'traditional' story forms rather than in experimentation as such. Both writers were particularly attracted to the mystery tale, probably because it offered a means by which they could structure and organise their common preoccupation with disorder, transgression and the breaking of limits. Many stories of Stevenson and Kipling move through a series of precisely engineered steps into the unknown and into new areas of consciousness. In this they are very much of their time, 'modern' in their traditionalism. Their stories can be distinguished very precisely from those of Poe because in his stories a pull towards disorder and chaos is suppressed. In the works of Stevenson and Kipling a tension is manifestly felt between a design imposed using the tight formal constraints of the short story and the underlying disorder and chaos of the subject matter.

Most of Arthur Morrison's *Tales of Mean Streets* first appeared in the 1880s in W. E. Henley's *Scots Observer*, subsequently *The National Observer*. Morrison thus offers a tangible link between the experimentalists and the traditionalists, joining with Crackanthorpe and Harland of *The Yellow Book* on one hand and with Kipling and Stevenson of *The National Observer* on the other.

Henley was a key figure for the growth of the short story as a prestigious literary form, as H. G. Wells testifies:

> The Nineties was a good and stimulating period for a short story writer. . . . *The National Observer* was at the climax of its career of heroic insistence upon lyrical brevity and a vivid finish. . . . Then came the generous opportunities of *The Yellow Book*, and *The National Observer* died only to give birth to *The New Review* [also edited by Henley]. No short story of the slightest distinction went for long unrecognised.[19]

Himself a minor poet, Henley encouraged a group of writers known variously as 'Mr Henley's truculent Fifth Form' (Henry Harland) and as 'Henley's Regatta'. Stevenson's friendship with Henley, though strained at times, led Stevenson to immortalise him as Long John Silver, a kinder fate than that which awaits most literary editors.

The short stories of Stevenson depend quite heavily on the reader's knowledge of romance tradition, while there is, paradoxically, no direct link between his writing and this tradition. Stevenson was not, that is, writing from within a flourishing folk tradition but was consciously adopting an archaic model for his work. His appropriation of the medieval romance form might be linked with Wilde's interest in the fairy tale. For both writers the sense of artifice, of deliberate re-vivification of the forms of an ancient genre, gives a typical *fin-de-siècle* flavour to their work. Stevenson's harking back to the medieval world can also be related to the Gothic Revival of the 1850s and 1860s. Such a passage as this, from 'The Sire de Maletroit's Door', might easily be set beside one of Rossetti's early paintings:

> The place terminated behind the altar in a round end, embossed and honeycombed with a superfluity of ornament in relief, and pierced by many little windows shaped like stars, trefoils or wheels. These windows were imperfectly glazed, so that the night air circulated freely in the chapel. The tapers, of which there must have been half a hundred burning on the altar, were unmercifully blown about; and the light went through many different phases of brilliancy and semi-eclipse. On the steps in front of the altar knelt a young girl richly attired as a bride.[20]

Stevenson wrote in 1884 that:

> No art does 'compete with life'. Man's one method, whether he reasons or creates, is to half-shut his eyes against the dazzle and confusion of reality. The arts, like arithmetic and geometry, turn away their eyes from the gross, coloured and mobile nature at our feet, and regard instead a certain figmentary abstraction.[21]

He urged this in direct reply to Henry James's celebrated assertion, in his article 'The Art of Fiction', published in *Longman's Magazine* in September 1884, that 'The only reason for the existence of a novel is that it *does* compete with life.' Stevenson's reply, which initiated a friendship between the two writers, was entitled 'A Humble Remonstrance' (*Longman's Magazine*, December 1884).

It is not surprising that Stevenson should contrast art – 'neat, finite, self-contained, rational, flowing, and emasculate' – and life – 'monstrous, infinite, illogical, abrupt and poignant' – in this way. Stevenson was not like the characteristic novelist who, according to James, was normally intent on multiplying 'his relations, his points of contact, with society'.[22] His was the romancer's and story writer's selective, exclusive view of fiction, a view he defended with adroit sophistication in letters and articles. He wrote in a further letter to James, for example:

> Where we differ, both as to the design of stories and the delineation of character, I begin to lament. Of course, I am not so dull as to ask you to desert your work; but . . . might you not cast your characters in a mould a little more abstract and academic . . . and pitch the incidents, I do not say in any stronger, but in a slightly more emphatic key.[23]

Few men can have asked James to make his characters more abstract; few would have dared to ask for more emphatic plotting. But one can see that Stevenson's requests are natural given the interest which he himself described to James in *typical* characters placed in an *extreme* situation rather than in specific individuals in normal conditions.

Having noted Stevenson's sophistication and extreme self-consciousness, it is all the more interesting to find that his impressive early romance 'The Sire de Maletroit's Door' (1882) conforms beneath its iridescent surface to the fundamental modes of the 'true' folk tale as described by Vladimir Propp in his pioneering work *Morphology of the Folk Tale* (first published in Russian in 1928). In essence, writes Propp, 'Morphologically, a tale (skázka) may be termed any development proceeding from villainy or a lack through intermediary functions to marriage.'[24] Propp distinguishes thirty-one 'functions' in the folk-tale: no tale of those he analysed contained more than thirty-one, which always appear in the same order. The tale will contain no more than seven characters. If we turn to 'The Sire de Maletroit's Door' we find Propp's 'functions' of the tale followed very closely. A 'member of the family absents himself from home'; 'an interdiction is addressed to the hero'; 'the interdiction is violated' and so on. We may read these terms into this passage from the opening of the story:

> He had put up his horse with due care, and supped with due deliberation; and then, in a very agreeable frame of mind, went out

to pay a visit in the grey of the evening. It was not a very wise proceeding on the young man's part. He would have done better to remain beside the fire or go decently to bed. For the town was full of the troops of Burgundy and England under a mixed command; and though Denis was there on safe-conduct, his safe-conduct was like to serve him little on a chance encounter.[25]

In this manner Stevenson follows, consciously or unconsciously, the rigid rules of folk-tale convention. However, we can go a stage further in our analysis of his texts if we go beyond Propp's syntagmic kind of structural analysis, in which the formal organisation of the text is described in terms of the chronological order of the linear sequence of elements in the text. An alternative mode of structural analysis is the paradigmatic. This would seek, in Levi-Straussean terms, to define the pattern, usually based on an *a priori*, binary principle of opposition, which underlies the folkloristic text. This pattern will not be sequential: the elements of the tale will be taken out of their given order and re-grouped following one or more analytic schema. The most important paradigmatic structure informing and shaping Stevenson's story can be located through study of the motifs of the maze, the door, and the circle. As the story opens the young hero Denis de Beaulieu (connected with place and space by his name) finds himself lost in a labyrinth of dark streets:

Denis was ill-acquainted with the intricate lanes of Chateau Landon; even by daylight he had found some trouble in picking his way; and in this absolute darkness he soon lost it altogether. He was certain of one thing only – to keep mounting the hill. . . . With this clue to go upon he stumbled and groped forward, now breathing more freely in open places where there was a good slice of sky overhead, now feeling along the wall in stifling closes. It is an eerie and mysterious position to be thus submerged in opaque blackness in an almost unknown town. The silence is terrifying in its possibilities.[26]

The image of the labyrinth suggests both the motive of the quest and also, and most predominantly, the fear of the unknown – in a silence 'terrifying in its possibilities'. A sense of potential is thus oddly combined with a fear of entanglement or entrapment. Also intriguing is Denis's one sure idea, to 'keep mounting the hill' in order to get home. When he has been walking for some time he comes to a lane which seems to have no issue except in a 'terrace with a bartizan wall' which looks 'as out of an embrasure' into a valley below. At this point a rapid speeding up of events occurs. Denis perceives the semblance of an opening/escape only to find himself in fact completely trapped when the one way out of the cul-de-sac is blocked by the sudden arrival of a party of drunken English soldiers. At the very last moment he finds, again, apparent release through the mysterious opening of a door in a porch behind him:

> To his surprise, it yielded behind his weight; and though he turned in a moment, continued to swing back on oiled and noiseless hinges, until it stood wide open on a black interior. . . . There was something obscure and underhand about this that was little to the young man's fancy. It looked like a snare.[27]

It is not difficult to provide a psychoanalytic reading through a consideration of the topography of this story. In classical Freudian analysis the house or building is seen as an analogue of the female body. Denis de Beaulieu's journey may be seen as a quest which only ends when he is finally united to Blanche de Maletroit after having braved many dangers. These do not in fact cease even when he has gained access to the house: only after a trial of virtue and patience does the patriarchal Sire de Maletroit give his blessing for the marriage. The story can thus be read as an initiation myth. The journey up the hill would then also fit into the psychoanalytic scheme. The story betrays considerable sexual fear and anxiety which speak through the silences and imaged spaces of the unknown in the text.

The sexual theme in this tale seems to be confirmed through a final transmutation which occurs at the close of the story when an image of an empty iron ring (again defining a space of fear and lack, a ring with which the Sire de Maletroit has previously threatened to kill Denis) merges with an image of the fullness of the rising sun: 'And still the daylight kept flooding insensibly out of the east, which was soon to grow incandescent and cast up that red-hot cannon-ball, the rising sun.'[28]

Stevenson is most famous for his Gothic tales, and the most famous of these is of course *Dr Jekyll and Mr Hyde*. In taking up the form of the Gothic tale of terror Stevenson was again consciously reviving a lapsed genre or tradition. His stance is again sophisticated and self-conscious: his stories are in no sense continuous with the late eighteenth- and early nineteenth-century Gothic tales, but rather conterminous with them.

Stevenson's stories abound in many of the trappings of earlier Gothic; the isolated house, of singular and sombre aspect, is perhaps the most important of these – reminding us of Otranto and Udolpho. The house is often equipped in the approved manner with a maze of surrounding pathways, each one of which seems to lead nowhere. Heavy doors swing back only to reveal atrocities and horrors, mysterious spiritual presences, or ghosts (in 'Thrawn Janet' for example).

Stevenson's Gothic tales go beyond their models in their explicit concern with limit. The romances – 'The Sire de Maletroit's Door', 'Providence and the Guitar', 'A Lodging for the Night' – act in the manner of all folk-tales. They expose a fear, then seek to naturalise and neutralise it, offering patterns of reassurance and miming defeat of that which is feared. Stevenson's Gothic tales are by contrast explicitly concerned with extremes of human potential: the narratives seek to push against the frontiers of our knowledge and apprehension of that which constitutes humanity. Humanity itself is a concept which is interrogated in the text of *Dr Jekyll and Mr Hyde*. Thus the main adversary of Jekyll/Hyde, Mr Utterson, the lawyer (is there also a play on his name?) is introduced in these terms:

> Mr Utterson the lawyer was a man of a rugged countenance, that was never lighted by a smile; cold, scanty and embarrassed in discourse; backward in sentiment; lean, long, dusty, dreary, and yet somehow lovable. At friendly meetings, and when the wine was to his taste, *something eminently human beaconed from his eye.* [my italics][29]

The 'something eminently human' in Utterson is linked precisely with his capacity for self-discipline and for limiting his pleasures:

> He was austere with himself; drank gin when he was alone, to mortify a taste for vintages; and though he enjoyed the theatre, had not crossed the doors of one for twenty years.

Jekyll/Hyde's *inhumanity* is associated with a desire to break those limits which structure our humanity and personality. Jekyll speaks of 'laying aside restraint' and 'plunging in shame' *in propria persona* before his 'spring headlong into the sea of liberty' in the person of Hyde.

Jekyll is attracted by the idea of the 'separation' of the warring elements of his nature, though this is a division which is of course purely imaginary, an unattainable ideal. As Jekyll himself writes in his narrative: 'I saw that, of the two natures that contended in the field of my consciousness, even if I could rightly be said to be either, it was only because I was radically both.'[30] And later, as Hyde, he experiences 'an unknown but not an innocent freedom of the soul. *I knew myself*, at the first breath of this new life, to be more wicked, tenfold more wicked, sold a slave to my original evil' (my italics).[31] In other words, evil cannot exist without man's consciousness of it, and may only be defined in terms of its opposite, good. Here Stevenson appears to set some kind of conceptual limit to Jekyll/Hyde's ambition and imaginings, but the drive towards the inhuman has so much energy in the text that the writer seems to be continually denying a limitation which we know rationally to exist. Thus one of the most powerful passages in the story describes an infamy committed by Hyde:

> All at once, I saw two figures: one a little man who was stumping along eastward at a good walk, and the other a girl of maybe eight or ten who was running as hard as she was able down a cross-street. Well, sir, the two ran into one another naturally enough at the corner; and then came the horrible part of the thing; for the man trampled calmly over the child's body and left her screaming on the ground. It sounds nothing to hear, but it was hellish to see. It wasn't like a man; it was like some damned Juggernaut.[32]

The word 'juggernaut' is a corruption of a name for Krishna, the god before whose image in a chariot devotees would throw themselves to be crushed to death in a mêlée, without life, without humanity or individuality. Its use in this context is painfully and strikingly appropriate.

Stevenson's adoption of the forms of the short story and romance – as opposed to the psychological novel, for example – can be accounted for in part by his characteristic themes and perspectives. Stevenson was not primarily interested in character-portrayal in the Jamesian sense. Indeed, he wrote that literature, 'so far as it imitates at all . . . , imitates not life but speech; not the facts of human destiny, but the emphasis and the suppressions with which the human actor tells of them'.[33] His fascination was with the moment of revelation, through some form of speech or language, of psychological crisis. However, we are made to feel that such moments could become part of the experience of us all. For as we have seen, and as Stevenson wrote in 'A Humble

Remonstrance', he felt that a writer should be occupied 'not so much in making stories true as in making them typical'. The crisis of Denis de Beaulieu is typical; so too, it is Stevenson's art to make us feel, is the moral crisis experienced by Jekyll. He makes the 'hero' Wiltshire's crisis in 'The Beach of Falesá' 'typical' in the same sense. This, like Jekyll's experience, is communicated through direct first-person narrative, with its attendant 'emphasis and suppressions'.

In 'The Beach of Falesá' the protagonist Wiltshire has to measure himself in terms of a fairly common colonial situation (typical, but not then much discussed in literature). The story is concerned not with the question of Wiltshire's individual character and decency, but rather to demonstrate the way in which a man set free from his native background and his own society finds happiness not in exploiting the natives of Falesá but in binding himself to them by the same kind of ties which have bound him in the past to his family and society at home.

The story opens as a romance, with an enchanting description of a South Sea island:

> I saw that island first when it was neither night nor morning. The moon was to the west, setting, but still broad and bright. To the east, and right amidships of the dawn, which was all pink, the day-star sparkled like a diamond. The land breeze blew in our faces, and smelt strong of wild lime and vanilla.[34]

The sense of mystery and romance is dispelled to a certain extent as we encounter for the first time some of the white settlers on the island:

> In the back room was old Captain Randall, squatting on the floor native fashion, fat and pale, naked to the waist, grey as a badger, and his eyes set with drink. His body was covered with grey hair and crawled over by flies: one was in the corner of his eye – he never heeded.[35]

Later in the story Stevenson deliberately sets out to undercut any *Treasure Island* expectations of island adventure. We find Wiltshire undercutting and exposing the falsity of the mysterious objects by means of which Case, the villain of the piece, has been frightening the native inhabitants:

> I went as far in as the bend, and, looking round the corner, saw a shining face. It was big and ugly, like a pantomime mask, and the brightness of it waxed and dwindled, and at times it smoked.

'Oho!' says I, 'luminous paint!'

And I must say I rather admired the man's ingenuity. With a box of tools and a few mighty simple contrivances he had made out to have a devil of a temple.[36]

However, the central theme of the story is Wiltshire's marriage. This takes place in a haphazard sort of way almost as soon as he arrives on the island. The forms of the marriage contract must be quoted:

> This is to certify that *Uma*, daughter of *Faavao*, of Falesá, island of ——, is illegally married to *Mr John Wiltshire* for one night, and Mr John Wiltshire is at liberty to send her to hell next morning.
>
> JOHN BLACKAMOAR
> Chaplain to the Hulks
>
> Extracted from the register
> by William T. Randall,
> Master Mariner[37]

The project of the story is to show Wiltshire's immediate impulse of remorse ('The more ashamed I was, the more hurry I was in to be gone') shaping and developing into something more substantial as his attachment to Uma grows. Impelled partly by his contempt for the sordid dealings of the other whites in Falesá, partly by private shame over the way he has tricked Uma, he demands a regular marriage to her at the very moment when he discovers that she is the cause of a taboo which is losing him trade. He takes Uma, an isolated individual rejected by her own people and binds her to him, setting up the basis for the development of the relationship which interests us throughout the rest of the story. By its close we perceive that within his limits Wiltshire has chosen to develop his sense of responsibility and of community. He is, with reservations, content, because he has recognised his ties and obligations to others. The story ends with this 'inner speech':

> My public-house? not a bit of it, nor ever likely. I'm stuck here, I fancy. I don't like to leave the kids, you see: and – there's no use talking – they're better here than what they would be in a white man's country, though Ben took the eldest up to Auckland, where he's being schooled with the best. But what bothers me is the girls.

They're only half-castes, of course; I know that as well as you do, and there's nobody thinks less of half-castes than I do; but they're mine, and about all I've got. I can't reconcile my mind to their taking up with Kanakas, and I'd like to know where I'm to find the whites?[38]

Stevenson's moral optimism is in striking contrast with the pessimism of Conrad when dealing with the same issues. In the tales in which Conrad explores the colonial situation he throws doubt on whether man's innate capacity for good is strong enough to hold up without the support of the complex codes of civilisation. Placed in a position where they experience no social restraints or constraints, men like Kurtz in *Heart of Darkness* experience moral disintegration. Stevenson, however, finds in the primary, most elemental bond between men and women the unchanging origin of a human or humane ideal of conduct. As men and women become bound together like Wiltshire and Uma they will develop a new concept of responsibility and of regard for each other.

Stevenson's romantic and Gothic tales can usefully be compared with those of Hardy, most of which were written in the 1880s and 1890s. Hardy's exploitation of the reading public's taste for the romantic and bizarre may be compared with Stevenson's integrity in the use of romance and Gothic forms. In Stevenson's case the forms have integrity because they act as appropriate vehicles to carry his imaginative and moral vision. Hardy on the other hand had, in John Wain's words, 'no special respect for the story as a literary form'.[39] He used the story as a means of recording material which might later be developed in a novel, and also wrote many stories as pot-boilers for the periodical market. In consequence, his tales, colourful and remarkable though they often are, remain fundamentally unsatisfactory: we have little sense in them of a developing sensibility shaping new versions of old forms. T. S. Eliot, indeed, has accused Hardy of morbid self-indulgence in his short stories. He cites 'Barbara of the House of Grebe', from the collection *A Group of Noble Dames*, as an example and writes of it:

This is not realism; it is as Hardy catalogues it, 'romance and fantasy' with which Hardy can do exactly what he wants to do. I do not object to horror: *Oedipus Rex* is a most horrible plot from which the last drop of horror is extracted by the dramatist: and among Hardy's contemporaries, Conrad's *Heart of Darkness* and James's *Turn of the Screw* are tales of horror. But there is horror in the real world;

and in these works of Sophocles, Conrad and James we are in a world of Good and Evil. In *Barbara of the House of Grebe* we are introduced into a world of pure Evil. The tale would seem 'to have been written solely to provide a satisfaction for some morbid emotion.[40]

He adds that Hardy indulges himself 'at the reader's expense' in this story.

Stevenson wrote of his young contemporary, somewhat quizzically:

Kipling is by far the most promising young man who has appeared since – ahem – I appeared. He amazes me by his precocity and various endowment. . . . At this rate his works will soon fill the habitable globe; and surely he was armed for better conflicts than these succinct sketches and flying leaves of verse?[41]

Kipling's development in the short story far exceeded what Stevenson could detect in those early 'succinct sketches', but it is worth registering that Kipling did indeed begin his career as a reporter and sketch-writer for *The Civil and Military Gazette* at Lahore in Northern India, fitting his sketches to a 2000-word limit and to a tight time schedule. In its own way Kipling's story art owes a great deal to the opportunities and constraints of newspaper production. It was in Lahore that he mastered the swift scene-setting which is a hallmark of his stories, and the staccato, near-epigrammatic character depiction which is so effective in his work.

Towards the close of *Kim*, written in 1901, is a passage which gives us a unique insight into the early Kipling. At the end of his adventures, young Kim has, in Kipling's words, an 'unnerved brain', and muses in a state of shock:

All that while he felt, though he could not put it into words, that his soul was out of gear with its surroundings – a cog-wheel unconnected with any machinery, just like the idle cog-wheel of a cheap Beheea sugar-crusher laid by in a corner. The breezes fanned over him, the parrots shrieked at him, the noises of the populated house behind – squabbles, orders, and reproofs – hit on dead ears.

'I am Kim. I am Kim. And what is Kim?' His soul repeated it again and again.

He did not want to cry – had never felt less like crying in his life – but of a sudden easy, stupid tears trickled down his nose, and with an almost audible click he felt the wheels of his being lock up anew on the world without. Things that rode meaningless on the eyeball an instant before slid into proper proportion. Roads were meant to be walked upon, houses to be lived in, cattle to be driven, fields to be tilled, and men and women to be talked to. They were all real and true – solidly planted upon the feet – perfectly comprehensible – clay of his clay, neither more nor less.[42]

This dualism, the movement between the feeling that the soul is 'out of gear' and then the sense of the 'wheels of being locking up anew' with the external world underpins Kipling's early fiction, and finds wider symbolic expression in his evocation of two worlds: the 'safe' Anglo-India of the empire builders, and 'native' India.

In Kipling's early fiction the Anglo-Indians are shown as having created to all intents and purposes their own world, self-sufficient in moral and spiritual – or quasi-spiritual – terms, offering a built-in sense of purpose and identity. Within the confines of this world the insider is safe, his place defined for him: he has no need to create his own sense of meaning in life. Once he steps outside this world however he will come to feel his identity questioned and the meaning of his life will become problematic, just as his role is problematic in Indian eyes. The Englishman's lapse into the native world thus works as a kind of extended image for the kind of mental lapse suffered by Kim when for a moment life seemed to lose its meaning and coherence.

By extension, the Anglo-Indian world comes to be associated with life, the Indian with death. This opposition can fruitfully be compared with the one we find in the work of Forster. Like Forster, Kipling associated the irrational, the mystical and sensual aspects of life with the Indians but for him these qualities have a negative charge. Hence such fearful images in his work as those in this extraordinary description of Indians asleep in the story 'The City of Dreadful Night'. Crowded, breathing, sleeping bodies are transformed into corpses:

On either side of the road lay corpses disposed on beds in fantastic attitudes – one hundred and seventy bodies of men. Some shrouded all in white with bound-up mouths. Some naked and black as ebony in the strong light; and one – that lay face upwards with dropped jaw, far away from the others – silvery white and ashen grey.

'A leper asleep; and the remainder wearied coolies, servants, small shopkeepers, and drivers from the hack-stand hard by. The scene – a main approach to Lahore city, and the night a warm one in August.'[43]

In Kipling's early Indian stories we are made aware continually of the rigid line separating English and Indian communities. The titles reflect this concern with limit – 'Beyond the Pale', 'The Gate of One Hundred Sorrows', 'At the End of the Passage', 'Through the Fire', 'The Limitations of Pambé Serang'. Members of both races are harshly punished if they cross over this boundary. One of the most horrific examples is to be found in the story 'Beyond the Pale', in which a young Indian girl/widow 'pays' for her affair with an Englishman when she has her 'roseleaf' hands amputated by her guardian. The man escapes more lightly in this case, with only a slight leg-wound. In 'Without Benefit of Clergy' an English man and Indian girl feel that they have been punished for their love when their son dies; subsequently the girl dies too because she refuses to leave her lover in order to escape from a fever-ridden town.

Such stories as these work towards a powerful affirmation of the view that contentment rests on close adherence to the rules and ceremonies of one's given society. To break with this society is to invite a punishment which may seem to the reader grotesque in its severity. The explanation for this lies in the fact that for Kipling the punishment, which is often almost an annihilation, is an image for something he feared deeply: the loss of the self. The self is defined by society, for Kipling, and when a man is removed from his proper social sphere he risks a fragmentation of his sense of identity. This is what happens to the protagonist of the story 'At the End of the Passage'. The man, an engineer, has been kept in near-isolation for months, and gradually begins to lose his integrity and his sanity. He is unable to sleep and in the last week of his life begins to be haunted by a spectre which is his double – 'the figure of myself':

> He approached the figure, which naturally kept at an unvarying distance from him, as is the case of all spectres that are born of overwork. It slid through the house and dissolved into swimming specks within the eyeball. . . . Hummil went about his business till even. When he came in to dinner he found himself sitting at the table. The vision rose and walked out hastily.[44]

Isolation has caused this man to lose that sense of self which is created and sustained in large part through our interaction with others. Hence the image of the double, suggesting a splitting and disintegration of the ego which in this case leads literally to the man's death, from fear: ' "He was scared to death," insisted Lowndes. "Look at those eyes! For pity's sake don't let him be buried with them open!" ' .[45]

Related forms of frenzy or insanity are examined in stories such as 'The Madness of Private Ortheris' or 'The Dream of Duncan Parrenness'. The first of these two stories contains a sensitive account of an early version of shell-shock, or exhaustion produced by the strain of 'sodgerin' ' (soldiering). The soldier is discovered having one of his 'fits', singing a parody of 'The Ramrod Corps', 'full of cheerful allusions to battle, murder, and sudden death'. In 'The Dream of Duncan Parrenness' the figure of the double is again associated with mental and emotional strain. Parrenness has spent a year out in India during which period he has indulged 'a thousand bad passions and desires'. He sees his double in a horrific waking dream:

> I, Duncan Parrenness, who was afraid of no man, was taken with a more deadly terror than I hold it has ever been the lot of mortal man to know. For I saw that his face was my very own, but marked and lined and scarred with the furrows of disease and much evil living.[46]

The link between social disorientation, social transgression and the collapse of the self is heavily underlined in these stories. From this point on Ortheris and Parrenness will seem to themselves divided beings, lacking inner integrity.

When Kipling first rose to fame he was acclaimed as a writer of the exotic. H. G. Wells has described 'his astonishing advent' on the scene: 'with a series of little blue–grey books, whose covers opened like window shutters to reveal the dusty sun-glare and blazing colours of the East'.[47] His stories focus on the unusual, on the bizarre, sometimes on the horrific. In this they resemble the stories of Stevenson, and some kind of link can also be posited with the earlier short and exotic forms of the romance and Gothic tale. The influence of the 'form' of newspaper work must also be noted in Kipling's early work however. And his interest in extreme situations also has a different emphasis from that of Stevenson and suggests an incipiently modern anxiety. It reflects not an interest in transcending human – and social – limitations, but a profound anxiety about the breakdown of the self, a breakdown which is viewed in wholly negative terms. Integration of self and society, the one defining the other, is Kipling's ideal. Conflict between the two, however, is seen as the norm, and the tension engendered by such conflict might be seen as the motive force of an art driven on, like that of James, by the 'imagination of disaster'.

Kipling's early tales form a distinct unit in his work and it is likely that their 'exotic' qualities, in particular, derive very largely from the opportunities which he found for rapid and widespread publication in popular magazines of the 1880s and 1890s. As conditions of publication changed, and this magazine market shrank, so Kipling's stories, seeming to reflect the age, dwindled in number but became more distanced and considered. His mature art will be considered in its historical context in the following chapter.

2 The Tale-Tellers: I

It has been suggested that in the 1880s and 1890s, the period when according to H. G. Wells 'short stories broke out everywhere', there were two distinct types of 'short story'. The prose poem and psychological sketch were early examples of 'short prose fiction', while the stories of Stevenson and Kipling pointed the way to a renewal of traditional short story forms. The lines of development of the short story and short prose fiction will be followed separately from this point; in chronological terms it makes sense to focus first on the traditional short story. This flourished in the early years of the twentieth century, while the seed sown by the prose poem and psychological sketch took longer to germinate, to flower eventually in modernist short fiction.

We can see the traditional short story or tale as a form developing in the work of the later Kipling, 'Saki' (H. H. Munro) and Somerset Maugham. It has been argued that the short story, as we are familiar with it in the late nineteenth century, is distinguished not so much by its 'antiquity' as by the element in it of a conscious revival of traditional forms. It has also been suggested that there is a connection between social unease or disjunction and a preference for the short story form. Both notions may shed light on the rapid development of the tale in the form of the exotic story in the Edwardian era. The salient fact about the writers mentioned above is that all three are writers of the empire, successors to the Stevenson who wrote 'The Beach of Falesá' and 'The Ebb-Tide'. At a time when the sun of empire was beginning to set in political terms, the 'native' or exotic found its way into English literature as a new arena for fantasy, replacing the romantic medieval *topos* of Morris and Rossetti. The remote settings of India, Africa and the Far East offered a distance in place which allowed for the release of certain areas of the imaginative and fantastic which could not be received into the literature of everyday life, especially in the form of the realist novel.

A new social class was created for the government of the British empire. Kipling and Saki belonged to this class and were consequently uncertain about their 'true' position in society. Born in India and Burma respectively, they belonged to two cultures but were fully accepted in neither. In England they formed part of a class composed in the main of new recruits to the upper middle class, still with a certain rawness of aspect. In the colonies such people banded together to form an artificially hermetic community, united in their attempt to affirm the status and power somewhat arbitrarily bestowed on them by the processes of history.

It is not surprising therefore to find that the basis of a story for Saki and Maugham was the anecdote. The anecdote relies for its effect on convention. It both appeals to and endorses a shared system of values: at its simplest level it appears as the 'in joke' and it may have a certain bravura quality, affirming group values a shade too emphatically. It will normally be told by a first-person narrator who guarantees both the tale and certain values associated with it.

The anecdote informs some of the early work of Kipling, who projects, as many critics have noted, a rather irritatingly knowing air in some of the stories of *Plain Tales from the Hills*. This could be referred to a need to over-compensate, to affirm absolutely one's place in a society where there are no absolutes. In stories of his middle and later periods, however, Kipling moved from anecdotal to mythical and fantastic modes. In an age of experiment in the short story form one would expect a writer such as Kipling, acknowledged as a master of the genre by the time he was thirty, to experiment widely. Among Kipling's later work we find many different types of short story: proto-science fiction ('As Easy as A.B.C.'); stories influenced by cinema technique ('Mrs Bathurst', 'My Son's Wife'); fables à la La Fontaine ('The Mother Hive'); more importantly, stories of the supernatural ('They', 'The Wish House', 'A Madonna of the Trenches'); also complex Jamesian studies of manners and motive ('Mary Postgate', 'Dayspring Mishandled').

In his elliptical autobiography *Something of Myself* (1937) Kipling wrote of his early discovery in writing *Plain Tales from the Hills* that

a tale from which pieces have been raked out is like a fire that has been poked. One does not know that the operation has been performed, but everyone feels the effect. Note, though, that the excised stuff must have been honestly written for inclusion. I found that when, to save trouble, I 'wrote short' *ab initio* much salt went out of the work.[1]

Kipling's description of his 'cutting' technique is illuminating. It suggests that he was in essence a 'metonymic' writer, first forming his narratives according to the 'law of combination along the axis of contiguity',[2] only subsequently cutting what seemed least expressive, in a symbolic sense, of his central theme. In consequence Kipling's stories often have lacunae which make them seem elliptical in a modernist manner. His stories have been described as modernist,[3] but this is inaccurate. The ellipses in the works of the modernists generally occur for an 'opposite' reason, when the author is combining the elements of his story according to the law of similarity, not contiguity, and sacrifices narrative continuity to symbolic order. The basic trope of the modernist story is metaphor, while Kipling's stories often centre around a synecdoche or metonymy, for example Bisesa's 'roseleaf hands' in 'Beyond the Pale' or Holden's Indian home in 'Without Benefit of Clergy', whose desolation at the close of the story mirrors a man's state of mind: 'He found that the rains had torn down the mud pillars of the gateway, and the heavy wooden gate that had guarded his life hung lazily from one hinge.'[4]

Stories with a plot tend to deal with limits and extremes of situation and human behaviour. In the case of Stevenson a fascination with the extreme signifies a desire to push beyond 'normal' states of being and to interrogate the concept of humanity. In Kipling's work an equally strong tendency to the extreme appears to stem from a desire to push to its limits the code of behaviour within which the 'real' author had been brought up. Kipling opposes this code to a bizarre or horrifying situation and dispassionately watches it crack, without, in the early stories, offering anything in its place. In the work written after 1900, he offers a sense of place as a corrective to breakdown and loss of the self. This trend is illustrated by two stories, one of 1904 and one of 1913. They furnish examples of the extraordinary unevenness of Kipling's work and offer a focal point for discussion of the 'flawed' quality of his writing.

'My Son's Wife' is the later of the two. The title immediately suggests a sense of possession, relationship and security, and this is a sense which gradually envelops the hero as the story progresses. The title phrase is sung by a woman who will become the protagonist's wife: it acts as the opening phrase for a new movement in his life. The story is a parable turning on the regeneration of the hero as he abandons town life and socialism – apparently inextricably linked – in favour of the countryside and conservative social values. Midmore changes from a man who had 'attached himself to the Immoderate Left' into a country squire possessed by the idea of possession:

> Everything his eyes opened upon was his very own to keep for ever. The carved four-post Chippendale bed, obviously worth hundreds; the wavy walnut William and Mary chairs – he had seen worse ones labelled twenty guineas apiece; the oval medallion mirror; the delicate eighteenth-century wire fireguard; the heavily brocaded curtains were his – all his.[5]

Vulgar materialism and an easy satire which takes the place of political understanding are apparent in this story. Moreover there is an over-assertiveness in some of the phrasing which seems to indicate a writer only half at ease with his material:

> Such pagan delights as these were followed by pagan sloth of evenings. . . . But Midmore preferred to lie out on a yellow silk couch, reading works of a debasing vulgarity; or, by invitation, to dine with the Sperrits and savages of their kidney.[6]

The over-insistent 'Englishness' of this passage suggests an observer writing of an alien culture, anxious to learn the rules and passwords which will make him acceptable within it. This strain – in both senses of the word – is there in Kipling, and yet ten years earlier he had recorded in 'They' a most delicate appreciation of English country life. 'They', of course, influenced T. S. Eliot in the writing of 'Burnt Norton'. In this story Kipling achieved the sure grasp of specific place and time which Eliot was later to prescribe for the 'intersection of the timeless moment' with time – 'In England and nowhere'.

'They' opens with a sweeping panorama of the Sussex countryside, which gradually closes in on the narrator and the reader. The form of a quest is embedded in the successive stages of the narrative, which leads the reader on as in a maze:

> One view called me to another; one hill-top to its fellow, half across the county . . .
> I found hidden villages where bees, the only things awake, boomed in eighty-foot lindens . . .
> I did not allow for the confusing veils of the woods. A quick turn plunged me first into a green cutting brim-full of liquid sunshine.[7]

This rich, atmospheric description is on an imaginative level quite different from that of 'My Son's Wife'. In 'They' the country house has full weight in the text, functioning as an image of accommodation between the forces of nature and of history:

> As the light beat across my face my fore-wheels took the turf of a great still lawn from which sprang horsemen ten feet high with levelled lances. . . . Across the lawn – the marshalled woods besieged it on three sides – stood an ancient house of lichened and weather-worn stone, with mullioned windows and roofs of rose-red tile. It was flanked by semi-circular walls, also rose-red, that closed the lawn on the fourth side, and at their feet a box hedge grew man-high. There were doves on the roofs about the slim brick chimneys.[8]

'They' is a story of the supernatural, and some critics have complained of its realistic social and physical setting which, they feel, jars with the supernatural elements of the tale. Yet one could argue that the intermeshing of the two is Kipling's precarious achievement. Motor cars and Ordnance Survey maps offer one way of approaching the house and its mysterious inhabitants but on an intersecting plane is the narrator's sighting of the ghost children in the wood and by the fountain; a sighting possible only for those who have themselves lost a child. The mingling of the two levels of 'reality' offers a triumph of control of tone:

> It was a long afternoon crowded with mad episodes that rose and dissolved like the dust of our wheels; cross-sections of remote and incomprehensible lives through which we raced at right angles; and I went home in the dusk, wearied out, to dream of the clashing horns of the cattle; round-eyed nuns walking in a garden of graves; pleasant tea-parties beneath shady trees, the carbolic-scented, grey-painted corridors of the County Institute; the steps of shy children in the wood, and the hands that clung to my knees as the motor began to move.[9]

'They' covers in the space of a few pages several weeks in time and a variety of incidents but the diverse elements of the story are held together by the presence of a characteristically static narrative voice, heavily adjectival and with few active verbs, creating a single 'time of narrative'.

A progression is discernible in Kipling's work from a youthful sense of *nada* and existential despair to a defining of the self through a sense of place which in turn makes possible the development of certain areas of the spiritual life. The intermeshing of levels of the 'real' and supernatural is perhaps Kipling's greatest contribution to the short story form. His metonymic cutting technique, akin to that of a film editor, forges stories which are fluid and restless in structure, never able to rest on a single perspective on reality and thus susceptible to the incorporation of elements of the supernatural and surreal.

The category of the supernatural needs a little more definition. It enters a significant number of Kipling's stories after 1900. In some cases he does no more than toy with fairly trite and superficial ideas of spiritualism or telepathy, in 'Wireless' for example and 'A Madonna of the Trenches'. In neither of these stories does the supernatural have any status in itself: it remains a curiosity and has no integral connection with the development of the tale. However in many of the finer stories (including 'They'), the use of the supernatural adds an extra dimension to the tale while contributing to thematic development. The introduction of something felt as alien to human experience throws into relief the normal, what is deep and enduring in human life.

The supernatural relates to things which cannot be explained by natural law, and by extension from this the term is used to refer to events caused either by a god or by occult beings. The term is used more loosely to denote simply that which exceeds the ordinary, i.e. the abnormal. The last is the sense most pertinent here. Though references to the occult and to the suspension of natural law occur frequently in the short story, they function in literary terms primarily as metaphors directing us to a sense of the strange or abnormal – they are not usually intended to be taken literally. The device of the 'wish house' in Kipling's story of that name functions like this.

The literature of the supernatural has its specialised vocabulary, which is a vocabulary of negation. The writer will frequently refer to the un-natural, the un-earthly, the in-tangible, the in-visible; also to the un-speakable, the un-utterable, the un-imaginable. The second category directs our attention to the idea of a potential which is sensed beyond the familiar areas of experience charted by language.

'The Wish House' (1924) fruitfully entwines natural and supernatural elements. The story is built on a fundamental contrast between the natural and supernatural, between the superstitious beliefs of the elderly women characters and their attitude to these beliefs. Grace Ashcroft, the main speaker of the story, believes that she has taken on herself all the hurt which would otherwise have fallen on the man she loved. This has been achieved by means of the 'wish house', which she first heard about from a little girl who claimed to have 'taken away' her headache:

> Sophy said there was a Wish 'Ouse in Wadloes Road – just a few streets off, on the way to our green-grocer's. All you 'ad to do, she said, was to ring the bell an' wish your wish through the slit o' the letter-box.[10]

The wish is granted by 'a Token', a wraith of the dead or the living, but, we are told, 'All you'll get at a Wish 'Ouse is leave to take some one else's trouble' – you cannot ask for anything for yourself. Grace Ashcroft has asked to take 'everythin' bad that's in store for my man . . . for love's sake', and since that time has traced a relation between the health and welfare of her ex-lover and the state of a sick leg she has had from the day she visited the wish house. Now she senses that she has not long to live, but insists that she wants no more than she has had from life. As long as 'de pain is taken into de reckonin' ', as long as she has kept Harry well at her expense, Grace is content. Her feeling stems from a realistic mixture of motives, in part altruistic, in part fiercely possessive – Grace wishes to feel that in taking on Harry's pain she has possessed him as no one else can. This mixture of motives fits in well with the down-to-earth, physical nature of her love for Harry: 'I couldn't ever get 'Arry – 'ow *could* I? I knowed it must go on burnin' till it burned me out.'[11] Throughout the story the elements of the uncanny are so deployed as to sharpen the reader's sense of the strongly and deeply human in the characters of the two elderly women speakers. The wish house itself is clearly uncanny, *unheimlich* – a suburbanised version of the deserted Gothic castle of earlier fiction:

> Fourteen, Wadloes Road, was the place – a liddle basement-kitchen 'ouse, in a row of twenty–thirty such, and tiddy strips o' walled garden in front – the paint off the front door, an' na'undone to na'un since ever so long. There wasn't 'ardly no one in the streets 'cept the cats. *'Twas* 'ot, too! I turned into the gate bold as brass; up de steps I went and' I ringed the front-door bell. She pealed loud, like it do in an empty house. When she'd all ceased, I 'eard a cheer, like, pushed back on de floor o' the kitchen.[12]

The apprehension of something inhuman is powerfully conveyed through the tone and vocabulary of Grace Ashcroft's speaking voice. Her voice is skilfully exploited as a narrative device: because Grace believes implicitly in the story she is telling, she convinces us. Paradoxically it is her acceptance of the uncanny which makes it possible for us to believe in it on one narrative level and makes us question it on another. For Grace's vivid maturity, her quality of acceptance, dominates the story, dwarfing the invocations of household ghosts and 'Tokens'. It is a maturity which is eminently natural, as Kipling stresses by repeatedly linking Grace and her natural environment:

> Mrs Ashcroft shook her head slowly – she never hurried – and went on stitching a sack-cloth lining into a list-bound rush tool-basket. Mrs Fettley laid out more patches in the spring light through the geraniums on the window-sill, and they were silent awhile.[13]

> A couple of jays squealed and skirmished through the undraped apple-trees in the garden. This time, the word was with Mrs Ashcroft, her elbows on the tea-table, and her sick leg propped on a stool.[14]

It is uncanny for the reader to hear Mrs Ashcroft detailing the connections between her bad leg and Harry's illnesses:

> 'That day,' Mrs Ashcroft went on, 'I'd stood on me feet nigh all the time, watching the doctor go in an' out; for they thought it might be 'is ribs, too. That made my boil break again, issuin' an' weeping. But it turned out 'twadn't ribs at all and 'Arry 'ad a good night. . . . It didn't hurt me that day, to speak of – seemed more to draw the strength out o' me like – and 'Arry 'ad another good night. That made me persevere. . . .'[15]

But Grace Ashcroft does not find it uncanny. It is natural for human beings to want to make sacrifices for those they love, and natural for them to make some sort of connection between pain which they suffer and some reward, either in this life or the next. Her attitude is simply the most positive we can adopt in the face of human suffering – 'It *do* count, don't it – de pain?'

The delicacy of 'The Wish House' is due in large part to Kipling's deft handling of the dialogue through which the story is conveyed. Mrs Ashcroft and Mrs Fettley speak 'precisely' in 'deep tones' and a contrapuntal effect is achieved through a stylistic trick of each speaker's picking up one of the closing words of the other:

> 'Nothin' was *said* to ye?' Mrs Fettley demanded.
> 'Na'un. She just breathed out – a sort of *A-ah*, like.'[16]

In structuring the story Kipling used cinematic cutting techniques with consummate skill. In snatches of dialogue the two women manage to reveal all the significant episodes of their lives, in a kind of montage effect. In less than twenty pages the life-span of the two women is covered, with no sense of artifice or strain. The story gives the impression of being finely honed: the art is primarily one of nicely judged omission. For example, Mrs Fettley's story is inferred from the closing lines of her recital, which are all that are given:

> Mrs Fettley had spoken very precisely for some time without interruption, before she wiped her eyes. 'And,' she concluded, 'they read 'is death-notice to me, out o' the paper last month. O' course it wadn't any o' *my* becomin' concerns – let be I 'adn't set eyes on him for so long.'[17]

Like other Kipling stories 'The Wish House' is indeed like a hugely truncated novel. It is quite characteristic of his work that he does not deal with single episodes, normally thought to be the staple of the story-teller, but deals elliptically with large and complex narratives, often covering a long time-span and involving many characters.

One of his very late stories, 'Dayspring Mishandled', offers one of the most intriguing examples of this elliptical method. The theme is Jamesian and the story operates on multiple levels of ambiguity. The 'dayspring mishandled' of the title refers to the youth, energy, talent and ability to love of the two young men who are at the centre of the story. They come together, as a result of lack of opportunities in the higher echelons of literature, to work for a financially rewarding 'Fictional Supply Syndicate'. In the course of time, one, Castorley, becomes a well-known literary critic; the other, Manallace, continues to produce hackwork, but earns enough money by it to support a woman whom he and Castorley have both loved. The lives of the two men continue to intertwine over the years, until a decisive evening when Castorley says something unforgivable about the woman involved. Manallace then devises an intricate plot to bring about the other man's downfall. He forges a Chaucer manuscript which Castorley 'discovers' and acclaims, subsequently receiving a title for his services to literature. It was Manallace's intention then to expose him, and he has merely been waiting for the appropriate moment. But Castorley's wife has not only guessed the truth about the manuscript but is even more anxious for her husband's downfall than is his erstwhile friend. The latter thus finds himself in a dilemma. He sees that the wife's cruelty, which is abhorrent to his sensibility, is merely a magnified image of his own, and he becomes more and more loath to put his plan of unmasking and revenge into action. In the end he becomes involved in a struggle with the wife to put off the day of revelation. Only with Castorley's death does he become safe, as the wife prepares happily to marry her lover, the dead man's surgeon.

The portrait of Castorley is an engaging, if slightly scathing, one of a literary critic complete with affected, slightly 'gamy', 'ninetyish speech:

> The freshness, the fun, the humanity, the fragrance of it all, cries – no, shouts – itself as Dan's work. Why 'Daiespringe mishandled' alone stamps it from Dan's mint. Plangent as doom, my dear boy – plangent as doom![18]

The portrait of Manallace is a study in obsession, an obsession which has acted as a displacement activity distracting him from failures in private and public life. The painstakingly detailed plot against Castorley and the hatred nurtured over years are both misplaced uses of energy, as Manallace realises at the close of the story when he also realises that he will be unable to 'redeem the time' he has wasted.

Waste of time and life are the major themes of the story, and are nowhere more sharply expressed than at the moment when Manallace sees his revenge turn back on itself, as he first sees the ugly image of his hatred in the wife of his colleague. He sees the futility of the purpose which has been for years his *raison d'être*. This moment is at the centre of the spider's web of the narrative of 'Dayspring Mishandled'. The narrative is elliptical and tortuous, a complex narrative order mirroring a slow process of self-discovery for Manallace.

Castorley reflects towards the close of 'Dayspring Mishandled': 'Life had always been one long innuendo'. The phrase doesn't quite fit our usual image of Kipling but it is suggestive in connection with his later work. Kipling's technique here is precisely one of innuendo. He did not fall into the trap of increased prolixity with the increased complexity of his subject matter but continually refined on the expressive substance of his stories while observing the need for verbal brevity in the short form. Sean O'Faolain has described the 'eloquence of form' which resulted, and, interestingly, singles out James as an example of a contemporary who failed to achieve such formal eloquence, who 'sprawled' in a manner unacceptable for the abbreviated form. The comparison is revealing, throwing into a sharper focus the special nature of Kipling's achievement.

The thrust of Kipling's art is to make the fantastic and strange familiar and to subdue them to human quality. Saki works in a different direction, towards transcendence and transformation of the familiar. Like Poe and Stevenson, Saki interrogates the concept of humanity but his tactics of alienation make him more closely akin to Swift. Most often Saki makes humanity strange to us ('defamiliarises' it), by invoking some sort of comparison or link with bestial life. In 'The Mappined Life', for example, human beings are likened to caged beasts, captive like the animals they watch in the Zoological Gardens, bound not by tangible bars of iron but by habits of thought and feeling:

> 'That is where our superior powers of self-deception come in,' said the niece; 'we are able to live our unreal, stupid little lives on our particular Mappin terrace, and persuade ourselves that we really are untrammelled men and women leading a reasonable existence in a reasonable sphere.'[19]

The image of the wild beast is pervasive in Saki's fiction: we hear it 'stamping its chained foot', like the beast in Virginia Woolf's *The Waves*, in stories such as 'Sredni Vashtar', 'Gabriel-Ernest', 'The Philanthropist and the Happy Cat' and 'The Interlopers'. The wild beast connotes both the 'joy of life' and the 'terror of unseen things', phrases conjoined in the line 'a stealthy linking of the joys of life with the terror of unseen things', from 'The Music on the Hill'. The beast figures expression of energy (which Saki calls 'liberty') and a falling into unknown modes of being: as such it operates as an image of desire. This becomes explicit in the famous story 'Sredni Vashtar', in which the household pet of a ten-year-old boy kills his feared and hated aunt. The pet is somewhat unusual – 'a large polecat–ferret'. Before the central incident we are told that the boy, Conradin, has ambivalent feelings about the ferret: he is 'dreadfully afraid of the lithe, sharp-fanged beast, but it was his most treasured possession'. When he finally realises what the ferret has accomplished – the murder of his aunt – 'a look of triumph began to blaze in his eyes that had only known the wistful patience of defeat'. Desire is fulfilled, the caged beast is literally and metaphorically set free, and now becomes beautiful, at one with the natural world:

> The great polecat–ferret made its way down to a small brook at the foot of the garden, drank for a moment, then crossed a little plank bridge and was lost to sight in the bushes.[20]

Pan, the deity representing nature and the expression of natural force, appears as a major agent in the story 'The Music on the Hill'. Embodying the ambivalence of desire he is described as both beautiful and cruel: 'across a thick tangle of undergrowth a boy's face was scowling at her, brown and beautiful, with unutterably evil eyes'.[21] When he seeks revenge on a girl who has stolen grapes from his shrine the outcome is presented as not just terrible but also stirring and in some way cathartic:

> The antlers drove straight at her breast, the acrid smell of the hunted animal was in her nostrils, but her eyes were filled with the horror of something she saw other than her oncoming death. And in her ears rang the echo of a boy's laughter, golden and equivocal.[22]

For Saki, the beast is in some respects more admirable than tame, civilised man. He suggests a side of man which has become repressed in civilised society, a part of his nature which is now 'unseen' and unknown but not necessarily harmful. The ideal seems to be a unification of the potential of the wild and the pretensions of the civilised – a unification as yet found only in the life of the humble cat:

> It is, indeed, no small triumph to have combined the untrammelled liberty of primeval savagery with the luxury which only a highly developed civilisation can command; to be lapped in the soft stuffs that commerce has gathered from the far ends of the world . . . and withal to be a free son of nature.[23]

Saki's indictment of human civilisation and his celebration of untrammelled 'nature' indicates a link with Nietzsche, the bulk of whose writings had been translated into English by 1909. The title of Saki's 1914 collection, *Beasts and Super-Beasts*, overtly suggests a connection, for the title is clearly an echo of, or an improvement on, that of Shaw's Nietzschean comedy *Man and Superman* (1903). Neither Shaw nor Saki followed Nietzsche's philosophy in a detailed or systematic fashion but the main drift of his thought is reflected in their work. For Saki the emphasis is on the negative side of Nietzschean philosophy: his scepticism over 'normal' civilised man's estimate of himself is very Nietzschean. This theme is powerfully expressed in two well-known stories, 'Tobermory' and 'Gabriel-Ernest'. In the first, a domestic cat miraculously learns to speak and demolishes the pretensions of a group of sophisticated house-party guests:

> Even in a delicate situation like the present, Agnes Resker could not endure to remain too long in the background.
> 'Why did I ever come down here?' she asked dramatically.
> Tobermory immediately accepted the opening.
> 'Judging by what you said to Mrs Cornett on the croquet-lawn yesterday, you were out for food. You described the Blemleys as the dullest people to stay with that you knew.'[24]

In 'Gabriel-Ernest' a young boy embodies the muffled, hidden duality of human nature. Neat, charming and civilised by day, 'sweet' according to his adopted aunt, the boy metamorphoses dramatically into a wolf at nightfall, 'a large wolf, blackish in colour, with gleaming fangs and cruel, yellow eyes'.

'The Story-Teller' can be taken as a tale emblematic of Saki's work. In this story about story-telling he takes very far the proposition, implicit in the rest of his work, that conventional behaviour is not always well adjusted to the real demands of existence. Two conflicting tales are told to an 'innocent' audience of young children. One – the conventional one – tells of a girl who was 'so good' that she was saved from a mad bull by rescuers who 'admired her moral character'. The second tells of a little girl who was so exceptionally good that she won three medals for good conduct; however their chinking betrayed her when she was hiding from a hungry wolf seeking his supper, and she was devoured 'to the last morsel'. The keynote of the second story is struck with the phrase 'horribly good' which the narrator applies to the girl. This instantly arouses the interest of the listening children and they subsequently express unconditional approval of the second story:
' "It is the *only* beautiful story I have ever heard," said Cyril.'[25] This

story within a story is a miniature of the kind of 'unmasking' story produced by Saki himself: the disturbing 'truth' it contains is validated by the response of the children.

In his short stories Saki frequently uses the frame of the practical joke for the purpose of unmasking, revealing something hidden beneath the surfaces of life. In his essay on Saki, Graham Greene comments that jokes, to be worth writing about, 'must bring forth something that is concealed or hidden'. Freud also linked the joke with the discovery of hidden meaning. In *Jokes and their Relation to the Unconscious* he related this kind of discovery to the operation of the unconscious:

> What happens is not that we know a moment beforehand what joke we are going to make, and that all it needs is to be clothed in words. We have an indefinable feeling, rather, which I can best compare with an *'absence'*, a sudden release of intellectual tension, and then all at once the joke is there – as a rule ready-clothed in words.[26]

As readers of Saki's stories we are placed in the position of the 'listener', the necessary second person who hears the joke (Freud points out that a joke is not perceived as funny by its author until it is told to someone else). To the reader, the witty 'trick ending' of a Saki story thus brings the pleasure of discovery: something is added to our perception of the world of the tale. The 'surprise ending' of the Saki story 'The Open Window' can usefully be compared in this respect with the endings of two celebrated stories, Maupassant's 'La Parure' and O. Henry's 'The Furnished Room'. Both these stories have been condemned for providing a final twist which adds nothing to the moral world of the tale. In 'La Parure' the lateness of the discovery that the crucial diamonds are made of paste does not accord with our perception of the shrewd nature of the husband and wife who have borrowed them, and the discovery cannot be said to have any moral or thematic relevance except in so far as it underlines a point which the author has already made about the vanity of appearance. In 'The Furnished Room', O. Henry makes a landlady withhold information about a girl who has committed suicide in one of her rooms. A young man arrives in search of the girl, rents the same room, and because the landlady has told him that no girl fitting his description has passed that way kills himself in a fit of depression. As Ian Reid has pointed out in a discussion of this story,[27] the withheld information is for the reader's benefit only, giving only an illusion of significance. Presumably the young man's reaction would have been the same whether or not the truth had been revealed to him.

In 'The Open Window' a young man pays a courtesy call in a neighbourhood in which he is taking a 'rest cure'. The lady to whom he has a letter of introduction is out and he converses instead with her niece. Diverting the conversation from her visitor's ailments, the niece tells the story of a tragedy which occurred in her family three years ago. Her uncle went out shooting with her aunt's two young brothers and the three never returned. The aunt still believes that one day they will come back and for that reason a french window always stands open in readiness for them, even on an October afternoon.

Dusk falls; the aunt arrives and begins to chatter about her husband and her brothers, her eyes 'constantly straying' to the open window in the room. Suddenly she breaks off. The visitor catches a glimpse of terror in the niece's eyes, swings round and sees 'In the deepening twilight three figures . . . walking across the lawn towards the window. . . . Noiselessly they neared the house.' Precipitately he breaks away from the room and quits the house: we are left to discover that the niece has been playing a practical joke on him – the story of the tragedy was invented as is the story she now begins to tell about her strange visitor. The story ends 'Romance at short notice was her speciality.'

An atmosphere of chill and gloom is sustained so effectively that the reader is by no means aware of the trick that is being played on the protagonist – and on him. The opening of the story prepares us for the intrusion of the supernatural, but not for the calm self-possession of the niece, so that we are not prepared for her bold takeover of the story. The joke she plays thus has two functions: it exposes the vain self-absorption and nervous debility of the protagonist and also exposes the complacency of the reader's expectations. The girl story-teller is another figure of the artist, a fabricator who bases her fables on her insight into others, who works for their confusion and our final illumination.

The practical joke works towards a moment of exposure in many of Saki's stories, 'The Quince Tree', 'Fur', 'The Yarkand Manner', 'The Phantom Luncheon', for example. For Saki the joke reveals a hidden function of character or behaviour, and its effect is cathartic and corrective. The joke, of course, is also used as a frame in some stories by Kipling, especially among the early Indian tales, though it also figures in such late stories as 'Dayspring Mishandled'. However, Kipling uses the practical joke less incisively than Saki: the emphasis is on the joke as a retributive rather than as a corrective device. The excellence of 'Dayspring Mishandled' lies precisely in the fact that the main character comes to repudiate his elaborate practical joke, realising that his motive for devising it has been one of revenge rather than proper regard for the welfare of his victim.

Perhaps no story-teller besides O. Henry has been so reviled as Somerset Maugham. Yet he remains obstinately there, incapable of being dismissed by anyone interested in the forms and distinctions of the short story. His inclusion in this study of tale-tellers could be justified simply because he is one of the most widely read of all English writers. More precise critical justification for a study of his work is provided by William Trevor. In an article on Maugham he writes:

> The one thing Maugham was *not* was second-rate: he was fifth-rate at his worst, and at his best he achieved the greatness that Mr Raphael[28] denies him. He remains, in fact, that strange – and quite rare – literary phenomenon, the writer who is both bad and brilliant. No twentieth-century short-story anthology makes much sense if Maugham isn't represented. 'The Hairless Mexican', 'The Kite', 'The Colonel's Lady', 'The Door of Opportunity' all are superb – and there are many others to challenge them.[29]

Before turning to the short story Maugham was a successful dramatist, and much of his best work reflects this earlier preoccupation. His most successful stories are told by a first-person narrator with a flair for dramatic presentation, able to set rapidly in motion events and character, without the strong commitment to authenticating background detail typical of the omniscient narrator in the novel. The stories tend, however, to be relatively lengthy and may approach the quality which has been described by Mary Doyle Springer[30] as being appropriate to the novella form: they are often 'degenerative tragedies' tracing the decay of a single individual over a period of time.

Maugham admired the dramatic quality which he perceived in the work of Maupassant:

> Such an author as Maupassant does not copy life; he arranges it in order the better to interest, excite and surprise. He does not aim at a transcription of life but at a dramatisation of it.[31]

He similarly 'arranges' the elements of his stories to heighten motion and movement so that the lines of dramatic action stand out hard and clear, predominating over character and mood. The stories display, in Roland Barthes' useful terminology, a marked dominance of 'functions' over 'indices', so that 'units of meaning which relate to "doing" predominate over those concerned with "being" '.[32]

The tragic aspect of Maugham's art seldom reaches its full potential. It could well be argued that this is due to *over*-dependence on a dramatic method. Maugham can concentrate too exclusively on the arresting incident or sequence, savouring its extraordinary quality without paying sufficient attention to causal relationships and character motivation. An interesting example of this can be found in the story 'Rain', in which Maugham focuses on the promising situation of a hell-fire preacher's reversion to sin, but fails to ground this reversion sufficiently in character and mood: the gesture towards a Freudian explanation of repression seems inadequate. In this sense Maugham does not progress far beyond the original notes for the story, in which the juxtaposition of the missionary and 'Sadie Thompson', and the idea of repression are already present:

> Mrs W. told me that her husband was a medical missionary, and as his district (the Gilberts) consisted of widely separated islands, he frequently had to go long journeys by canoe. The sea was often rough and his journeys were not without danger. . . . She spoke of the depravity of the natives in a voice nothing could hush, but with a vehement, unctuous horror . . .

> Miss Thompson. Plump, pretty in a coarse fashion, perhaps not more than twenty-seven: she wore a white dress and a large white hat, and large white boots from which her calves, in white cotton stockings, bulged.[33]

'The Colonel's Lady' is a more successful story because in it character is developed beyond the bare minimum needed for the telling of a sensational tale. The colonel's wife of the title has had an affair with a younger man. Many years after it has ended she celebrates it in a book of verse which has an overnight success, becoming a publishing sensation. However, the wife is no stereotyped adulteress. She is convincingly presented as a middle-aged woman of sensibility, considerately playing down the fame her book has brought her in order to promote the comfort and maintain the *amour propre* of her husband. Similarly, he is no 'Colonel Blimp' figure: when he discovers the truth behind his wife's literary achievement he determines to make no allusion to it – painful though silence is to him – for fear of unnecessarily distressing his wife.

A link which Maugham insists on in 'The Colonel's Lady' and in other stories is that between artistic creation and repression. It would seem that he endorses a Freudian theory of art as the sublimated expression of repressed emotion. The idea links up with the image of the artist or writer as the pathologist of human emotion which seems to underlie his work.

Maugham followed Kipling's use of an exotic setting to intensify the reader's apprehension of exotic or rare emotion. The unusual, the extreme – particularly when found hidden beneath the surface of everyday life – are recurrent themes. In 'The Letter', for example, adultery and murder are studied in a setting of deceptive mildness:

> Her face was no longer human, it was distorted with cruelty, and rage and pain. You would never have thought that this quiet, refined woman was capable of such fiendish passion. . . . Then they heard a voice calling from another room, a loud, friendly, cheerful voice. It was Mrs Joyce.
> 'Come along, Leslie darling, your room's ready. You must be dropping with sleep.'
> Mrs Crosbie's features gradually composed themselves. Those passions, so clearly delineated, were smoothed away.[34]

Sexual jealousy is the theme of 'The Letter' and 'The Force of Circumstance'. 'The Book Bag' is yet another story of extreme human feeling, in this case an incestuous love leading to suicide. 'The Pool' is a story of a destructive and degrading passion which again ends in suicide. Maugham saw himself primarily as a pathologist of human feeling and is seldom concerned to portray 'normal' feeling and response: his interest is in abnormal or unbalanced states produced by unusual circumstances and pressures. His stance in studying such states follows a clinical model, and it is perhaps not irrelevant to remember that, like Chekhov, he had first trained as a doctor. His detached, objective prose style is specifically modelled on that of Maupassant.

Though Maugham is famed for his story-telling abilities, in fact he rarely uses the surprise or trick ending. His plots are dramatic, even melodramatic, but the reader always senses what the conclusion must be at a point about half-way through the story. From this point on he watches the unfolding of the narrative with a kind of detached fascination, assimilating to himself something of the author's clinically objective stance. The reader's greatest involvement in the story will tend to be with the narrator, and this is one of the distinctive features of Maugham's art. His preference for a first-person narrator is well known. In the preface to the collected edition of his stories he explained the usefulness of such a narrator-figure to him. His explanation also sheds light on the role of the first-person narrator in the work of Kipling and Saki. A first-person narrator ensures credibility – 'when someone tells you what he states happened to himself you are more likely to believe that he is telling the truth than when he tells you what happened to somebody else'. A first-person narrator guarantees the truth of the action, creating an illusion which it is particularly important to establish quickly in the short story form. Such a narrator must not, however, be identified with the author: he is a character like any other and he may, as Maugham points out in his preface, also be the hero. Most interestingly, Maugham writes that the use of the first-person narrator has 'the merit from the story-teller's point of view that he need only tell you what he knows for a fact and can leave to your imagination what he doesn't or couldn't know'. Here the emphasis on 'fact' is disingenuous, for as Maugham himself has written in *Points of View* (1958) 'to copy life has never been the artist's business'. The artist 'sacrifices verisimilitude' to the effect he wants to produce, and, to this end, will manipulate naturalism as an artistic convention just like any other. Maugham's restriction of his role, however, to the presentation of 'facts', has wider implications. It turns out indeed to be an appeal to the imagination of the reader, an invitation to the reader to join the writer in the creation of the text. Maugham echoes Poe's suggestion of the particularly close involvement of the reader in the short story form. Close reading of his work shows that it is indeed through understatement and omission that Maugham engages the interest of his reader: it is this quality which marks his best work. An example is 'The Kite', a story of a possessive mother and an unsuccessful marriage.

The main actors in this drama are efficiently characterised at the outset. Mrs Sunbury, the hero's mother, is 'very refined', neat, sharp and over-possessive. The father is small, quiet and self-effacing – 'Every morning for twenty-four years Samuel Sunbury had taken the same train to the City, except of course on Sundays and during his fortnight's holiday at the seaside.' Herbert, the son, a good-looking child, is rigorously brought up to be 'like a little gentleman'. Into this exclusive world walks Betty, an energetic young woman who prevails on Herbert with her 'red lips' and permanent waves, becoming his fiancée and then his wife.

The ensuing battle for possession of Herbert is lifted above the level of anecdote or farce by Maugham's reticence. He moves adeptly at this point in the story from the level of analysis to that of symbol. The course of the actors' feelings and desires is presented in dramatic form through a battle for possession of a kite. Flying this kite in the park is a hobby for both Herbert and his parents. Significantly it is a childish activity, deprecated by Betty who 'says it's a kid's game anyway and I ought to be ashamed of myself, flying a kite at my age'. Both Herbert and his parents are immature, and the kite figures a childish dream of escape from the world, a refusal to admit Freud's 'reality principle'. At the same time, the sense of freedom given by the kite is not undercut or devalued by the author: 'the kite took the air beautifully, and as he watched it rise his heart was filled with exultation. It was grand to see that little black thing soaring so sweetly.'[35] Betty's final destruction of the kite may seem inevitable, but is not endorsed by simple-minded psychologising.

Maugham's work illustrates particularly clearly the uses to which a first-person narrator can be put in short fiction. First-person narration has the ring of authenticity and enables the author to establish the validity of his story in a short space of time. It also offers a 'natural' pretext for the omissions and temporal dislocations which are common features of short fiction. Moreover the absence of omniscient narration and reliance on a single narrative voice offers scope for a more direct and dramatically charged relationship between reader and writer. In this respect Kipling, Saki and Maugham were all, to a greater or lesser degree, pioneers of direct, colloquial narrative style in the short story.

Kipling, Saki and Maugham each extended the range of the short story. Only Maugham was directly influenced by Freud, whose *Interpretation of Dreams* was not translated into English until 1913. However, the pre-Freudian Edwardian era was still an age of unmasking, of seeking the skeleton hidden in the Victorian family cupboard. This spirit is reflected in the themes and structure of the stories of these writers. All three use the short story to unmask, exploiting the fact that the story usually has only one peripeteiac moment, which draws its impact from isolation. Saki and Maugham in particular exploit the self-consciously fictive element in short story telling, building their stories around façades which are later dismantled or questioned. Kipling, less sure of the existence of an empirical 'reality' behind any façade, may invoke the supernatural to undermine our sense of an achieved, final reality in a story. More perhaps than any other short story writer, Kipling has the ability continually to change his point of reference, so that his stories always seem to be, in Borges's words, 'tokens of something else'.[36]

3 Moments of Being: Modernist Short Fiction

The modernist short story grew out of the psychological sketch of the 1890s. Like the psychological sketch it is more properly called a type of short fiction for one of its leading characteristics is a rejection of 'story' in the accepted sense. Modernist short fiction writers distrusted the well-wrought tale for a variety of reasons. Most importantly they argued that the pleasing shape and coherence of the traditional short story represented a falsification of the discrete and heterogeneous nature of experience. Such stories relied on a too-ready and facile identification of causal relationships. And the achieved and rounded finality of the tale was distrusted, for 'story' in this sense seemed to convey the misleading notion of something finished, absolute, and wholly understood.

The emphasis of modernist short fiction was on a single moment of intense or significant experience. It was not generally thought desirable to break down experience into smaller units still, for example units of language: such a breakdown could theoretically proceed infinitely, leading to a complete degradation of meaning and value. So the 'epiphany' or 'blazing moment' came to form the structural core of modernist short fiction (and, it will be argued, of many modernist novels). This stress on the fleeting moment is consistent with the prevailingly relativist philosophy inherited by modernist writers.

It was because of a general interest in the 'significant moment' that short fiction came to prominence in the modernist period. The short form is clearly suited to the presentation of a single incident, with a central 'moment of significance'. It is *the* form by which to convey 'mood' and in consequence it usually has a time-scale no longer than a single day. In general terms one might say that in the early twentieth century the unit of fiction moved from the year to the day – one may compare the traditional time-span of *Emma* and *The Ambassadors* with that of *Ulysses*, *Mrs Dalloway*, *Death in the Afternoon*. Experiments in the form of the short story, which Elizabeth Bowen has called the 'ideal reflector' of the day, played a crucial part in this transition.

The notion of character was also undergoing change and this shift too can be related to the rise of the story. The idea of character as a fixed and fully knowable identity – what Lawrence famously called the 'old stable ego of the character' – was abandoned by many writers of the post-Freudian era. In its stead came a sense of external personality as an ever-changing, infinitely adjustable 'envelope' surrounding the real self, neither ego nor id, but a transcendent essence rarely felt or apprehended either by a given individual or by those around him. It became the task of the writer to express his sense of the tensions between external and internal identity and to reveal those moments when one most nearly approaches awareness of his inner self. The short story, or fiction, is perhaps better suited, formally, to such a concept of character than the novel. By reason of its brevity and the ambivalence which it can maintain towards past and future it may better embody the twentieth-century sense of the opacity and elusiveness of human character. The short story or fiction may present a discrete moment or unit of experience, with suggestions of possible links with past and future events and experiences, but an ambivalent attitude towards these links can be maintained for they will always extend beyond the confines of the story.

Modernist short fiction was adapted to the expression of a relativist philosophy, and this bias is further reflected in a characteristic narrative strategy. Writers such as Joyce, Virginia Woolf and Katherine Mansfield were among the first to develop, initially in their short fiction, the 'indirect free' style of narration in which the voice of the narrator is modulated so that it appears to merge with that of a character of the fiction. The author thus avoids direct omniscient commentary and remains more closely within the orbit of particular characters and their experience. Close reading of these writers will demonstrate the operation and effect of this narrative style.

Our understanding of modernist short fiction must finally be influenced by our awareness of its role in a particular comtemporary literary context. In the modernist period the short form came to have, for the first time in its history, a status almost equivalent to that of the novel. Many prose writers began their career with short fiction and continued to find the form congenial. It is indeed noticeable that several modernist novels had their origin in a short prose piece, the most famous example being *Ulysses*, first conceived as a story for Joyce's collection *Dubliners* to be entitled 'Mr Hunter's Day'. One could argue that there is a sense in which *Ulysses* as it now exists is an extended short fiction. It pivots on a single 'event', the encounter between Stephen and Bloom which takes place about two thirds of the way through the book. The rest of *Ulysses* consists of an extended briefing for this meeting, designed to give us its context without stepping outside its terms of reference. Joyce thus seeks to embody in the novel form a relativism more commonly found in the short story. Some of the novels of Hemingway are, it can be argued, similarly extensions or extrapolations from the base form of the short fiction. Virginia Woolf recorded the moment when she found the method of *Jacob's Room* in the concept of her previous short stories 'taking hands and dancing'. This argument leads to the point at which it begins to seem that the modernist short fiction is the paradigmatic form of early twentieth-century literature, best able to express a fragmented sensibility. The aptness of the form has been well described by Nadine Gordimer:

> Each of us has a thousand lives and a novel gives a character only one. *For the sake of the form.* The novelist may juggle about with chronology and throw narrative overboard; all the time his characters have the reader by the hand, there is a consistency of relationship throughout the experience that cannot and does not convey the quality of human life, where contact is more like the flash of fire-flies, in and out, now here, now there, in darkness. Short story writers see by the light of the flash; theirs is the art of the only thing one can be sure of – the present moment. Ideally, they have learned to do without explanation of what went before, and what happens beyond this point.[1]

This sheds some light on the widespread use of the short fiction form by the early modernist writers, and their elaboration of this form in the novel. The conventional novel is above all else cohesive, as Gordimer suggests. The great modernist texts of the early years of the century – *Nostromo*, *Ulysses*, *To the Lighthouse*, *The Waves* – are distinguished by their lack of cohesiveness on the level of narrative, their heterogeneous, unstable quality. They are not like the fashionable experimental novels castigated by Gordimer, which are 'juggling about' with chronology and so on, but exist rather as montages or collages of short stories, interlocking but not merging within a deliberately arbitrary frame. Or as Katherine Mansfield put it when describing Dorothy Richardson's *Pilgrimage*, the novels are 'nests of stories' which continually recede, eluding formal capture within the confines of narrative.

The short fiction of Joyce, Virginia Woolf and Katherine Mansfield can be directly related to the 'plotless' story of the 1890s and to the prose poem of the same period. All three writers acknowledged the influence of Symbolism on their work, and in modernist short fiction as much as in modernist poetry the assumptions of Symbolism flowered. However, the complementary tradition of realism also influenced the apparently 'plotless' quality of Joyce's fiction. A Zola-esque interest in 'the trivial' can be detected in his well-known definition of the epiphany:

> This triviality made him think of collecting many such moments together in a book of epiphanies. By an epiphany he meant a sudden spiritual manifestation, whether in the vulgarity of speech or of gesture or in a memorable phase of the mind itself. He believed that it was for the man of letters to record these epiphanies with extreme care, seeing that they themselves are the most delicate and evanescent of moments.[2]

A conflict between realist and symbolist modes can indeed be located in Joyce's early short fiction and is betrayed by a curious juxtaposition of terms in this passage in which Joyce confounds the 'man of letters' and he who 'records'. Joyce implies that the writer both creates and reports the reality which we see embodied in the text, and the distinction between the reality of language and reality 'out there' is thus elided. This epistemological confusion is mirrored in the unstable narrative forms of *Dubliners*. Throughout 'Eveline', for example, we are unsure whether the perceptions evoked are those of the girl herself or the narrator. A brief quotation will illustrate this hovering narrative technique, mingling third person and indirect free forms apparently at random:

> But in her new home, in a distant unknown country, it would not be like that. Then she would be married – she, Eveline. People would treat her with respect then. She would not be treated as her mother had been. Even now, though she was over nineteen, she sometimes felt herself in danger of her father's violence. . . . And now she had nobody to protect her. Ernest was dead and Harry, who

was in the church decorating business, was nearly always down somewhere in the country. Besides, the invariable squabble for money on Saturday nights had begun to weary her unspeakably.[3]

Joyce's short stories are characterised by deletions which work with his manipulation of narrative point of view to enhance our sense of the 'unknowability' of human character and experience. The most obvious deletion is that of the conventional beginning and ending of a story. This technique, used by both Joyce and Katherine Mansfield, has usually been considered Chekhovian but it is as likely that these writers adopted it from the work of English story-writers of the nineties – for example Wilde, Symons and George Moore. The abruptness with which the texts of *Dubliners* begin and end appears to reflect the author's reluctance to follow conventional structures of meaning. Joyce's objection to 'story' in this sense was expressed in an early fiction review:

This little volume is a collection of stories dealing chiefly with Indian life. The reader will find the first five stories – the adventures of Prince Aga Mirza – the more entertaining part of the book, if he is to any extent interested in tales of Indian magic. The appeal, however, of such stories is, frankly, sensational. . . . The people who regulate the demand for fiction are being day by day so restricted by the civilisation they have helped to build up that they are not unlike the men of Mandeville's time, for whom enchantments, and monsters, and deeds of prowess were so liberally purveyed.[4]

The forms of the 'sensational' are closely linked with the forms and restrictions of contemporary life.

In *Ulysses* Joyce falls back on story, on myth and the marvellous, but having 're-told', however elliptically, the story of the *Odyssey* he omits its conclusion, leaving critics dangling inelegantly in mid-air speculating about the future of the Blooms' marriage. The inconclusive structure of *Ulysses* can be found on a smaller scale in many of the stories of *Dubliners*, for example 'A Little Cloud', which resembles *Ulysses* in subject matter. This short fiction concerns a single day in the life of a young middle-aged man. We are dropped into the story with the deictic sentence: 'Eight years before he had seen his friend off at the North Wall and wished him God-speed.'[5] We follow Little Chandler through his reunion with an old friend Gallagher, his late return home and his re-appraisal of his home and family. We learn little about this anti-hero in factual material terms, little about his past or possible future. In his marriage Little Chandler seems to waver between the poles of sentimental affection and alienation, and we can hardly tell from the conclusion of the story what will be the outcome of his reconsideration of his wife:

> Little Chandler felt his cheeks suffused with shame and he stood back out of the lamplight. He listened while the paroxysm of the child's sobbing grew less and less; and tears of remorse started to his eyes.[6]

The technique of deletion reflects the thematic concerns of *Dubliners*. 'The Sisters' perhaps shows Joyce's most radical use of this technique. Most striking is the displacement which takes place in the title of the story, in which a 'false' subject is substituted for the real one, which is the story of 'the brother', Father Flynn the priest. 'The Sisters' is also characterised by frequent use of ellipses, as in the following passage:

> 'No, I wouldn't say he was exactly ... but there was something queer ... there was something uncanny about him. I'll tell you my opinion ...'
> He began to puff at his pipe, no doubt arranging his opinion in his mind. Tiresome old fool! When we knew him first he used to be rather interesting, talking of faints and worms; but I soon grew tired of him and his endless stories about the distillery.
> 'I have my own theory about it,' he said. 'I think it was one of those ... peculiar cases ... But it's hard to say ...'[7]

The ellipsis signals something odd, outside normal experience – the 'something' being the estranged sensibility of the priest. With reference to this state Joyce places us as readers in the same position as the character-observers: like them we only half-comprehend, are compelled to guess and piece together the man's story from odd images and half-finished phrases:

> 'It was that chalice he broke ... That was the beginning of it. Of course, they say it was all right, that it contained nothing, I mean. But still ... They say it was the boy's fault. But poor James was so nervous, God be merciful to him!'
> 'And was that it?' said my aunt. 'I heard something ...'[8]

'The Sisters' focuses clearly on a theme which underlies many of the stories of *Dubliners*. Its chief concern is the elusive quality of knowledge and the story itself is structured rather like a maze, built of information and misinformation. The boy at the centre is surrounded by the deceptions and suppressions of adults. He himself has already learnt to protect himself from others by dissimulation – 'I knew that I was under observation, so I continued eating as if the news had not interested me.' The external world is puzzling and impenetrable to him – for example he cannot reconcile the priest's death and the bright sunlight of the day following it. Surrounded by information which he cannot order, he has to learn to attend to the relations between appearances and discovers too that knowledge is disclosed as much through the interstices of language as through that which is actually spoken. So he tries to piece together the truth about his friend the priest, finding that he must pay attention to silence as well as to that which is said – 'I puzzled my head to extract meaning from his unfinished sentences' as he says, referring to the speeches of 'Old Cotter'. Yet the 'truth' about the priest eludes him because there are irrecoverable gaps in his knowledge. The boy cannot remember 'the end' of his puzzling dream about the priest, and in exactly the same manner the ending of 'The Sisters' is elided for us as readers, leaving us with a sense of baffled and halted perception:

> Eliza resumed:
> 'Wide-awake and laughing-like to himself ... So then, of course, when they saw that, that made them think that there was something gone wrong with him ...'[9]

All this would seem to lead to the conclusion that Joyce presents in *Dubliners* a strong sense of the indeterminacy of human experience and of the relativity of truth. Yet, one remembers, Joyce spoke of 'recording' his epiphanies and he also spoke of the need for a style of 'scrupulous meanness' for his stories. Both terms suggest an empirical ideal at odds with the idea of relativism. It could be argued that empiricism and relativism co-exist rather uneasily in *Dubliners*, except in the last, most celebrated story, 'The Dead'. 'The Dead' is cast in indirect free form from the opening sentence which reflects the thoughts of 'Lily': 'Lily, the caretaker's daughter, was literally run off her feet. . . . It was well for her she had not to attend to the ladies also.'[10] The style is adapted to the thoughts and habits of the characters. The joint consciousness of the Misses Morkan, for example, is suggested through flat repetitive rhythms:

This was Mary Jane's idea and she had also suggested apple sauce for the goose, but Aunt Kate had said that plain roast goose without any apple sauce had always been good enough for her and she hoped she might never eat worse.[11]

The substance of the fiction is refracted through the consciousness of Gabriel Conroy, an internal exile in the world of Dublin. The style is attuned to Gabriel's literary but also provincial consciousness – it is easy to miss the specifically Irish locutions with which Joyce endows a man who is no aspirant Dedalus:

Was she sincere? Had she really any life of her own behind all her propagandism? There had never been any ill-feeling between them until that night. It unnerved him to think that she would be at the supper-table, looking up at him while he spoke with her critical quizzing eyes. Perhaps she would not be sorry to see him fail in his speech.[12]

The story culminates with a famous meditation inspired by the story of Gabriel's wife's love for another man:

Generous tears filled Gabriel's eyes. He had never felt that himself towards any woman, but he knew that such a feeling must be love. The tears gathered more thickly in his eyes and in the partial darkness he imagined he saw the form of a young man standing under a dripping tree. Other forms were near. His soul had approached that region where dwell the vast hosts of the dead. He was conscious of, but could not apprehend, their wayward and flickering existence. His own identity was fading out into a grey impalpable world: the solid world itself, which these dead had one time reared and lived in, was dissolving and dwindling.[13]

The language is no longer Gabriel's, but nor is it that of a narrator firmly distinguished from the characters of the fiction. The perceptions expressed seem to grow out of the rendered experience of the characters: the conclusion does not step outside the terms of reference of their common sensibility, and so 'The Dead' preserves its narrative integrity.

The narrative has this integrity because Joyce avoids the presence of an omniscient narrator but he does not in practice relinquish any of his control over the narrative. He simply directs it in more covert ways through the organisation of the text, through juxtapositions of characters, events, images and thought patterns. Thus 'The Dead' gives the impression of an indeterminacy which is by definition not possible for the writer, whose decision to write in itself indicates that he has placed a meaning and value on his material.

The stories of *Dubliners* are structured around an epiphany which is often 'false' in the sense that expectations are set up in relation to the crucial moment which are then denied. The stories 'Araby', 'Eveline', 'Counterparts', 'Clay', 'Ivy Day in the Committee Room' all centre on moments of disappointment or denial which do not merely embody, as critics have suggested, Joyce's sense of the frustration or 'paralysis' inherent in Dublin life. For such a movement towards denial is found not only in the stories of Joyce but also in many of those of Katherine Mansfield and Hemingway and it constitutes in itself a salient feature of modernist short fiction. It reflects again the thrust of this fiction against what were felt to be the trite and outworn forms of the exotic or romantic. Joyce's 'Araby' singles out the blandishments of the exotic, suggested in terms which remind us of the 'enchantments' of Mandeville or perhaps of Kipling. These suggestions are indeed said to cast an 'enchantment' over the narrator which is broken only by the slow fiasco of his visit to the bazaar. The story ends on a critical note of self-reproach, the narrator seeing himself as 'a creature driven and derided by vanity' – even his sense of his folly involves him in vanity and self-delusion.

The epiphany or moment of vision tends to be more positive in the short fictions of Virginia Woolf. It is important as a structural focus in both her short fictions and her novels. The short fiction of Virginia Woolf is intimately connected with her novels, but has received comparatively little critical attention. According to Leonard Woolf, she was in the habit of writing short stories 'all through her life', with two periods of particular intensity in early 1920 and again in 1925. During the first period she had just finished the long and essentially traditional novel *Night and Day*. This had been adversely reviewed by, among others, Katherine Mansfield. Virginia Woolf was much influenced by Katherine Mansfield's approach to fiction at about this time,[14] and it seems likely that her acknowledged rival's review of *Night and Day* was at least one stimulus which moved Virginia Woolf further towards both experiment and short fiction in the years immediately preceding the publication of *Jacob's Room* (1922).

T. S. Eliot described the short pieces collected in *Monday or Tuesday* (1921) as 'experimental prose'. They seem today more experimental than the novels, linking quite closely with the work of Gertrude Stein in *Tender Buttons*. An example might be this passage from 'A Haunted House':

> But they had found it in the drawing-room. Not that one could ever see them. The window panes reflected apples, reflected roses; all the leaves were green in the glass. If they moved in the drawing-room, the apple only turned its yellow side. Yet, the moment after, if the door was opened, spread about the floor, hung upon the walls, pendant from the ceiling – what? My hands were empty. The shadow of a thrush crossed the carpet; from the deepest wells of silence the wood pigeon drew its bubble of sound. 'Safe, safe, safe,' the pulse of the house beat softly. 'The treasure buried; the room ...' the pulse stopped short. Oh, was that the buried treasure?[15]

In *Tender Buttons*, Gertrude Stein wanted to 'abolish' the noun as an arbitrary signifier and to put in its place many associational words carrying 'sound sense', which would together approach more nearly the essential quality of the thing described. This is also Virginia Woolf's method in her short fiction. In 'A Haunted House' the author patiently evokes a value which she does not name until the closing of the story as 'the light in the heart'. This evocation is cumulative, achieved through repetition of imagery and an apparent redundancy of verbal and adverbial description. An element of strong rhythmical patterning can be seen in one phrase which occurs no less than six times, each time slightly modified:

the pulse of the house beat softly
the pulse stopped short
the pulse of the house beat gladly
gently knocking like the pulse of a heart
the heart of the house beats proudly
the pulse of the house beats wildly

The value of 'the light in the heart' is defined both by presence and absence. It is set against images of joy and fulfilment – 'the wood pigeons bubbling with content', 'the apples . . . in the loft' – and then against barrenness and darkness – 'But the trees spun darkness for a wandering beam of sun', 'The wind drives straightly', 'Wild beams of moonlight cross both floor and wall'. Presence and absence intertwine most tellingly in the final paragraph, when tangible light is shown to be imaginary and the intangible to be real:

> 'Long years–' he sighs. 'Again you found me.' 'Here,' she murmurs, 'sleeping; in the garden reading; laughing, rolling apples in the loft. Here we left our treasure–' Stooping, their light lifts the lids upon my eyes. 'Safe! safe! safe!' the pulse of the house beats wildly. Waking, I cry 'Oh, is this *your* buried treasure? The light in the heart.'[16]

In 'Monday or Tuesday' Virginia Woolf similarly leads the reader towards a perception she is reluctant to name directly. The sketch is predicated on the assumption of an inherent opposition between the diversity and indeterminacy of human experience and the felt human need for order and a sense of absolute truth:

> Desiring truth, awaiting it, laboriously distilling a few words, for ever desiring – (a cry starts to the left, another to the right. Wheels strike divergently. Omnibuses conglomerate in conflict) – for ever desiring – (the clock asseverates with twelve distinct strokes that it is midday; light sheds gold scales; children swarm) – for ever desiring truth. Red is the dome; coins hang on the trees; smoke trails from the chimneys; bark, shout, cry 'Iron for sale' – and truth?[17]

Towards the close of this fiction, or prose poem, the act of reading (or writing) is summoned up and set against both the intuition of order and the experience of disorder:

> Now to recollect by the fireside on the white square of marble. From ivory depths words rising shed their blackness, blossom and penetrate. Fallen the book; in the flame, in the smoke, in the momentary sparks – or now voyaging, the marble square pendant, minarets beneath and the Indian seas, while space rushes blue and stars glint – truth? or now, content with closeness?
> Lazy and indifferent the heron returns; the sky veils her stars; then bares them.[18]

Words flower on an empty page and solidify into presence, 'blossom and penetrate', encompassing both the 'flame and smoke' of confusion and the 'glint' of truth. The closing lines of the story mime the final truth without directly stating it. We must not be 'content with closeness' (closure); the text refuses to seal itself up and we are left with a sense of endless dialectic between two aspects of human experience.

This technique of circling round a truth or intuition which the author is reluctant to name and thereby to limit also characterises Virginia Woolf's novels. In their wider structure we must in the same way look to the images and organisation of the text in order to discover the 'buried' (unnamed) 'treasure' within.

This fundamental structural movement in Virginia Woolf's fiction may be connected with her feminism, her determination to be a female writer (the 'first great lesson' for a woman writer, she wrote in *A Room of One's Own*, is to forget 'that she is a woman, so that her pages [are] full of that curious sexual quality which comes only when sex is unconscious of itself').[19] It can be argued that in general, women tend to have more immediate access than men to 'inner speech', as opposed to outer, socialised speech.[20] The syntax of inner speech is simplified by the elimination of the subject for we already 'know what we are thinking about'. What is left is predication. Both Virginia Woolf and Gertrude Stein show a marked tendency to avoid the substantive and to recreate substantive meanings by imagery and sensory particularisation.

That Virginia Woolf's short fiction provided her with the structure of her mature novels is clearly indicated in her notes for *Jacob's Room* (1922). In a diary entry of 1920 she wrote, just after finishing 'An Unwritten Novel' (one of the fictions for *Monday or Tuesday*):

> Whether I'm sufficiently mistress of things – that's the doubt; but conceive (?) *Mark on the Wall*, *K.G.* and *Unwritten Novel* taking hands and dancing in unity. What the unity shall be I have yet to discover; the theme is a blank to me; but I see immense possibilities in the form I hit upon more or less by chance two weeks ago.[21]

It is interesting to note that she speaks of the difficulty of finding a 'unity' in this form. It has been argued earlier that the experimental novel lacks a certain kind of cohesiveness which is natural, indeed essential to the realist novel: perhaps the unity which is finally imposed in the experimental novel is always in a sense arbitrary. We might remember Virginia Woolf's well-known comment on the meaning of the lighthouse in *To the Lighthouse*:

> I meant *nothing* by The Lighthouse. One has to have a central line down the middle of the book to hold the design together. I saw that

all sorts of feelings would accrue to this, but I refused to think them out, and trusted that people would make it the deposit for their own emotions.[22]

The mythical structure of *Ulysses* can be viewed in an analogous way.

Just as *Jacob's Room* evolved directly out of Virginia Woolf's experiments in short fiction, so *Mrs Dalloway* grew out of an idea for a series of interlocking short texts:

> Oct 6th 1922.   Thoughts upon beginning a book to
> be called, perhaps, At Home: or The Party:
> This is to be a short book consisting of six or seven
> chapters, each complete separately.
> Yet there must be some sort of fusion!
> And all must converge upon the party at the end.[23]

In the end this plan was abandoned and the novel itself radically altered in the course of its writing. It was 'fused' much more closely around the character of Clarissa Dalloway. Yet *Mrs Dalloway* still retains elements of the modernist story, focusing on a day in the life of its protagonist rather in the manner of 'Bliss', a story by Katherine Mansfield which is close in theme. And when Virginia Woolf returned to write the 'six or seven chapters' she had originally had in mind, after the completion of *Mrs Dalloway*, she wrote:

> – and then I shall be free. Free at least to write out one or two more stories which have accumulated. I am less and less sure that they are stories, or what they are. Only I do feel fairly sure that I am grazing as near as I can to my own ideas, and getting a tolerable shape for them.[24]

The implication is that it is the short fiction which is the basic, the apt form or mould into which to pour one's ideas and sensations. There may be a clue to one of the reasons for this in Virginia Woolf's emphasis, in the letter to Roger Fry quoted earlier, on 'design'. This suggests that the novel is very consciously being viewed spatially by the author, as well as being conceived of linearly in terms of chronology.

The arts of painting and literature were closely connected in Virginia Woolf's mind. In a review of E. M. Forster's *Aspects of the Novel* she made a plea for a greater emphasis on aesthetic patterning in the novel, and rejected, implicitly, his liberal-humanist position *vis à vis* the form. She emphasised her point by making a comparison with visual art:

But the assumption that fiction is more intimately and humbly attached to the service of human beings than the other arts leads to a further position which Mr. Forster's book again illustrates. It is unnecessary to dwell upon her aesthetic functions because they are so feeble that they can safely be ignored. Thus, though it is impossible to imagine a book on painting in which not a word should be said about the medium in which a painter works, a wise and brilliant book, like Mr. Forster's, can be written about fiction without saying more than a sentence or two about the medium in which a novelist works. Almost nothing is said about words.[25]

The short story can approach the art of painting more nearly than the novel. An analogy with visual art highlights some of the distinctions between the short story and novel forms. The painterly analogy for the novel must, ultimately, break down, for in our response to a painting we are predominantly involved with space: our response to the novel involves us primarily with time. However, the analogy between a short story and a painting is much closer because, as Poe remarked, the short story is read over a relatively short period of time and can therefore more readily be grasped as an aesthetic whole. Its 'spatial' and structural elements can be exploited for aesthetic effect in ways not possible over the longer time-course of the novel. In this respect, the short story is more author-directed than the novel. There is less potential, during the time taken over its reading, for the imagination of the reader to play unforeseen tricks with the text, subjectively conflating, transposing, mis-remembering scenes, landscapes and images. The actual process of reading cannot 'interfere' so much with the text. The modernist impulse to short-circuit the sense of process and chronicity dominant in prose fiction thus found one of its most characteristic outlets in the short form.

The writings of Gertrude Stein provide us with the missing term in the structure of modernist short fiction, apart from Woolf's notion, derived from Fry, of 'spatial form'. This is movement. Stein identified the character of her own special epoch as 'a space of time filled with moving', a description which catches exactly the quality of her own best writing. It suggests the strong sense of spatiality discussed above, but does not stop there leaving us with the idea of the modernist fiction as a purely static object. This element of movement can be linked philosophically with what Gertrude Stein called the 'continuous present' or 'immediate existing'. Her stress on the immediate moment came directly from her teacher, the philosopher William James, who wrote that while we are contemplating the present 'it has melted in our grasp . . . gone in the instant of becoming'. James's philosophy was close to that of Henri Bergson, who influenced the thinking of both Virginia Woolf and Katherine Mansfield with his concept of *la durée*. The *durée* is the continuous present which is not known until it is past but to which the artist, like the child, has special access. Gertrude Stein defined her sense of *la durée* in her critical writings:

> At any moment that you are conscious of knowing anything, memory plays no part. When any of you feels anybody else, memory doesn't come into it. You have the sense of the immediate. Remember that my immediate forebears were people like Meredith, Thomas Hardy and so forth, and you will see what a struggle it was to do this thing. This [*The Making of Americans*] was one of my first efforts to give the appearance of one time-knowledge, and not to make it a narrative story. This is what I mean by immediacy of description.[26]

The consequence of the decision to pursue the 'immediate' was the necessary abolition of all that mediated, that made the text 'a tale that was told', a story of the past. 'Stories' concealed the quality of the immediate present by the very nature of their formal, condensing power:

> Do not bother. Do not bother about a story oh do not bother. Inevitably one has to know how a story ends even if it does not. Fred Annday's story does not end but that is because there is no more interest in it. And in a way yes in a way that is yes that is always so. I can tell this story as I go. I like to tell a story so.[27]

Gertrude Stein wrote this at the end of her five-chapter 'novel' or novella *The Superstitions of Fred Anneday, Annday, Anday A Novel of Real Life* (1934). Here she proposes a fiction of the present and makes a crucial distinction between *narrative* and *narration*. 'Narrative' was mediate story-telling; narration was her own immediate fictive art.

The ideal of movement also led Gertrude Stein to 'abandon' the noun and adjective in favour of the verb and adverb. For:

> As I say a noun is a name of a thing, and therefore slowly as you feel what is inside that thing you do not call it by the name by which it is known. Everybody knows that by the way they do when they are in

love and a writer should always have that intensity of emotion about whatever is the object about which he writes.

Verbs and adverbs are more interesting. In the first place they have one very nice quality and that is they can be so mistaken. . . . Besides being able to be mistaken and to make mistakes verbs can change to look like themselves or to look like something else, they are, so to speak on the move and adverbs move with them and each of them find themselves not at all annoying but very often very much mistaken.[28]

Here is an example of Gertrude Stein's writing 'so to speak on the move', from one of the portraits written in 1909:

Matisse

One was quite certain that for a long part of his being one being living he had been trying to be certain that he was wrong in doing what he was doing and then when he could not come to be certain that he had been wrong in doing what he had been doing, when he had completely convinced himself that he would not come to be certain that he had been wrong in doing what he had been doing he was really certain that he was a great one and he certainly was a great one. Certainly every one could be certain of this thing that this one is a great one.[29]

Illustrative or narrative effects are jettisoned in Gertrude Stein's work in favour of a prose of subtle 'insistence' (repetition with variation) which will convey the shadowy, slight changes of sight, sound and sense which 'make difference',[30] make reality, make our world as continuously perceiving human beings. However, it seems that this subtle insistence cannot be extended beyond a certain point if we are to remain adequately receptive to its discriminations. This explains Gertrude Stein's relative failure in longer works such as *The Making of Americans*: it also of course implies a limitation in her theory of literature, a refusal to recognise the 'reality' in practical terms of pre-conceived ideas in our lives. Some of the short prose pieces which make up *Tender Buttons* – normally considered one of Stein's most unsatisfactory, impenetrable productions – seem for these and other reasons to be among her most successful writings. 'A Red Hat', 'A Blue Coat', 'A Purse' can stand beside Pound's hokku poems

('In a Station of the Métro' for example) in purity of effect and form. In *Tender Buttons*, in the portraits written between 1909 and 1930, and in certain other pieces of experimental short prose Gertrude Stein found, or created, the most accommodating forms for her linguistic and philosophical interests.

In order to examine closely the qualities of Gertrude Stein's experimental short prose one cannot do better than study in some detail 'The Autobiography of Rose' (1937). This piece is one of several in which Gertrude Stein tried to push experimentation in short fiction to a limit. These pieces go beyond a concern with the 'significant moment' to a study of the mechanisms of language itself, anticipating by thirty years the work of 'experimentalists' such as Beckett and John Barth. As the title of 'The Autobiography of Rose' deftly suggests, the piece is concerned with problems of language, naming and identity. Gertrude Stein was throughout her career preoccupied with the different ways in which we can establish an authentic relationship with existing reality. Following her teacher William James, she speculated about the status of the child's early perceptions, those antedating the acquisition of language and memory. Were these fresh perceptions closer to 'reality' than those of the adult? What relationship did they have to the child's sense of identity?

In 'The Autobiography of Rose' we are shown that the child Rose knows 'herself' as 'Rose' through language: language gives a sense of identity. Her sense of her self apart from her name (her sense of entity) is less secure:

> How does she know her name is Rose. She knows her name is Rose because they call her Rose. If they did not call her Rose would her name be Rose. Oh yes she knows her name is Rose.[31]

This instability is explored further:

> Let us make believe that her name is not Rose. And if her name is not Rose what would be her autobiography. It would not be the autobiography of Rose because her name would not be Rose. But it is the autobiography of Rose even if her name is not Rose oh yes indeed it is the autobiography of Rose.

As readers we are called on to experience the same problems of identity as Rose. We, like her, 'know' that her name is Rose because other people (in our case the author) have told us so. By authorial sleight of hand we are then made to subtract the name of Rose from that entity which before it had *identity* did not exist for us: we conjure Rose's inner being from the empty spaces on the page.

In the third section of the piece the importance of events in creating identity/entity is negated. For in terms of imaginative potential all events exist and are experienced: it is only chance which determines those which shall actually exist:

> Hay can dam the water. And Rose, Rose with her father and her mother can be caught by all that water but Rose and her mother and her father were caught by all that water.

In section four we are told that Rose's name has nothing to do with:

> playing checkers and being beaten by her grandmother, oh no that had nothing to do with her name being Rose.
> Rose does know the difference between summer and winter and this has something to do with her name being Rose. It has something to do with her name being Rose.

Like any word, Rose/rose takes on meaning in relation to difference. Here it is the difference between summer and winter which plays its part in defining the nature of a rose. The specific example illustrates the general truth that language is constituted as a system of differences. Rose's strongest perception of her entity, as opposed to her language-given identity, is also realised in terms of difference, or negation:

> Rose could look at herself and when she saw herself and she knew her name was Rose she could look at herself and not see that her name is Rose. Oh yes she could. She could see that perhaps her name was not Rose.

The arbitrariness of language, the lack of any necessary connection between signifier and signified, is stressed in section six, which demonstrates the way in which language is built up autonomously, self-referentially:

> THE AUTOBIOGRAPHY OF ROSE

> It is taller to be taller
> Is it older to be older

Is it younger to be younger
Is it older to be older
Is it taller to be taller

In section seven the divorce between language and reality is taken to its furthest practical limit. Stein presents us with a linguistic unit which in itself makes perfect sense but which is meaningless for the reader without some gesture towards a concrete, empirical reality 'out there':

THE AUTOBIOGRAPHY OF ROSE

A glass pen oh yes a glass pen
Would Rose prefer a little dog named Pépé or a glass pen . . .
. . . And now everybody prepare.
Rose is to be offered one.
Which one.
Which one is Rose to be offered the glass pen or a little dog named Pépé. Which one. This one. And which is this one. Ah which is this one.

This stress on the 'solipsistic' nature of language has the effect of making us mistrustful of the fixed notions of identity associated with language, naming and narrative. By contrast, Stein turns *us* towards the meaning of entity. In section eight, the longest in the piece, the entity of Rose is evoked as nearly as possible and placed firmly in the present. In Stein's view we exist most fully in moments of pure responsiveness free from ratiocination. Our habits of mind, moving between the twin poles of memory and expectation, continually blunt and blur our present experience:

The autobiography of Rose is that she was young. And when she was young oh yes when she was young she said she had been young and that is quite certain she had been young. Was she regretting that she had been young so young, was she regretting anything. If she was regretting anything she was not young, how young can you be to be young.

In the ninth section of the piece the purity of immediate perception is linked with the concept of entity. Our fullest sense of self comes in those moments when we forget identity and indeed all fixed mental categories:

And as autumn does not follow winter, autumn comes first and as spring very often does not follow autumn winter comes first and as summer very often comes after what is the matter with Rose knowing it most. She does know it most. That is the autobiography of Rose not that she knows it the most.

In the last section the reiterated title THE AUTOBIOGRAPHY OF ROSE is finally placed as itself problematic:

THE AUTOBIOGRAPHY OF ROSE

Rose. What can she remember. Can she remember Rose. Can she. I am wondering.

Can Rose remember Rose, and thus have an autobiography? Not if Rose *is* Rose, located in the immediate present. Rose, like Alice B. Toklas, can only have her autobiography through a medium, through the artist Gertrude Stein, who will undertake to mediate on her behalf between reality and language, entity and identity.

Stein's importance in the development of short fiction is due also to the part she played as literary mentor for Ernest Hemingway. Her influence was strong at the time when Hemingway was writing *In Our Time* (1923), the collection which established his reputation. Some of Hemingway's finest work is in the short fiction form: his novels may suffer from simple repetitiveness rather than Steinian 'insistence'. For Hemingway, the short prose form was not more limited than the novel. Like the novel, it could aspire to a condition of 'potential totality', the state defined by Paul Hernadi in his study of the novel form – 'Not everything is, but everything could be included within the scope of the unobstructed horizon.'[32] Or in Hemingway's own words:

If a writer of prose knows enough about what he is writing about, he omits things that he knows and the reader, if the writer is writing truly enough, will have a feeling of those things as strongly as though the writer had stated them. The dignity of movement of an ice-berg is due to only one eighth of it being above water.[33]

Economy of form and style unite in Hemingway and it is difficult to disentangle his concern for a new prose style from his impulse towards the short fiction form. Like Katherine Mansfield, he had an acute sense of the unexplored potentialities of prose and like Ezra Pound he felt that good prose was more difficult to write than good poetry. His best writing gives an extraordinary sense of weight and strain, of every word bearing all possible stress. He discussed the issue of prose in *Green Hills of Africa*:

> 'The kind of writing that can be done. How far prose can be carried if anyone is serious enough and has luck. There is a fourth and fifth dimension that can be gotten.'
> 'You believe it?'
> 'I know it.'
> 'And if a writer can get this?'
> 'Then nothing else matters. It is more important than anything he can do. The chances are, of course, that he will fail. But there is a chance that he succeeds.'
> 'But that is poetry you are talking about.'
> 'No. It is much more difficult than poetry. It is a prose that has never been written. But it can be written, without tricks and without cheating. With nothing that will go bad afterwards.'[34]

The achievement of Hemingway can be considered initially via close reading of the well-known story 'A Clean, Well-Lighted Place'. Its theme is Conradian, while its setting is stylised almost in the manner of a sketch of the 1890s. The 'place' of the title is a café and the story revolves round two waiters and one old man. The old man is deaf, at least eighty, and, we learn, tried to kill himself 'last week'. One waiter tends to identify with the old man, while the younger, married waiter is anxious to get him out of the café and close up for the night.

One theme of the story is of solitude versus community, if only the sense of community engendered by the café society. The deeper theme is related, for the story is about nothing, *nada*, the sense that life is meaningless. The old man is particularly exposed to this feeling because of his solitude: his limited contact with others takes away from his sense of self and erodes his sense of the meaning and significance of life.

In the second paragraph of the story the younger waiter, asking why the old man has tried to kill himself, is told:

> 'He was in despair.'
> 'What about?'
> 'Nothing.'

'How do you know it was nothing?'
'He has plenty of money.'[35]

The word 'nothing' is of course double-edged: the sense is not only that the man has no obvious material problems, but also that he is in despair over a sense of nothing, *nada*. The first waiter empathises with the old man and describes similar feelings which he himself experiences:

What did he fear? It was not fear or dread. It was a nothing that he knew too well. It was all a nothing and man was a nothing too. It was only that and light was all it needed and a certain cleanness and order. Some lived in it and never felt it but he knew it all was nada y pués nada y nada y pués nada.

Against this sense of despair, the story offers us 'a clean, well-lighted place'. This modest place, a café, offers an ethic, a way to live. It is described four times, with Steinian 'insistence':

It was late and everyone had left the café except an old man who sat in the shadow the leaves of the tree made against the electric light.

They sat together at a table that was close against the wall near the door of the café and looked at the terrace where the tables were all empty except where the old man sat in the shadow of the leaves of the tree that moved slightly in the wind.

This is a clean and pleasant café. It is well lighted. The light is very good and also, now, there are shadows of the leaves.

It is the light of course but it is necessary that the place be clean and pleasant. You do not want music. Certainly you do not want music.

The café offers light which literally gives substance to our impressions, endowing them with form and colour. The fact that the café is clean and well ordered testifies to the power of the human mind to create order out of the potential chaos of impressions. And the shifting shadows of leaves offer a third necessary element in the construction of the café, a suggestion of external beauty to which the human mind can respond.

Hemingway's story is close to one of Katherine Mansfield's, 'Miss Brill', which chronicles the breaking of a withered spinster's frail hold on the external social world. Hemingway's story is also like that of Mansfield in employing covert symbolism which cuts across the apparently smooth narrative surface of the text. For example, at the beginning of 'A Clean, Well-Lighted Place' drink is paralleled with dew and thus becomes an inverted image of redemption, the old man's increasing need for it measuring the extent of his despair – a mortal sin in Catholic countries:

> 'You should have killed yourself last week,' he said to the deaf man. The old man motioned with his finger. 'A little more,' he said. The waiter poured on into the glass so that the brandy slopped over and ran down the stem into the top saucer of the pile. 'Thank you,' the old man said.

If the use of indirect free form by such writers as Joyce, Virginia Woolf and Katherine Mansfield marked a major step towards the elimination of an authoritative narrator-figure distinct from the characters of fiction, the experiments of Hemingway, Katherine Mansfield, and later Samuel Beckett, with dialogue and monologue take us one stage further, removing even the sense of authorial intervention implied by the use of the third-person pronoun and anterior tense. Hemingway achieves an extraordinary sense of immediacy in such moments as this from 'A Clean, Well-Lighted Place':

> 'How did he do it?'
> 'He hung himself with a rope.'
> 'Who cut him down?'
> 'His niece.'
> 'Why did they do it?'
> 'Fear for his soul.'
> 'How much money has he got?'
> 'He's got plenty.'
> 'He must be eighty years old.'
> 'Anyway I should say he was eighty.'

Hemingway and Katherine Mansfield shared a belief that prose was an under-exploited medium, an 'undiscovered country still'. The short fictions of Katherine Mansfield have been reserved for consideration until the close of this chapter as she is the only one among the writers considered to have devoted herself exclusively to the short fiction form. Her fictions, like those of Joyce and Virginia Woolf, are founded on Symbolist principles. Her early notebooks show that she developed a consciously Symbolist aesthetic from her reading of Pater, Wilde and in particular Arthur Symons. She also borrowed the techniques of French Symbolist poetry for her early prose-poems and sketches. She developed the short fiction form deliberately, introducing into it Symbolist poetic techniques like those employed by T. S. Eliot and Ezra Pound. It says a good deal about Katherine Mansfield's conception of the short 'story' form that we find her writing to Virginia Woolf to explain that 'The Love Song of J. Alfred Prufrock' was 'really a short story'. The idea points to the lyrical concentration of her work.

Katherine Mansfield's fictions are built on a technique of suggestion. The themes are not stated directly but conveyed obliquely through concrete images. The idea of the concrete image can be extended in this context to mean the entire composition of a fiction and not just a single motif.

The strength of Katherine Mansfield's Symbolist technique can be fully appreciated only through close reading. 'The Escape' (1920) is, like her other fictions, a total image, a carefully composed expressive appearance in which each naturalistic detail also functions symbolically, contributing to the expression of a mood or state of mind. The central image is that of the journey, but while this determines the story's narrative structure we know nothing of the purpose of the journey, its setting in place, or the names or appearance of the two travellers.

To demonstrate the complex unity of the story, structure and imagery must be considered as they unfold together. The first paragraph establishes with economy the characteristics of the two main actors. The woman's nervous, overwrought state is indicated by the exaggerated, repetitive speech patterns of her stylised interior monologue. The man seems by contrast lazy and easy-going, forgetful of the time and unable to organise bills and trains.

As the woman surveys in retrospect a scene at the station where the couple missed their train, the details she recalls act as objective correlatives to convey her morbid sensibility. She remembers the children at the windows of the train as 'hideous', recalls the 'glare' and 'the flies' and people who seemed to gather round oppressively. She has been almost overcome by one detail: 'the woman who'd held up that baby with that awful, awful head. . . . "Oh, to care as I care –" '.[36] But, we realise, she cares not for the woman, nor for the baby, but for herself. Her narcissism is underlined in the next paragraph, when we return to the present and she comforts herself, 'pitifully, as though she were saying to somebody else "I know, my darling," she pressed the handkerchief to her eyes'.

On our perception of her narcissism the narrative shifts over to the husband's point of view. He looks at the bag from which his wife has taken her handkerchief and surveys its contents, all of which are thematic motifs in themselves – powder puff, rouge stick, a bundle of letters, pills 'like seeds', a broken cigarette, a mirror, 'white ivory tablets' of notepaper. 'He thought: "In Egypt she would be buried with those things".' But it is spiritual death which is evoked in the imagery of the next section of the story.

The external landscape is presented mainly through the woman's eyes, and she sees only squalid, straggling houses and the boils on the back of the driver's neck – though the narrator also intervenes briefly to point to the beauty which she does not see. The wind then starts 'in front of the carriage a whirling, twirling snatch of dust that settled on their clothes *like the finest ash*' (my italics). Dust and ash are associated with mortality and the death of the body, also with spiritual states of aridity and sterility. It is the suggestion that the springs of the life of the spirit are dried up that is important here.

The emotional distress of the couple is contrasted with the glee of a troop of ragged children who appear 'shrieking and giggling', coming downhill in the opposite direction. The children are 'sunbleached' and natural. They have gathered flowers which they offer to the couple, but they have gathered them artlessly, without any care for effect, mixing different types of flower – 'any kind of flowers' – some of them already faded. This natural offering, mixed as life itself, is immediately rejected by the woman who has already been established as one who prefers the artificial to the natural. She flings the flowers back at the children who experience a 'queer' (unnatural) shock.

Before the carriage reaches the summit of the hill tension is increased by a final detail. The man makes as if to smoke but the woman stops him – ' "If you could imagine," she said, "the anguish I suffer when that smoke comes floating across my face". . . .' The smoke, like the powder, raises more dust.

The turning point comes when the woman realises that her parasol has been knocked out of the carriage. At this she is 'simply beside herself': 'My parasol. It's gone. The parasol that belonged to my mother. The parasol that I prize more than – more than ...' (Katherine Mansfield's ellipsis). The parasol is the literal embodiment of the fragile protective shell to which the woman clings, the artifice which she sets between herself and the world, herself and her husband, herself and her deeper self. 'Spitefully', therefore, she insists on going to look for the parasol, refusing help for 'if I don't escape from you for a minute I shall go mad'.

In this speech is embodied the central paradox of the fiction for in the next section we see how it is the husband, and not the wife, who 'escapes' from the present, or rather, transcends it.

As the woman moves away the man 'stretches himself out'; a constraint is lifted. He is motionless, and the sun beats down on him: 'The wind sighed in the valley and was quiet. He felt himself, lying there, a hollow man, a parched, withered man, as it were, of ashes. And the sea sounded, "Hish, hish".' In these lines the author invokes images suggesting spiritual death. The man feels himself to be a man of ashes, his spirit turned to dust. His spring of life is parched and withered and he lies helpless, feeling 'hollow' because he is a body without a spirit. His lying in the valley where the wind sighs also has Biblical associations – we recall the valley of dry bones of Ezekiel. But as Eliot tells us in 'Ash Wednesday', the question is 'shall these bones live?'. In the passage quoted above we realise that the man, unlike his wife, is aware of his state, a precondition of redemption or rebirth. He also notices the beauty of the sea. These intimations prepare us for what follows:

> It was then that he saw the tree, that he was conscious of its presence just inside a garden gate. It was an immense tree with a round, thick silver stem and a great arc of copper leaves that gave back the light and yet were sombre. . . . As he looked at the tree he felt his breathing die away and he became part of the silence. It seemed to grow, it seemed to expand in the quivering heat until the great carved leaves hid the sky, and yet it was motionless.

The tree is beautiful and has the quality of inalienable presence that enables the man to lose himself in contemplation of it. He feels for a moment at one with the external world. Yet there is something behind the tree – 'a whiteness, a softness, an opaque mass, half-hidden – with delicate pillars'. It is from behind the tree that a voice rises in song, at first also part of the peace and silence, but gradually 'as the voice rose, soft, dreaming, gentle, he knew that it would come floating to him from the hidden leaves and his peace was shattered'. It is through the human art of song – as opposed to the artifice associated with his wife – that the man's moment of vision is deepened and his consciousness extended:

What was happening to him? Something stirred in his breast. Something dark, something unbearable and dreadful pushed in his bosom, and like a great weed it floated, rocked . . . it was warm, stifling.

The great weed which floats and rocks suggests both more and less than the man's general spiritual malaise. It indicates his relationship with his wife as the specific situation from which he cannot 'escape'. Yet the relationship between husband and wife is symbolic of the wider net of circumstance within which the human spirit is held. From this there can be no escape as such, only the possibility of transcendence. It is in this sense that the man 'escapes', as he contemplates the tree and listens to the song during his 'timeless moment':

He tried to struggle, to tear at it, and at the same moment – all was over. Deep, deep, he sank into the silence, staring at the tree and waiting for the voice that came floating, falling, until he felt himself enfolded.

The man comes to full consciousness of his position, of the exhaustion of his spirit and the impasse reached with his wife. But in the same moment the beauty of the tree and of the woman's voice make their way into his heart as surely as 'the weed' and are accepted not as passing distractions, but as having as much validity as his suffering. The man transcends his subjective misery because he sees and admits as equally existent the beauty of the external world and of art. Such a moment of vision is the quintessence of modernist short fiction.

4 The Tale-Tellers: II

The three writers who most strongly continued the tradition of tale-telling in the period 1930–60 were the Irishmen Frank O'Connor and Sean O'Faolain, and T. F. Powys who was Welsh by descent. To an extent, the strength of the traditional story in Ireland in this period can be ascribed to the influence of the Celtic revival of the twenties and thirties. T. F. Powys's Celtic affinities are, however, tenuous: his major importance lies in his 'ruralism', which influenced a group of minor story-writers of whom perhaps the best known is H. E. Bates. Powys opposed mechanisation, literally, and mechanism, philosophically, and retired to the country to adopt a mode of life tainted as little as possible by the inroads of modern thought and technology.

O'Connor and O'Faolain strongly disapproved of the uses to which the short story had been put by the modernists. They rejected the extreme self-reflexiveness of writers such as Joyce, made manifest first of all on the level of language. O'Connor strongly criticised Joyce's work, for in it he felt a point had been reached at which:

> style ceases to be a relationship between author and reader and becomes a relationship of a magical kind between author and object. It is not an attempt at communicating the experience to the reader, who is supposed to be present only by courtesy, but at equating the prose with the experience.[1]

Joyce, on the other hand, had written to his brother as he was about to embark on *Dubliners* that his aim was:

> to give people some kind of intellectual pleasure or spiritual enjoyment by converting the bread of everyday life into something that has a permanent artistic life of its own . . . for their mental, moral, and spiritual uplift.[2]

Related issues seem to have become confused: the question of the desirability of the artist's being able to communicate, and the question of just what it is that he should communicate. O'Connor and O'Faolain both felt that there were limits to the value of subjective explorations of language. In their view, through an intensely cultivated subjectivity a writer such as Joyce might lose not only his audience but also his subject. Rather than following closely the contours of human experience, he might distort it beyond recovery, failing to recognise the ways in which human experience, like the language which reflects and defines it, is necessarily and, in Joyce's word, ineluctably, compounded of the general and the conventional as well as the subjective and particular.

In an early essay on Joyce, O'Faolain addressed himself to the vexed question of the generalising power of language. He took an unfashionably positive view of the communal, traditional aspects of language:

> Yet it is this continuity . . . that makes words so rich and overteeming, and here [with Joyce] we find the artist declaring that this quality which makes words so rich and full of nuance is exactly the quality that makes of language an imposition that counters his free expression at every step. Thus a man like Joyce would appear to be like an heir who chafes at a will because of the qualifications it contains. But there are qualifications to the whole of the phenomenon of existence and it seems a desperate thing that a man should thus rebel against what is not merely inevitable but inexorable.[3]

And as with language, so with plot. Writers such as Joyce and Katherine Mansfield had rejected the 'plotty story' because it seemed to depend too heavily on conventional assumptions about the meaning and value of human experience. By contrast, O'Connor and O'Faolain argued for the restitution of the kind of story which imposed a recognisable pattern on experience. The terms of their argument are far removed from the rational humanism of later critics like Lionel Trilling, who argued for the value of plot in *Sincerity and Authenticity* (1972). Trilling asserted that tales were told not by idiots but by 'a rational consciousness which perceives in things the processes that are their reason and which derives from this perception a principle of conduct, a way of living among things'.[4] For O'Connor and O'Faolain plot had a more basic, pre-moral, myth-making power. Their ideas must be seen in the context of the Celtic revival, with its emphasis on the dependence of all great art on folk tradition. More specifically, the theories of Yeats pointed a way forward for these young story-tellers who were disenchanted with the modernist enterprise:

The artist, when he has lived for a long time in his own mind with the example of other artists as deliberate as himself, gets into a world of ideas pure and simple. He becomes very highly individualised and at last by sheer pursuit of perfection becomes sterile. Folk imagination on the other hand creates endless images of which there are no ideas. Its stories ignore the moral law and every other law, they are successions of pictures like those seen by children in the fire. You find a type of these two kinds of invention . . . in the civilization that comes from town and in the forms of life that one finds in the country. . . . In the country . . . you find people who are hardly individualised to any great extent. They live through the same round of duty and they think about life and death as their fathers have told them, but in speech, in the telling of tales, in all that has to do with the play of imagery, they have an endless abundance.[5]

Yeats's summary hints at some of the contradictions which we will find in the work of O'Connor and O'Faolain. His emphasis on the power of the imagination, on its capacity to invent stories which do not 'impose' on reality but which may free us from it, constitutes one of the key defences of the story-telling impulse. Yet there is some conflict between the idea of the folk who are 'hardly individualised to any great extent', and the fertility, and hence presumably the individual quality, of their imagination. (Yeats claimed that while he was collecting stories from the people of Ireland he found that 'not one story is like another'.) The conflict is adumbrated in the limited number of true folk-tales to which we have access, in which a powerful tendency towards myth and mythopoeia cuts across what we can discern of the play of the individual, anarchic imagination. In the work of O'Connor and O'Faolain we feel, similarly, that the 'lonely voice' of the individual story-teller is often struggling under the weight of Irish mythology and typology. Irish folk tradition is in some ways a source of strength in their work; but their relation to 'tradition' is by no means stable.

Frank O'Connor strove consciously to forge a link between his own work and Irish folk tradition. He was steeped in the legends and mythology of Ireland: long before he began to write he had mastered Modern Irish and Old Irish, and through his translations, some of which were published in *The Fountain of Magic* (1939), he had made a practical effort to transmit something of the 'mysterious' Irish past to the present. He was closely connected with the Celtic revival through his friendship with Yeats, and became one of the directors of the Abbey Theatre, founded to 'build up a Celtic and Irish school of dramatic literature'. With these allegiances, it is not surprising that he formulated a literary theory in which an absolute dichotomy was established between the art of Yeats, with its supposed base in popular tradition, and the art of Joyce, the 'sterile' art of the townee. For O'Connor, in artistic terms, Joyce was the 'antithesis' to Yeats's 'thesis'. Thesis stood for the tradition of folk life, of nature with her abundant creativity and the 'deliberate . . . suspension of the critical faculty to justify a blind indulgence in intuition'. Antithesis represented the exclusive art life, sterile because it was not married to nature. Antithesis was not communal: it involved at best communication between a solitary reader and writer. Paradoxically, O'Connor recognised that this solitary relationship was that on which the art of the future would depend, and he had few illusions about folk readings or the oral transmission of his tales. He therefore placed a corresponding emphasis on the nature of the relationship which the modern artist should create between reader and writer. Hence his denial of multivalence, the quality which makes most modernist and postmodernist texts so attractive to the contemporary reader. For O'Connor, the primary task of the writer was to keep the lines of communication clear. He should write so directly that the reader would not be required to investigate the meanings of words beyond the purposes of immediate recognition. The writer, in other words, should communicate rather than express, relate rather than imply – 'tell us in plain words' as Molly Bloom would put it.

At the start of his career, O'Connor was placed in an unenviable position as the putative heir of Joyce, and this may account for the strongly anti-Joycean bias of his aesthetic. O'Connor used his aesthetic as a strategy, not a programme, as a means of freeing himself from particular pressures and of pushing his art in a desired direction. It is noticeable that throughout his career he used his critical writings in this way, as statements of intent which do not necessarily correlate with his practice as a writer. Thus his best known critical work, the study of the short story *The Lonely Voice* (1963) focuses on the individual 'voice' of the isolated story-teller – a perspective which seems at odds with the seemingly inextricable mingling of communal and individual concerns in O'Connor's own stories.

O'Connor's stories are informed by two dominant myths: the myth of

Ireland and the 'myth' of the family. The two structures are linked through the concept of authority which is central to both, authority which is usually both desired and feared by the protagonists of the stories. The myth of Ireland is poised on a paradox: the Ireland of the past is also the Ireland of the future, offering an image of an ideal society which will support the individual while at the same time allowing him full freedom for development. Contemporary Ireland gives cause for nothing but despondency: the growth of the individual is, in O'Connor's view, stunted and atrophied through the suffocating power of fossilised institutions. In stories such as 'The Miser' and 'The Holy Door', the Church is described in terms of 'deception' and professionalism: the letter without the spirit. The corruption of the law is treated with a mixture of irony and bitterness in stories such as 'Legal Aid' and 'Peasants'. But it is the institutions which have become corrupt, not the values which originally animated them. For the older generation, these values are still accessible through conventional channels: it is the young who find themselves cut off from the old ways without finding new paths to follow. This is the dilemma explored in the story 'Uprooted'. Tom and Ned Keating, the sons of peasants, have become, respectively, a priest and a teacher. Tom has managed to accommodate himself to his new life, partly because he is by nature 'boisterous' and extroverted, partly because he lives a life which is largely ordered and regulated for him. Ned, by contrast, feels himself to be adrift:

> He no longer knew why he had come to the city, but it was not for the sake of the bed-sitting-room in Rathmines, the oblong of dusty garden outside the window, the trams clanging up and down. . . . Half humorously, half despairingly, he would sometimes clutch his head in his hands and admit to himself that he had no notion of what he wanted . . . he felt that only when he had to work with his hands for a living and was no longer sure of his bed would he find out what all his ideals and emotions meant and where he could fit them into the scheme of his life.[6]

The story is structured round a visit the brothers pay to their parents. a visit which brings to a head Ned's sense of confusion. He finds that nothing at home has changed, and feels at first a renewed sense of attraction to the simplicity and stability of his parents' life:

> Nothing was changed in the tall, bare, whitewashed kitchen. The

harness hung in the same place on the wall, the rosary on the same nail in the fireplace, by the stool where their mother usually sat; table under the window, churn against the back door, stair without banisters mounting straight to the attic door that yawned in the wall – all seemed as unchanging as the sea outside.

During his visit, Ned meets a country girl and walks home with her in the rain, moving into the past as he takes shelter under her black shawl:

The rain was a mild, persistent drizzle and a strong wind was blowing. Everything had darkened and grown lonely and, with his head in the blinding folds of the shawl, which reeked of turf-smoke, Ned felt as if he had dropped out of Time's pocket.

Ned finds the girl attractive, and his desire to yield to her, or to what she represents, is indicated through the image of falling into unconsciousness and the notion of escape from the processes of history. Yet Ned recognises that the anachronistic shawl is 'blinding'. The blindness and the unconsciousness are states which he cannot share. It is Ned's misfortune that he sees, and the paradox of his position is that it is because he is alienated from the life of the country that he can define its qualities for us. His self-awareness is foregrounded at the close of the story as he 'places' the lost country of his childhood through a self-consciously artistic metaphor:

Through the apple-green light over Carriganassa ran long streaks of crimson, so still they might have been enamelled. Magic, magic, magic! He saw it as in a child's picture-book with all its colours intolerably bright; something he had outgrown and could never return to, while the world he aspired to was as remote and intangible as it had seemed even in the despair of youth.

'Uprooted' is shaped as a lament for a traditional way of life, and also for traditional ways of thought and feeling which are no longer accessible to Ned. In 'The Majesty of the Law' O'Connor is still more deeply concerned with the loss of certain codes of thought and belief. As the title indicates, O'Connor is here preoccupied with an institution which he sees as second only to the Church in its fall into decay and corruption. Here he seems to suggest that the legal system is by its nature antagonistic to the values it should enshrine. The 'majesty' of the law (and the word suggests something English, alien and imperialistic) is opposed to the dignity of a single peasant, and the reader is unwittingly drawn into the conflict through the use of a trick ending – one of the very few cases in which the use of such an ending can be fully justified. The author withholds certain information from us in order to expose the inadequacy of our conceptions in certain key areas. The story is so structured that as readers we find ourselves identified with the unthinking force of the law: only at the point when we perceive this have we been educated beyond our preconceptions in the way O'Connor intends.

The story trembles on the brink of sentimentality. It is one of O'Connor's most powerful, emotionally, but the emotion is finally contained as valid nostalgia. The writer's engagement with the subject is evident in the warm tonalities of visual descriptions such as this:

> And again they became lost in conversation. The light grew thick and coloured and, wheeling about the kitchen before it disappeared, became tinged with gold; the kitchen itself sank into cool greyness with cold light on the cups and basins and plates of the dresser. From the ash tree a thrush began to sing. The open hearth gathered brightness till its light was a warm, even splash of crimson in the twilight.

Interior and exterior landscape merge in a harmony which reflects that which runs through the life of the old peasant, Dan.

Most of the 'space' of the story is taken up with what appears to be a purely social visit as a young country sergeant calls on an old man whom we guess he must have known all his life. The question of civility is brought to the fore almost immediately as the two men negotiate their way around a difficult problem. Dan would think it insulting to his guest not to offer him whisky, which is however illegally distilled:

> 'Musha, Dan, I think sometimes 'twas a great mistake of the law to set its hand against it.'
> Dan shook his head. His eyes answered for him, but it was not in nature for a man to criticise the occupation of a guest in his own home . . .
> 'Them that makes the laws have their own good reasons.'
> 'All the same, Dan, all the same, 'Tis a hard law.'
> The sergeant would not be outdone in generosity. Politeness required him not to yield to the old man's defence of his superiors and their mysterious ways.

The question lapses, and the talk meanders until in the gathering gloom the sergeant rises and makes ready for a ceremonial leave-taking. When he has almost reached the gate, he turns back, breaking narrative and behavioural codes. And it is only at this point that we realise that the hours he has spent with the old man, discussing the old ways, have been spent with the intention of a complex and delicate courtesy. The sergeant is calling on Dan with a purpose which he will not confuse with his social and neighbourly obligations. He must spend more time than he normally would with the old man, and have all but left his house, before he can ask the question to which he already knows the answer. Dan will not pay the fine he has incurred by attacking another man: 'No, 'tisn't the money so much as giving that fellow the satisfaction of paying. Because he angered me, sergeant.' In consequence, Dan must go to prison: a situation which might involve, to say the least, some social stigma were it not, again, handled and coded with the utmost care. Exploiting a range of verbal nuance, the two men establish an appropriate tone for negotiation:

> 'But, as a matter of fact,' said the old man emphatically, 'the day that would be most convenient to me would be Friday after dinner, because I have some messages to do in town, and I wouldn't have the journey for nothing.'
> 'Friday will do grand,' said the sergeant.

The story ends some days later as Dan finally leaves his home. The word prison has not been explicitly mentioned: it is deliberately placed as the last word of the story in order to shock the reader into awareness of a discrepancy between the way Dan sees the situation and the actual humiliation which awaits him.

'The Majesty of the Law' is, then, partly about the ways in which we can create reality through language and imagination. The thrust of the story is towards identification with a traditional way of life which makes full allowance for the values of speech and imagination (and hence by implication makes allowance for the value of story-telling). Dan is the representative of this tradition, and his subtlety and developed sensibility are thrown into relief through his confrontation with the operations of the law. In a sense we are presented here with another Yeatsian distinction, another version of 'thesis' and 'anti-thesis'. Thesis might stand in this case for the organic life of tradition, antithesis for the impersonal, mechanical mode of operation of the modern state.

O'Connor closely connected the oppressions of Church and State and the restrictions of Irish family life. Like Sean O'Faolain, he blamed the 'pious elders' of the Irish Church for the widespread ignorance of sex which, apparently, led many into false relationships and disastrous marriages. O'Connor wrote in 'The Holy Door' that the Irish as a race 'combined a strong grasp of the truths of religion with a hazy notion of the facts of life', and many of his stories deal with the consequences. Yet in these stories – 'News for the Church', 'The House that Johnny Built' for example – O'Connor's powers do not seem to be fully engaged. His finest stories of family life focus on the relationships between parents and children on a more fundamental, archetypal level. Such stories often have analogues in classical myth – 'My Da' for example is, like *Ulysses*, another variant on the story of Odysseus. There are also analogues and sources in folk tradition, as O'Connor seems to recognise with his use of titles such as 'The Babes in the Wood' and 'The Stepmother'. Finally, O'Connor draws on the sexual paradigms established by Freud, though it is difficult to say to what extent he regards these as, in Vaihinger's terms, 'useful fictions' rather than as scientifically verifiable insights. 'My Oedipus Complex' nicely demonstrates this ambivalence. It has been treated as a serious indictment of the Oedipal structure of Irish family life. The story can be read in classically Freudian terms: an eldest son is passionately attracted to his dominant mother and when his father, who has been absent in the war, returns, he suffers from acute jealousy, spars with the father and vies for the mother's attention and love. Finally, he gives up hope of 'possessing' the mother, transfers attention to his father and begins to construct his masculine identity by modelling himself on him.

But the story also reverses the Oedipus complex, for it turns on a joke: before the father's return Larry used to share his mother's bed, and his expulsion from it constituted one of the most serious losses in the campaign against the father. At the close of the story the father is driven from his wife's bed by the endless cries of 'Sonny', a second son – and defeated by one son, he takes refuge with another, making his way penitently into Larry's bed. Surely O'Connor is gently tilting at Freud, and at over-schematic views of family relations.

However, the theme of the absent father is taken seriously enough in many stories: it is almost an obsession. In 'My Da' Stevie Leary, the victim of an absent father, is transformed by the father's near-magical return. He has been fatherless from a baby and has grown up to be effeminate, as the following description makes clear: it also suggests the way in which his mother has only made things worse by instituting adverse comparisons with the father he has never known and whom he has had no opportunity to emulate:

> Even his own mother hadn't much to say for him. 'Ah, he'll never be the man his father was, ma'am,' she'd say mournfully, over-right the kid himself. . . . He was a big overgrown streel of a boy with a fat round idiotic face and a rosy complexion, a walk that was more of a slide, and a shrill scolding old-woman's voice.

On his return to Ireland, Frankie, the father, re-institutes 'the masculine principle' in family life. He beats his wife and ignores Stevie, but this only contributes to his masculine mystique. As the narrator, a neighbour's child, relates:

> A little later Frankie went to bed himself, leaving his wife lying on the floor – dead, no doubt. Mother wanted to go in to her, but Father stopped that at once.
> 'Now,' he said oracularly, 'there's a man in the house,' and for years afterwards I found myself at intervals trying to analyse the finality of that pronouncement.

After his father's departure – as abrupt as his return – Stevie seems to fall into decline. But this is only the narrow verdict of popular opinion, and the narrator passes on information which prepares us for a different judgement. The two solid pieces of advice Stevie's father has given him are that he should attend night school and join the public library. Stevie has followed this programme assiduously, and eventually discovers a vocation for the priesthood. At the end of the story we are given the modern equivalent of a transformation scene. The narrator presents the new Stevie, formed by a brief parental visit which has given shape to his life:

> And suddenly it struck me with the force of a revelation that fathers had their good points after all. That evening I dropped in on the Learys. I wanted to see Stevie again. I had realized after Mass that, like the Delurys, I had for years been living with a shadow-Stevie, a comic kid who had disappeared ages ago under our eyes without our noticing. I wasn't surprised to meet for the first time an unusually intelligent and sensitive young man.

O'Connor's emphasis on the importance of the father–son relationship is clearly consonant with Freudian theory, though O'Connor
would certainly view his relationship with Freud in terms of a
coincidence of interest rather than in terms of deeper indebtedness. It
is worth pursuing the Freudian parallel a little further, however, for it
may help us to a clearer understanding of O'Connor's interest in the
'absent father'. Freud, we remember, firmly linked the authority of the
father with external and social structures of authority:

> The function of the father is gradually transferred from his
> individual person to his social position, to his image in the son
> (conscience), to God, to the various agencies and agents which teach
> the son to become a mature and restrained member of his society.[7]

It may be that O'Connor's interest in the father does not derive simply
from the determinants of his own family situation.[8] It could be viewed
as symptomatic of a wider sense of lost or ebbing power and authority
in society at large.

'The Babes in the Wood', one of O'Connor's later stories, seems to
make the connection more explicitly. The major focus is, again, on the
plight of a fatherless child. In this story there is no first-person narrator
to distance us from the child's suffering, as there is in 'My Da'. We are
presented very directly with a boy's need for a reassuring father-figure:

> Terry looked up at the reproach in his voice and then threw
> himself blindly about his knees and buried his face in his trousers. Mr
> Walker laughed and patted Terry's shoulder. His voice was quite
> different when he spoke again.
> 'Cheer up, Terry,' he said. 'We'll have good times yet.'
> 'Come along now, Terry,' his aunt said in a brisk official voice that
> terrified him.
> 'What's wrong, old man?' Mr Walker asked.
> 'I want to stay with you,' Terry whispered, beginning to sob.

This boy, Terry, is surrounded by parent-figures none of whom fills
their role satisfactorily. There is his mother, always known as his aunt,
who visits him only infrequently – 'She didn't come half often enough
to suit Terry.' There is Mrs Early, the old woman with whom he lives,
but she lacks motherly, or even grandmotherly, charm – 'Mrs Early
was a rough, deaf, scolding old woman'. Only one father-figure
appears, the 'Mr Walker' who, as his unreal name suggests, is a

potential bigamist who will never marry Terry's 'aunt' and bring them both safely to England.

At one point in the story it is stressed that the English, with their lax Protestant ways, would make no difficulty over Terry's living with his real mother, particularly if she could marry and provide him with his much-needed father. It is the strict *moeurs* of Irish, Catholic, rural life which have decreed that Terry must live at a distance: this becomes even more vital when the mother is at last married. She is now ready to have 'proper children', a respectable family. The double-think about the sanctity of Irish family life is emphasised, and it is made clear that it is typical of a retrograde and repressive society. We feel the whole weight of this society behind the unhappiness of one small boy.

Eventually, Terry finds consolation in his friendship with a nine-year-old girl who is also illegitimate. The two are drawn together through their common awareness that there is something 'wrong' with them.

> 'What's wrong with us?'
> That was a question that Florrie had often asked herself, but she was too proud to show a small boy like Terry that she hadn't discovered the answer.
> 'Everything,' she sighed.

As the children confirm their bond the story shifts onto the level of dream or fairy-tale. Impossible promises are made, guarantees of eternal loyalty which will compensate for all that has been lost. As dusk falls and the children fall asleep in each other's arms – in a wood – the author makes a clear appeal to the world of the original *Babes in the Wood*:

> 'If you'll swear to be always in with me I'll be your girl again. Will you?'
> 'I will,' said Terry.
> She put her arms about him and he fell asleep, but she remained solemnly holding him, looking at him with detached and curious eyes. He was hers at last. There were no more rivals. She fell asleep too and did not notice the evening train go up the valley. It was all lit up. The evenings were drawing in.

The shift to the world of the fairy-tale does not carry a final weight of conviction, however. And the felt disjunction between the 'real' world of O'Connor's story, with its contingent social pressures, and the world of the fairy-tale, reflects a perennial ambivalence in his work. O'Connor believed passionately in the power of the imagination and in the power of the word to compensate for the miseries of existence. However, he seems to see this power, increasingly, as a consolatory rather than as a transforming one. It might be said that his best stories dramatise a loss of belief in the transforming powers of the imagination. 'The Majesty of the Law', for example, anticipates defeat for a vision of life so intense that it could, almost, transform reality. Many of his other stories – 'The Long Road to Ummera', 'Peasants', for example – betray a sense of loss and separation from traditional ways of thought and feeling. O'Connor dramatises his sense of a weakening hold on the mythology he prizes so dearly.

The work of Sean O'Faolain also has an elegiac quality: his writing is pervaded by a sense of nostalgia for a civilisation which is past. Like O'Connor, O'Faolain was drawn early in his career to Yeats's Romantic–Celtic vision and to the attractive image of Ireland as a beggar nation dressed in the last rags of a noble folk tradition. But despite his interest in tradition and Irish folk history, O'Faolain is in a sense a less 'Irish' writer than O'Connor. Ireland has from the start presented him with problems of identification and commitment which O'Connor does not seem to have experienced. In his autobiography, O'Faolain has described the doubts which assailed him when he was on the point of returning to Ireland in 1931. He had been reading James, and the master's indictment of nineteenth-century American civilisation had made a forceful impression on him. Would he find in Ireland the same 'coldness, the thinness, the blankness' of civilisation which was, according to James, inimical to the development of the artist? James's 'accumulation of history and custom' might be present in Ireland, noted O'Faolain, 'in a folk sense but not in [the] urbane sense'.[9] O'Faolain's appreciation of the value of folk tradition has always been qualified by his feeling for urban, and urbane, values, and this in turn has led him to experiment more widely than O'Connor with the short story form. His stories are less closely tied in the structural sense to folk models (compare O'Connor's frequent use of the journey or quest motif, his fondness for the semi-magical 'apparition' of character, his investment of character with archetypal rather than individual significance). The structure of O'Faolain's stories is most often episodic, and inclusive rather than exclusive, particularly in terms of the delineation of character. It could even be argued that in their fullness and specificity his stories – in particular the later ones – aspire to the condition of the novel. O'Faolain would perhaps prefer to call such later stories 'tales', in accordance with a distinction he made in a preface to a 1966 collection:

> A short story is concentrated stuff. . . . A Tale is quite different. Like a small plane [as opposed to the 'kite' of the short story] it is more free, carries a bit more cargo, roves farther, has time and space for more complex characterization, more changes of mood, more incidents and scenes, even more plot.[10]

Interestingly, despite his cosmopolitan stance and wider range of subject matter, O'Faolain is a more romantic writer than O'Connor. He recognised this quality in his early work, and analysed it with critical acuity:

> [The stories] are very romantic, as their weighted style shows. I should have to change my nature if I were to change the style, which is full of romantic words, such as 'dawn', 'onwards', 'youth', 'world', 'adamant' or 'dusk'; of metaphors and abstractions; or personalizations and sensations which belong to the author rather than to the characters.[11]

This romantic quality persists in his latest stories (or tales): for example in 'The Planets of the Years' from the collection *The Talking Trees* (1971) we find such sentences and cadences as these:

> 'Slieve Callan,' she murmured, and I saw its whiteness rising like music under the low clouds moving imperceptibly from twenty miles away across the wrinkled Shannon.

> How gently the lighted snow kept touching that window-pane, melting and vanishing, and, like love, endlessly returning across the planets of the years.

Such romanticism is, as O'Faolain himself points out, largely a matter of narrative voice: it is released through the use of 'stress words' and 'personalizations and sensations' belonging to the implied author. And it is the presence of a consistently romantic narrative voice which gives to O'Faolain's work its unity and charm. While it was O'Connor who called for a return of the sense that 'a man was speaking to men' in the short story, it was O'Faolain who restored the teller to the tale as O'Connor intended. He achieved that sense of 'communicated personality' which is curiously absent in O'Connor's work.

Like O'Connor, O'Faolain's major theme is the 'question of Ireland', though his interest in the question is frequently expressed in terms of disaffection and doubt. For O'Faolain, the glory of Ireland was something of a necessary myth, to be placed very firmly in the past. He has tended to concentrate on an analysis of contemporary troubles, not untouched by the emergence of a new mythology, however:

> Out of Ireland, have we come.
> Great hatred, little room,
> Maimed us at the start . . .[12]

Political determinism takes the place of Fate in O'Faolain's early stories, providing the framework within which he will seek to 'find [a sense of] order in the seeming chaos of Life'.[13]

'Midsummer Night Madness' is the most interesting of these stories. Set in Ireland during the Troubles, it has a polished allegorical superstructure which is continually threatened by a sense of the muddy complexities of a contingent situation. The allegory is clear, almost painfully so. The story centres on a decayed landowner of English descent, 'Old Henn', and a tinker girl Gypsy, the last in a long line of his 'lady loves'. The girl has become pregnant by him, and instead of relinquishing his responsibility as he has done so often in the past, Old Henn is forced by the local IRA commandant to marry her (the battalion is stationed in Henn's home, against his wishes). The couple are described leaving Ireland for their honeymoon:

> The woman, in a massive hat with a scarlet feather, had flaunted her way to her carriage – the old man, her husband, hobbling and shuffling along yards behind her. His travelling coat almost completely hid him, its tail touching the ground, its coat-collar up about his ears.[14]

The grotesque union is heavily emblematic. The degenerate English landowner, in being forced to marry a representative of the class most victimised and outlawed by his kind, is being impelled to make some reparation for the 'rape' of Ireland – a land which offered 'a marvellous but a lost opportunity' as he himself puts it.

The honeymoon description constitutes the last paragraph of the story, and imposes a retrospective order on the confusion of impressions we have gathered from it. The main body of the tale deals with the earlier visit of an unnamed first-person narrator to Henn Hall. As he is working for the IRA, we would expect the narrator to loathe Henn and all he stands for, but his responses are more fluid than our expectations. His subtle perceptions endow the story with a richness which exceeds the strict requirements of the allegorical frame.

During the visit the narrator comes to recognise the historical 'rage' of the Anglo-Irish, seeing 'for the first time how deep the hate on [Henn's] side could be, as deep as the hate on ours'. He recognises, in other words, that Henn is as much the product of the historical moment, and of historical process, as any member of the IRA. Listening to Henn, he has to acknowledge too that some kind of ideal, however limited, has guided the behaviour of most of the colonists:

> 'I believed in things once,' he said. 'I had ideas about the people, the people on my land. I thought I'd get them to do things with their land – I was ready to help them with loans and advice. I'd tell them how to drain it, how to grow more variety of vegetables.'[15]

He concedes the 'fatal' passivity of the Irish, exemplified in the lax behaviour of the local IRA commandant:

> At that Stevey burst into a terrible profane rage, but he caught my eye and fell silent. He knew my thought – if he had not been so inactive for the past four months the Tans would not be roaring their way so daringly through his territory now.[16]

In comparison with the boorish commandant, the narrator finds Old Henn positively attractive. And here we feel the real richness of the story, which is rooted in the play of the narrator's individual sensibility and in his recorded past. He has grown up in the district, and remembers Henn and his home as they were in their prime:

> It was a wonderful old house to look at, and often we looked at it from far off, sitting up on its own high hill, its two gable chimneys like two cocked ears . . . it must have been visible for miles to anyone driving westward to Crookstown along the valley, following the little river and its dark line of woods.[17]

Henn's house is, almost, a 'great good place', offering an ideal of grace and civilisation. Even in its decay it offers the narrator a rare experience of beauty and charm; indeed it is because it is now in decay that Henn's house exerts so powerful a hold over his imagination:

> But as I looked I saw, too, how the clouds were gathering like pale flowers over the inky sky and even as I dropped silently downhill the first drops beat the fronded layers above. On my left, high as two men, rose the estate walls that had once kept the whole countryside at bay but could not now (gapped and crumbling as they were) keep a fox out or a chicken in. I passed two great entrance-gates sunken in the weeds. Then the pale ghostlike pillars of the third gate came in view across a gap in the tunnel where the rain was beating down the dust.[18]

A self-confessed 'romantic', the narrator is susceptible to a dying fall and is, we feel, never so close to English civilisation as when he feels it in decline, a fit subject for clergy like the Celtic civilisation it had supplanted.

In 'Midsummer Night Madness' we sense some disjunction between the mythic framework of the story and the wayward, 'lonely voice' or sensibility of the narrator. It may be useful in this respect to compare the story with 'No Country for Old Men', published in 1962. The theme is rather similar, but O'Faolain approaches it very differently. He subordinates narrative to dramatic presentation, externalising, as it were, the burden of the 'lonely voice'. 'No Country for Old Men' is, it is true, introduced by a frame narrator, but he rapidly fades into the background. His function is to create a false sense of security at the opening of the story through what might be described as his 'urbane' acceptance of the IRA, his facile assimilation of their values:

> Joe and Freddy had sent the son racing back across the border in the Jaguar. They then took over the van and the dead boy. We took off our hats to Joe O'Ducie and Freddy Gilpin and we let it be known to them both that there would be a public dinner at the Dolphin waiting for them when they came out of jail.[19]

The narrator has no direct knowledge of the incident at the heart of the story and, initially, misrepresents what has happened. His tangential relationship to the action reflects his marginal value as a moral guide or commentator.

In the key episode the narrator becomes, as it were, a character. Joe O'Ducie is a substitute or stand-in for the narrator: fat, wealthy and corrupt, 'building up his country' by doing a healthy trade in corsets, having long forgotten the Republican principles which animated his youth. Joe is confronted with three versions of his former self: his son, a member of the IRA; a second, unnamed youth who has died for the cause; and a contemporary, Freddy, who has not yet lost completely the principles of his youth. It is Freddy who articulates the theme of this and many other of O'Faolain's stories. He meditates on the loss of youth and attendant attrition of feeling, and finishes his speech with a sentence which reverberates far beyond its immediate context (a reference to the legend of Faust): 'There's no magic strong enough to cheat the world.'[20] 'Magic' might be associated with the troubled romanticism of O'Faolain's early stories, and with the related impulse to mythologise the condition of Ireland. In 'No Country for Old Men' O'Faolain suggests that romantic idealism is a quality necessarily associated with youth, and that it will wither and decay under the pressure of a man's dealings with 'the world, the flesh and the devil'. The dead youth of Joe and Freddy is figured as the corpse of the young man they must carry on their backs until they reach the Irish border – rather as one might carry a dead part of oneself. The boy is described in appropriately romantic terms, having a 'pallid brow' and 'dark and glossy' hair. The idea of 'magic' is then undercut in comic fashion as Freddy the *philosophe* recalls the 'tricks and jokes shop' he was reduced to running when he left the IRA and approached the grim realities of life in Manchester:

> you know the sort of thing – false noses, imitation ink blobs, stink bombs, card tricks, little celluloid babies that squirt water when you squash 'em, nutcrackers in the shape of a woman's legs . . . cockroaches to drop in a fellow's beer.[21]

It is the burden of the story that 'magic' must yield to what Freddy calls 'the long humiliation of life', but from his understanding of this fact Freddy derives some comfort. Like Yeats in the poem from which the story takes its title, O'Faolain offers understanding, and the ability to 'place' experience, as compensation for the loss of 'wonder':

> Caught in that sensual music all neglect
> Monuments of unageing intellect . . .[22]

O'Faolain's best stories, like those of O'Connor, tend to dramatise loss. This becomes particularly interesting when the theme of a story is story-telling itself, as it is, in a sense, in O'Connor's 'The Majesty of the Law', and as it is more directly in O'Faolain's 'The Silence of the Valley' and 'Angels and Ministers of Grace'. A consideration of the latter two stories will illuminate O'Faolain's changing relationship to the story-telling tradition.

In 'The Silence of the Valley', O'Faolain addresses directly the relationship between story-telling and a traditional way of life. He presents this relationship as axiomatic. The ability to tell a story depends on a sense of life's intelligibility, on a sense that one inhabits a manageable and comprehensible universe. This is the sense possessed by the dead cobbler who has, through his famed ability to tell stories, moulded the life of the people in his valley. The last of a long line of tale-tellers, the cobbler has – just – been able to accommodate contemporary developments to his imaginative world:

> the priest too was pulling his pipe and telling her about the dead cobbler, and how every night in winter his cottage used to be full of men coming to hear his views on Hitler and Mussolini and the prophecies of Saint Columcille which foretold that the last battle of the last world-war would be fought at Ballylickey Bridge. The others began to listen as he retold some of the cobbler's more earthy stories that were as innocent and sweaty as any Norse or Celtic yarn of the Golden Age.[23]

Just as Hitler rubs shoulders with figures from the 'Golden Age', so pagan and religious elements mingle in the mind of the cobbler. Both Christianity and pagan myth are as it were aspects of a single, indivisible, primordial 'story' – and this is an interpretation which the local priest is happy to accept. He himself is closely associated with two of the symbols of paganism running through the story – the eel and the salmon, both by pagan tradition sacred – and at one point is described in terms which seem more appropriate to paganism as a 'necromancer'.

The story-teller's gift, his understanding, is seen as eminently natural, perhaps as dependent on a certain natural, unselfconscious quality. The story opens with a description of the 'silence of the valley', broken intermittently by natural sounds:

> In the summer a fisherman will hear the tinkle of the ghost of one of those falls only if he steals among the mirrored reeds under the pent

of the cliffs, and withholds the plash of his oars. These tiny muted sounds will awe and delight him by the vacancy out of which they creep, intermittently.[24]

The voice of the cobbler is equated, by implication, with such natural 'speech', in a later passage which offers clear parallels with that quoted above. As the priest visits the cottage of the dead man he becomes aware 'for the first time in his life, of the silence of this moor'. We are told that:

> Always up to now he had thought of this cottage as a place full of the cobbler's satirical talk, his wife's echoes and contradictions. Somebody had once told the old man that he was not only the valley's storyteller but its 'gossip-columnist'. . . . He realized that this cottage would be completely silent from now on.[25]

His awareness of the loss of the cobbler's speech precipitates in the priest 'a sudden poignant sensation of autumn', although it is in fact bright May. This is meant to trigger our sense of the death of tradition, the theme which occupies the middle section of the story.

In relation to this theme, the characters of the story may be divided into two groups. First, there are those who are still living a 'primitive' way of life, and who are locked in tradition, living as it were in a time-warp. O'Faolain uses disturbing images of entrapment to evoke their situation: for example, as a group of outsiders travel back to the hotel from the cobbler's cottage, they feel that the mountains are trying to 'bar their way', and, as they struggle back to the hotel, 'it was as if they were cycling not through space but through a maw of Time that would never move'.[26] The second group consists of the guests at the hotel, representatives of civilisation who are all aware of the values of tradition although they are cut off from a primitive way of life. Much space is devoted to their appreciation of tradition, and to the disputes which arise as they consider ways in which traditional standards might be retained and assimilated to progress:

> 'I worship these mountains and these lakes and these simple Gaelic people because they alone still possess . . .'
> 'But you were angry last night when I defended primitive life. You wanted sea-planes on the lake and tourists from Manchester in Austin Sevens parked in front of . . .'
> 'I have already explained to you,' he reproved her, 'that to be

natural doesn't mean that we must be primitive! That's the romantic illusion. What I mean to say is – that is in very simple words of course . . .'

And his dark face buttoned up and he became ill-disposed again as he laboured to resolve his own contradictions.[27]

What the guests are unable to realise is that their attitude to tradition is marred by a fatal self-consciousness, and that it is this which divides them irretrievably from such people as the old cobbler. It is, it seems, not only that their lives are more complex than those of the 'folk', but that their knowledge of the world is more complex and full of 'contradictions'. As a result, no 'story' can make their life whole: it can only offer an image of potential harmony. For the disputants quoted above, truth must be sought in the pages of Darwin and Lamarck, not in the springs of narrative.

'The Silence of the Valley' is thus something of a paradox: a successful story which deals with the loss or breakdown of story. The text is held together by a sense of elegy appropriate to the diverse characters. The peasants feel a sense of direct personal loss over the death of the old cobbler, which can merge easily enough with the more sophisticated melancholy of the guests at the hotel, who mourn a passing tradition. Thus far the story might be compared with O'Connor's 'The Majesty of the Law', were it not for the fact that the voices of the hotel guests reverberate, troubling the surface of O'Faolain's story and leaving us with a sense of something unresolved. It is as though, through these characters, O'Faolain has questioned fundamentally the basis of his story but has been unable to find any satisfactory 'answer' to his question. In consequence we are left with a sense of a silence, an absence, at the heart of the story.

In 'Angels and Ministers of Grace', published fifteen years later, there is no such absence. In general, the lines of O'Faolain's later stories are more confident, as we have seen in 'No Country for Old Men'. With O'Faolain's sudden realisation, described in 1958, that 'Ireland had not adjusted herself to the life about her in the least little bit', it is as though a difficulty, both formal and moral, over the appropriate form for the short story had been resolved. From this time O'Faolain tended to view the difficulties faced by such characters as those in 'The Silence of the Valley' as essentially false, the product of lazy habits of thought rather than of any fundamental change in the 'quality of life'. With this restored feeling for the continuity of human experience came a renewed belief in the relevance and value of story-telling, nowhere more gaily celebrated than in 'Angels and Ministers of Grace'.

Jacky Neason is told by his doctor to rest his heart for a couple of months. He takes this advice, rather ruefully, and retires to bed, clutching *A Catholic Dictionary* as a substitute for the encyclopaedia the doctor has recommended as light reading. Jacky, who has not been to church for five years, becomes absorbed in the *Dictionary*, and becomes fascinated by certain doctrinal questions: how did the devil tempt Adam and Eve if they were innocent? How can a thousand angels stand on the point of a needle? He discusses these issues with his neighbour, a teacher, and manages by his scepticism to unsettle his stolid friend. In consequence, while Jacky gradually becomes bored with the *Dictionary*, the teacher, the priest, a neighbouring monk and Jesuit all become perplexed by the issues he has raised, to the extent that they can hardly carry on with their pedagogic and pastoral duties. The story has a double thrust. First Jacky, like a sensible man, gives up the *Dictionary* as a bad job, dismissing it as fiction. His lighthearted stance is contrasted with the unnecessary gloom of those who make the mistake of taking it seriously:

> 'Forget it!' said Jacky. 'Eileen!' he roared. 'Bring up the bottle of whisky.'
> 'No thanks,' said Milo, getting up gloomily and putting the obscure volume under his arm. 'Father Milvey is coming around to my place tonight and I'll have to have a jar with him'. He looked down miserably at Jacky. 'You're looking fine!'[28]

Secondly, Jacky picks up a copy of *The Arabian Nights*, in the *Dictionary*'s place. He begins to read, and reads on until far into the night. The story ends:

> He raised his eyes to the night sky. It was a fine, sweet, open-faced night in May. A star among the many stars beamed at him. There are more things in Heaven. . . . With renewed relish he returned to the Grand Vizier's daughter. His glass was full.[29]

'Angels and Ministers of Grace' offers a celebration of the power of narrative, and the reference to *The Arabian Nights* is particularly interesting. O'Faolain manages to present Jacky's interest in ancient narratives as the most natural thing in the world – indeed it is after reading the stories that Jacky notices, for the first time, the beauty of the external world. We feel no disjunction between Jacky's world and that of Scheherazade, and this seems to reflect the author's sense of ease, a feeling, ultimately, of continuity with the springs of narrative. Such ease contrasts markedly with the tension expressed in the work of later post-modernist writers who have tried to return to the springs of narrative. It is significant, for example, that John Barth has also written about Scheherazade – but his tone and stance differ widely from that of O'Faolain.

The title of O'Faolain's story refers to Hamlet's cry as he encounters his dead father:

> Angels and ministers of grace defend us! . . .
> Thou com'st in such a questionable shape
> That I will speak to thee: I'll call thee Hamlet,
> King, father . . .
>
> (*Hamlet* I. iv. 39–45)

It is clear that the 'angels and ministers of grace' which must defend Jacky are Scheherazade's stories, and, it transpires, it is in some sense against a ghostly or symbolic 'father' that they must defend him. Jacky must be protected from that excessive preoccupation with authority in the form of Church or State which O'Faolain regarded as the vice of the Irish, and the source of their 'squint-thinking'.

Like O'Connor and O'Faolain, T. F. Powys was occupied by questions of order and authority, but unlike them he sought an answer to the 'seeming chaos of Life' in religious terms. He was a religious allegorist, writing in the tradition of Chaucer and Bunyan and often using the techniques of medieval plays and fables. Most of his fables and stories were written before 1930 but they were not published until the thirties and forties, by which time he was poised to influence a younger generation of storywriters. Powys's 'ruralism' has already been mentioned in this context: it was this aspect of his work which had the greatest impact on subsequent writers. Like his brothers John Cowper and Llewelyn Powys, he celebrated the traditional values of rural England at a time when these were unfashionable. Living in relative isolation at East Chaldon in Dorset, he emphasised the virtues of life in a small pastoral community. Not surprisingly, one of the first critics to praise his work was F. R. Leavis, who encountered his writing around the time when he was expounding the values of the English rural tradition in *For Continuity*, and, with Denys Thompson, in *Culture and Environment*.

Powys's retreat from twentieth-century urban life may be linked with his search for religious truth. He was not associated with the Church in any orthodox sense, and shrank away from fixed forms of belief. His concept of God was protean – sometimes in his work 'God' is equated simply with consciousness, less frequently God is identified with moral power. Powys shifted his ground on principle, as it were, believing that fixed ideas could only stand in the way of the kind of truth he was after. As he wrote in 1918, 'I am without a belief, a belief is too easy a road to God' (*Soliloquies of a Hermit*).

Powys's religious consciousness was thus predicated on an ancient paradox – 'Lord, I believe. Help thou my unbelief' – and perhaps it was because his thought was founded on paradox that he was drawn to the allegorical mode. Allegory, as recent critics have emphasised, is itself a problematic form. We can no longer say that allegories are founded on a fixed, stable view of the world: rather we might say that the use of the allegorical form suggests a longing for such a fixed, stable view. The allegorist is drawn to pattern, repetition and the ordering of human experience, but he can do no more than offer a sense of order which will frequently be betrayed by the dynamics of his text. Allegory is a more unstable mode than earlier critics have thought, offering a paradigm of desire, rather than of belief.

We can appreciate Powys's stories most fully, then, if we are alert to their contradictions and suspicious of neat formulations and fixed 'meanings'. Apart from their religious complexity, Powys's stories offer a rich analysis of human desires and weaknesses, and, in particular, an analysis of human sexual drives. 'The Bucket and the Rope' deals directly with the sexual theme. This is a true fable in that the protagonists of the story are the inanimate objects of the title, taking part in a simple dialogue which reveals much more about the human 'hero', Mr Dendy. The telling of the story from the point of view of the bucket and rope creates an effect of defamiliarisation, and forces us to a reappraisal of our own attitudes to sexuality. In particular, the bucket and rope lead us to question the idea of monogamy and sexual possessiveness: in their view Mr Dendy's young wife is doing no more than create and dispense joy as she gives herself to another young man outside marriage. Their misreading of Mr Dendy's attitude makes Powys's point with comic effectiveness – they think he must be hiding himself to watch the guilty couple 'for the pleasure of witnessing the kindness of his wife'.

The true ambivalence of the story lies in the presentation of the wife, first described in these terms: 'Anyone could see that she had the sweetest of natures, that would be unlikely, for fear of being cruel, to refuse anything a man might ask of her.'[30] It has perhaps not been sufficiently stressed that women in Powys's fiction are at once angelic and demonic. Apparently 'sweet' and docile, they have an underlying sexual drive which is stronger than that of any man, and it is they who are in a sense 'blamed' for all sexual transgressions. On the one hand Powys seems to approve of women's vitality and ability to love, and he seeks to endorse in pagan fashion the 'play' of love wherever it may appear. But, ultimately, conventional morality, even superstition, seem to get the better of him, and so he figures as a reluctant misogynist, fearing and blaming the power of women. This passage from 'The Key of the Field' is indicative:

> If Lily had a fault – and she was so well-grown and comely a girl that anyone might expect her to wish to be a wanton – it was that her heart was responsive to the slightest touch of love, though she seemed kinder to her uncle than to any other man.

Mr Dendy of 'The Bucket and the Rope' finally hangs himself because of his wife's infidelity, but we tend to have a double response to this. On the one hand, we can see his death as an understandable tragedy for which his wife is responsible; on the other, we can see it as the foolish action of a man unable (like most of us) to take the 'larger view' of human tides of feeling.

In a sense, love is Mr Dendy's undoing, and love is certainly viewed with distrust in many of Powys's stories. His best-known novel, *Mr Weston's Good Wine* (1927), turns on the contrast between the 'light wine' of love, suitable for the prime of life, and the dark wine of death, offering far greater comfort for those who are ready to accept it. The story 'Darkness and Nathaniel' is structured around a rather similar contrast between light and darkness. Light is associated with the fleeting pleasures of the body, with colour, warmth, birdsong and the promise of love:

> Nathaniel never felt alone when light was with him. Abroad in the daytime he would watch a rabbit or a child at play with the same gladness. Nathaniel's friend was always promising him pleasure in some kind of manner – by means of a sunbeam or a little candle.
>
> 'Oh! Nathaniel,' Light seemed to say, 'live and enjoy yourself, you

are not dead yet, and one day you will be happy. Even if your beard is ragged, you cannot fail to find presently a young woman who will not be frightened by it.'

Nathaniel is a poor man whose wife and children have left him. He lives a frugal and harmless existence, sustained by the promise of Light. He is continually led to expect 'merry company', or an encounter with some 'lively wanton', but these promises are never fulfilled. One evening he finds himself sitting alone in the darkness which he fears. Despair comes to him 'creeping like a snake along the muddy lanes' – a typical Powysian introduction of a Biblical reference in homely, unpretentious fashion. Then Darkness speaks, berating him for his love of fickle Light, 'a liar and a meddler'. Light and love are well enough 'for the day', says Darkness, but it is in darkness that one discovers 'what is profound, lasting and sublime'. The story or fable ends much like *Mr Weston's Good Wine*. Darkness answers Nathaniel's final questions:

'I give eternal longings,' replied Darkness, 'and after that true happiness.'
'And what is true happiness?' asked Nathaniel.
'Death', replied Darkness.

'Darkness and Nathaniel' could be viewed as in some ways more successful than *Mr Weston's Good Wine*: the force of Powys's vision is more strongly felt in the short story form, which offers fewer narrative disjunctions and digressions. Yet 'Darkness and Nathaniel' does not deal in simple or unrelieved contrasts: like all Powys's work it is more subtle than summary makes it appear. To give just one example, the lyrical impulse of the story is clearly with Light, not Darkness, a projection as it were of man's inescapable involvement with the 'things of light and day'.

Powys's empathy with a range of human feeling and reluctance to commit himself to a final point of view is most marked in a series of meditative fables: 'The Stone and Mr Thomas', 'Mr Pim and the Holy Crumb', 'The Corpse and the Flea', 'John Pardy and the Waves'. 'The Stone and Mr Thomas' is one of his most opaque stories. Like 'The Bucket and the Rope' and 'Darkness and Nathaniel' it takes a dialectical form, recording a spirited dialogue between the skull of Mr Thomas, dead these fifty years, and the stone which heads his grave. Conflict arises because Mr Thomas is, in the view of the stone, far too keenly aware of his own importance: 'Though Mr Thomas's skull was all that was left of him, it was the more ready to believe itself to be of the utmost importance, just as the whole body used to believe in the days when he lived.' The stone attempts to deflate Mr Thomas's pride, assuring him that his life is worth nothing in comparison with the 'life' of a stone: 'You, Mr Thomas, were formed in the womb of your mother for my sake; you lived your short life and you went your way only to give me a final, a distinctive, a long existence.' Mr Thomas is warned in doom-laden tones that 'God only made the earth as a cemetery for man to corrupt in': man's mortality and insignificance are stressed as a corrective to presumption.

On one level the stone's reduction of human pretensions seems reasonable, but then Mr Thomas's memories of human existence cut across his antagonist's logic. The transient pleasures of human life are endowed with a seemingly irreducible power:

> What of those peaceful days that I spent in rowing my little boat under the white cliffs? Are they gone so early? I behold now the dark blue colour of the sea, so rich, so heavy, while above the hot lustful sun ravished all comers with its love. Did not the beauty of those summer days sink deep within me, when the seaweed, far down in the dark colour of the water, moved here and there swaying delicately, with so fantastic a loveliness, that a man's soul could melt in the very beauty that the eyes saw?

'The Stone and Mr Thomas' finally resists interpretation to the extent that it is not possible for the reader to 'resolve' the dispute between the stone and Mr Thomas. On the one hand, the stone appears to be correct in his analysis of an excess of human egotism; the narrative seems to confirm this through a final juxtaposition of 'old bones' (here Mr Thomas's skull) and 'crushed beetle', both said to make excellent dung for spring onions. On the other hand, the stone is only a stone – able to speak but unable to experience the higher emotions. And it is suggested, through changes in narrative tone more than anything else, that in moments of intense awareness man is a vessel for 'the moods of God', transcending self through identification with the external world.

Powys tends to thwart readerly expectations by means of sudden changes of narrative tone or perspective. The dialectical structure of many of his stories seems to promise a 'final solution' which is almost always denied us. In his comparatively few 'long short stories', Powys would seem to have more space for an exploration of religious or ethical contradictions. However, such longer stories, for example 'The Only Penitent', are marked by the same ambiguous and elusive quality as the fables. A certain narrative opacity seems to be the necessary correlate of Powys's religious unorthodoxy.

In 'The Only Penitent', an Anglo-Protestant clergyman is suddenly drawn to the idea of confession, thinking, as he wanders about the fields of his parish, that he sees the animals – frogs and rooks – congregating to confess their sins, and leaving the 'congregation' with a lighter heart. The way in which Mr Hayhoe receives his 'call' to implement the rite of confession is presented comically, and we are left in no doubt that he is wildly misinterpreting the behaviour of the animals. Yet Mr Hayhoe is a virtuous man, or at least is initially presented as such: 'He lived but humbly: that is, he never thought of how he dined, or dressed, or spoke, having only one idea in his life – to love all men.' As Mr Hayhoe becomes more engrossed in the idea of the confessional, his motives come under greater suspicion. He and his wife begin to take a vicarious interest in the sins of the villagers, hoping, however ingenuously, that enough sins will have been committed for the confessional to be a success:

> 'But perhaps no one has sinned,' said Priscilla.
> 'Oh! I am sure someone must have,' cried Mr Hayhoe.

Later, Mr Hayhoe is forced to admit that there may have been some egotism in his desire to install himself as village confessor; he then realises that there is egotism even in such self-deprecation.

So the vicar's goodness is not so simple in its causes and effects as would at first appear. And, ironically, one of the first results of his announcement about the confessional is that the villagers of Madder, like their vicar, begin to take a new and somewhat suspect interest in sin:

> All kinds of doings, that had before been but ordinary acts, were now regarded with suspicion, and all wondered what ought to be confessed. Each thing that was done – even to the picking of a few daisies, or the darning of a stocking – might hide in it a secret sin that could be told to Mr Hayhoe. And so, with this added interest in the matter, the delight in all manner of naughtiness increased apace.

The summer days pass, and no one comes forward to the confessional. Mr Hayhoe, the most virtuous man in the village, becomes sick and ill as he ponders the failure of his plan – but the sturdy villagers carry on with their round of carnal pleasures. And again we sense a typically Powysian ambivalence. The strength of the villagers, and their ability to enjoy life, is enthusiastically presented and again seen as somehow self-vindicating. The behaviour of Mr Hayhoe seems by contrast perverse.

As each Sunday passes, the emptiness of the vicar's confessional increases the reader's suspense about the anticipated arrival of the 'only penitent'. The climax of the story is heralded by an apocalyptic storm, and the sudden appearance in the church of 'Tinker Jar'. Aloof, impenetrable and wayward in his dealings with men, he comes only rarely to the village of Madder, to be greeted by the fear and scorn of the villagers. On this day he has come to Mr Hayhoe to repent, needing, he says, the forgiveness of a mortal man. He 'confesses' that he has crucified his own son and brought all woe into the world. He concludes his confession: ' "I destroy all men with a sword," said Jar. "I cast them down into the pit, they become nothing." ' Mr Hayhoe, who has already taken the opportunity to point out that 'Tinker Jar' has created 'joy and love' as well as destruction, seizes on the last word, 'nothing'. As soon as Tinker Jar confirms that it is annihilation and not eternal life which awaits man after death, the vicar 'boldly' forgives Tinker Jar his sin.

The conclusion is unorthodox, to say the least, in religious terms, and it is also interesting to note how un-Nietzschean the story is. Powys's debt to Nietzsche has often been remarked, but it is surely superficial. The real bent of Powys's thought is slower, deeper, more truly provincial. It is, if anywhere, in a kind of Anglo-Saxon stoicism and acceptance of annihilation that Powys's stories find a point of rest, not in any doctrine of 'eternal recurrence'.

Most of Powys's stories and fables are haunted by images of order and significance, but these remain mere images or possibilities. 'Bottle's Path' might stand as a paradigm for Powys's allegories. In this story a man tries night after night under the moon and stars to trace a fixed path through a field full of waving hay, but each morning the hay, like the sea, has rippled back into place, obliterating all signs of his human efforts and endeavours. 'I believe I went all wrong', Mr Bottle has to conclude.

The work of O'Connor, O'Faolain and T. F. Powys is marked by a concern for order and a desire to make sense of the world through story or myth. Though the relationship of these three writers to the story-telling tradition differs radically in some respects, they share an important characteristic. For them, as for Stevenson and Kipling before them, there can be no simple relationship to the tale-telling tradition. As exponents of the modern short story, a form sophisticated and highly literary from its inception, they can only look back self-consciously to a past offering a hypothetically organic 'world of story' which has now vanished. This is the world evoked by Walter Benjamin: he is writing about 'every real story':

> It contains, openly or covertly, something useful. The usefulness may in one case, consist in a moral; in another, in some practical advice; in a third, in a proverb or maxim. In every case the storyteller is a man who has counsel for his readers. But if today 'having counsel' is beginning to have an old-fashioned ring, this is because the communicability of experience is decreasing. . . . Counsel woven into the fabric of real life is wisdom. The art of storytelling is reaching its end because the epic side of truth, wisdom, is dying out.[31]

While it is impossible to 'prove' Benjamin's thesis in any empirical, historical sense, the feeling of loss which he describes, and the sense of a troubled distance between the writer and the mainsprings of his art, are characteristic of this generation of 'tale-tellers'. In formal terms, Powys is the least self-conscious of these writers, but his studied realism and rejection of the urban present are symptomatic of some unease.

5 The Free Story

Writing of the short story and the cinema, both 'young' arts in which she found intriguing similarities, Elizabeth Bowen suggested in 1937 that:

> The new literature, whether written or visual, is an affair of reflexes, of immediate susceptibility, of associations not examined by reason: it does not attempt a synthesis. Narrative of any length involves continuity, sometimes a forced continuity: it is here that the novel too often becomes invalid.[1]

In the same essay she coined the term 'free story', and defined that freedom in terms of lack of a sponsoring tradition. For her the free story was utterly divorced from folk narrative tradition: it was, literally, a new art, the 'child of this century'. It is not clear whether she made any distinction between the free story and modernist short fiction: the reference to the 'lack of a sponsoring tradition' suggests that the two new forms merged in her mind. Indeed, it appears that the free story has not yet been adequately distinguished from modernist short fiction, though the two types can be clearly separated in chronological and formal terms.

The free story must be treated as a separate entity, distinct from modernist short fiction, because although it too comes under the broad category of short fiction rather than short story (I retain the term 'free story' for purely historical reasons), it is in experimental terms a retrogressive form. The free story does not go beyond, but rather turns its back on, many of the barriers broken by the modernists. Perhaps the question of characterisation is the most important here. Symbolist and modernist short fiction had interrogated the concept of a coherent, historical character, whereas the free story may often pivot on the exploration of character in the traditional sense. Characters are seen as internally coherent and consistent in time: human beings are valued for their 'character' in the sense of their uniqueness and idiosyncrasy.

Such a concern for the contingent and specific extends into other areas of the free story. Character and locale, for example, are usually closely delineated by free story writers, who are attracted to the particular rather than the general. They rarely use description for symbolic purposes: the emphasis is on the particular, concrete subject. So V. S. Pritchett writes that the short story is for him: 'a form which depends on intensifying the subject, stamping a climate on it, getting the essence of it.'[2] The free story also shows far more response to social pressures than does modernist short fiction. This shift in emphasis may be ascribed in part to the impact of the Second World War, which affected civilian life as the First World War did not. It is significant that immediately after the war, when Elizabeth Bowen, V. S. Pritchett and Graham Greene joined in a debate on the question 'Why Do I Write?',[3] their major preoccupation was with the writer's relationship to society. All three writers affirmed the importance of this relationship, in an unequivocal manner which would have startled their modernist precursors.

Such aspects of the free story would suggest that it has closer affinities with the novel than with, say, a lyric poem. The interest in social issues, in particular, seems to link the free story with the novel form, and this may account for the number of novelists who, when writing in the short form, have turned to the free story. Angus Wilson and Joyce Cary are examples. Yet these novelists are rarely completely successful in this, and for the free story as for other short story and fiction forms, it remains true that there are only certain writers who, in Elizabeth Bowen's words, 'show in this form a special, unique release of their faculties', and who, by their gifts, give the form 'new direction and force'. Such writers are almost invariably writers in the short form before they are novelists: this is true of V. S. Pritchett and William Sansom, and, I suggest, of Bowen herself. As her first biographer has indicated, in the 'judgement of posterity' it seems likely that her short fiction will be valued above her novels.[4]

The free story comes into the category of short fiction rather than short story because, despite the name Elizabeth Bowen gave it, it is not primarily biased towards narrative. Plot, in so far as it exists, is there to reveal character – the art of the free story writer is, in Pritchett's words, to catch people at the moment when, through action or speech, 'the inner life exposes itself unguardedly'. Plot is not there, as it often is in the short story proper, for didactic purposes, nor is it there to express through its own structure a metaphysical truth. Like modernist short fiction, the free story is thus typically inconclusive as narrative. Elizabeth Bowen has written:

The art of the short story permits a break at what in the novel would be the crux of the plot: the short story, free from the *longueurs* of the novel is also exempt from the novel's conclusiveness – too often forced and false: it may thus more nearly than the novel approach aesthetic and moral truth.[5]

The contention that 'aesthetic and moral truth' are by definition shifting and relative links the free story with Impressionist painting. Scene and vision are still more important in the free story than in modernist short fiction, and it is not coincidence that the principal writers considered in this chapter all wished initially to paint rather than to write. Elizabeth Bowen studied painting for a short while before turning to short fiction; V. S. Pritchett has described his early passion for that most evanescent medium, watercolour; and William Sansom has described himself as a 'painter *manqué*'. The analogy between the free story and Impressionism can be pressed quite far. Like the Impressionists, the free story writers were committed to sensation and perception, and their work is marked by a heightened sensitivity to colour, light and atmosphere. Light takes on an almost mystical significance, the recurrent image of light moving on water suggesting the evanescent nature of human perception and experience. Using a similar image, V. S. Pritchett described the art of Chekhov: 'He is asserting that life is a fish that cannot be netted by mood or doctrine, but continually glides away between sun and shadow.'[6]

The shifting, interpenetrating relations between subject and object are a central concern of free story writers, though it must be emphasised that in this Impressionist form both subject and object have a status and coherence denied them by modernist and post-modernist writers. Thus there is no great apprehension of, or desire for, the merging of subject and object: interrelation and interaction between the two create the magnetic field in which the free story flourishes. Here Elizabeth Bowen presents a typically tense encounter between subject and object:

She was house-proud, and led this new friend with a touch of emotion up the path to the porch, across the ambitious raw garden. Davina, however, looked neither to right nor left: indoors, she did give one glance of surprise rather than pleasure round the Harvey living-room, artfully pale and bare, where through steel-framed windows blue–pink afternoon light flooded the walls and waxy expanse of floor. . . . Ranged round the cold brick hearth, three low chairs with sailcloth cushions invited a confidence everything else forbade.[7]

Such an encounter produces a relationship between subject and object from which we can extrapolate a vision of society: the encounter is not intended to create a mood in the Symbolist or modernist sense.

A further analogy which might be pursued is that between the free story and film. Elizabeth Bowen described techniques which she felt had been taken over from the cinema: 'oblique narration, cutting, the unlikely placing of emphasis'.[8] Verbal equivalents of these techniques are used in the free story, and metonymic cutting devices, in particular, enable the free story writers to combine the brevity prescribed by the early modernists with a wider range of social reference.

The free story writers' interest in character has been emphasised, and in fact Freudian theory provides much of the underpinning for their work. Freud's writings were not widely known in England until the twenties and thirties, and it was then, rather than in the early modernist period, that his influence was most widely felt in literature. The Freudian model of the super-ego, ego and id did not seem, initially, to conflict with the notion of a relatively fixed identity; whereas the diagnostic aspects of his work, and in particular the idea that the unconscious self could be revealed through such mechanisms as the lapsus, the dream and the joke, had particular relevance for short fiction writers. Elizabeth Bowen elaborates:

Man has to live how he can: overlooked and dwarfed he makes himself his own theatre. Is the drama inside heroic or pathological? Outward acts have often an inside magnitude. The short story, with its shorter span than the novel's, with its freedom from forced complexity, its possible lucidness, is able, like the poetic drama, to measure man by his aspirations and dreams and place him alone on that stage which, inwardly, every man is conscious of occupying alone.[9]

V. S. Pritchett also stresses the idea of 'revelation' when he writes that his characters 'live for projecting the fantasies of their inner, imaginative life and the energies that keep them going'.[10]

Revelation, vision – such terms point forward to a Surrealist quality which we will find in the free story of the war years. Another analogy with visual art – but the free story is itself so slippery of definition that often the best means of conveying a quality or aspect of the form is by such analogy. Perhaps Elizabeth Bowen has best summed-up the qualities of the form – though not without recourse to metaphor:

> This century's emotion . . . makes a half-conscious artist of every feeling man. Peaks of common experience soar past an altitude-line into poetry. There is also a level immediately below this, on which life is being more and more constantly lived, at which emotion crystallises without going icy, from which a fairly wide view is at command. This level the short story is likely to make its own.[11]

If in this context we substitute 'free story' for short story, and equate the poetic 'peaks of emotion' with the epiphany of modernist short fiction, we may have a fairly clear picture of the place, range and scope of the free story.

The 'discrepancy between fact or circumstance and feeling and the romantic will', a phrase used by Elizabeth Bowen in an essay in *Collected Impressions* (1950), identifies the central conflict in her short fiction, as in her novels. Usually this conflict is focused through the juxtaposition of the romantic consciousness of an adolescent and the jaded awareness of the adults who surround him or her. The world of adulthood, of 'maturity', is presented as almost uniformly diminished and disappointing. In Elizabeth Bowen's fiction the adult finds it impossible to recover the grand forms and dreams of childhood. A character in the story 'The Disinherited' thus articulates a common perception: 'One is empowered to live fully: occasion does not offer.' The theme of disillusion – a form of revelation – is clearly well suited to the short fiction form, and need not be seen in wholly negative terms. As Elizabeth Bowen writes:

> Even stories which end in the air, which are comments on or pointers to futility, imply that men and women are too big or too good for the futility in which they are involved. Even to objectify futility is something.[12]

The process of attrition which she sees in the maturing of the individual is mirrored for her on a wider historical scale. Modern life is presented as characteristically 'dwarfed', and the architectural imagery which appears frequently in her fiction develops our sense of a change in scale, a loss of the grand style in a modern world. 'Over-looked and dwarfed' man can find his theatre, his appropriate setting, in imagination only.

'Ann Lee's' is the title story of a collection published as early as 1926. It is interesting because it is a story 'about' a character in a sense that would not be possible in modernist short fiction. Ann Lee is viewed externally, and revealed, in as much as she is revealed, through her actions and speech, which are located in a particular social setting. Her social and professional status is delineated very precisely: she runs a hat shop in the 'miserable back streets' which lie behind Sloane Square, yet she is vulgarly described by one of her clientèle as 'practically a lady', and another speaks of her as 'not the sort of person, somehow, that one could ask to reduce her things'. Ann Lee is first seen framed in a doorway, and the painterly images of the door and mirror run through the story, so that characters are often found or 'frozen' in revealing attitudes. Appearance speaks for the characters, just as does environment. Elizabeth Bowen frequently uses a character's setting metonymically: environment is seen as an attribute of personality, effect rather than cause of being. So the exterior of Ann Lee's shop suggests a particular charm:

> Grey-painted woodwork framed a window over which her legend was inscribed in far-apart black letters: 'ANN LEE – HATS.' In the window there were always just two hats; one on a stand, one lying on a cushion; and a black curtain with a violet border hung behind to make a background for the hats. In the two upper storeys, perhaps, Ann Lee lived mysteriously, but this no known customer had ever inquired, and the black gauze curtains were impenetrable from without.

Ann Lee holds out the promise of romance to the two idle young women who have come to her shop. Themselves graceless and inept, they feel that in possessing one of Ann Lee's hats they will partake of some of her mystery and charm. Social divisions are overturned as these society women are placed in the position of supplicants, their eager manner contrasting with Ann Lee's serenity:

> These were the hats one dreamed about – no, even in a dream one had never directly beheld them; they glimmered rather on the margin of one's dreams. With trembling hands she reached out in

Ann Lee's direction to receive them. Ann Lee smiled deprecatingly upon her and them, then went away to fetch some more.

Up to this point the story has been concerned with certain codes of behaviour, which have been questioned through the simple juxtaposition of Ann Lee, whose poverty 'sets off' her economic and aesthetic independence, and the two clients, consumers who devote their life to the spending of the money of others. The level of the story is deepened through the introduction of a sub-plot. Just before the two women leave the shop a stranger comes in, letting in a sudden draught of cold air. He is instantly recognised as a type by one of the women, Miss Ames:

> As a matter of fact she was recognising him; not as his particular self but as an Incident. He – It – crops up periodically in the path of any young woman who has had a bit of a career.

This 'recognition' tells us something about both Miss Ames and Ann Lee: now Ann Lee seems to lose some of her Madonna-like quality. However, the oblique, glancing conclusion of the fiction gives us more insight into the implacability of character which protects her despite her ambiguous social position. As the visitors make their way back to Sloane Square, the stranger stumbles past them in the fog, sobbing. Ann Lee has certainly been firm:

> A square man, sunk deep into an overcoat, scudded across their patch of visibility. By putting out a hand they could have touched him. He went by them blindly; his breath sobbed and panted. It was by his breath that they knew how terrible it had been – terrible.
> Passing them quite blindly, he stabbed his way on into the fog.

'Ann Lee's', despite its brevity, deals with Jamesian themes; in particular with the complex relations between money, morality and taste. Its structure is loose and episodic: there is an almost conscious asymmetry in the fiction with its rushed sub-plot, which reminds us of Elizabeth Bowen's note on the 'unlikely placing of emphasis' in new fiction.

'The Little Girl's Room' (1934) could also be traced back to James, with its emphasis on the violence which may lurk in the mind of even the most docile of young girls. It may be useful too to compare this fiction with Katherine Mansfield's 'The Doll's House', in order to illustrate more clearly the differences between the modernist and the 'free' forms of short fiction.

In reading 'The Little Girl's Room' our first response is to the author's delicate handling of social nuance. We are taken into a very specific, and very English, social setting, which cannot be adequately characterised by the use of a simple label such as middle-middle class. The little girl of the title lives with her step-grandmother in a house of muffled and oppressive luxury. The décor establishes the tone of a household in which opulence is at war with good taste:

> So the child came to Mrs Letherton-Channing's house, where one had the impression of dignified exile, where British integrity seemed to have camped on a Tuscan hill, where English mid-summer did not exceed Italian April – roses wearing into July an air of delicate pre-maturity – and high noon reflected upon the ceilings a sheen of ilex and olive. Here the very guests seemed expatriate, and coal-fires, ruddy ghosts of themselves, roared under mantles crusted and swagged with glazed Della Robbia lemons and bluish pears. Clara Ellis, who was at least sincerely malicious, professed to adore this little Italy from Wigmore Street.

Likewise, respectability clashes with vulgarity. As Geraldine enters a room we are told that: 'At first Clara Ellis frowned: talk of a first-rate scandalous quality had been held up.'

Against this background Geraldine stands out clearly, a neglected child who has become passively selfish and malicious by default. Her isolation from other children, added to the fact that every initiative of hers is immediately overtaken by her grandmother (as the author puts it, 'Each young tendril put out found a wire waiting'), has made it impossible for her to develop her character through the normal channels of expression. Only in her daydreams can repressed fears and desires find some kind of outlet:

> She asked, 'General Littlecote,': they replied: '*He is massacred too.*' She saw his foolish old face lie in blood on a staircase, and spread out her hand to her side, in terror, close to her thumping heart. Her cheeks blazed. The rope of excitement she had been playing out guardedly, sparingly, now fled through her fingers, burning. She began to shout '*I defy – !*' and stamped on the mild carpet.

The narrative line of 'The Little Girl's Room' could be said to be marred by the inclusion in the fiction of some adventitious material, particularly in the light of Bowen's own indictment of work in which 'some adventitious emotion starts to deform the story'. Yet her fiction progresses adventitiously, and in this differs sharply from modernist short fiction, which is deliberately shaped round a central symbolic intention. Her writing progresses to a considerable extent by means of casual association, and it is thanks to this process that we are given in 'The Little Girl's Room' such delights as Miss Weekes, the 'resident lady gardener':

> [She] remained in outlook resolutely Old English. She whistled; the smock and breeches in which she worked were an offence to Mrs Letherton-Channing, who had engaged her to look after the frames and hot-houses, not expecting her to emerge from these. She had discovered that Miss Weekes morris-danced, that she did rush-work, that she participated in every possible movement to build Jerusalem in this pleasant and green part of Berkshire.

What haunts us, finally, about this particular short fiction is the atmosphere produced by the interaction of a particular character and her environment. In Geraldine, Elizabeth Bowen is concerned with a specific, a special, case, and it is the flavour of the contingent and specific which marks the story. There is no suggestion that the central figure is to be considered symbolic in a wider sense.

Katherine Mansfield's 'The Doll's House' is, like 'The Little Girl's Room', centred in the consciousness of a young girl sensing for the first time some of the pressures of adult life. 'The Doll's House' is set in New Zealand, but many have read it without realising that the setting is not English, for in Katherine Mansfield's fiction there is no place for the kind of exact social reference and placing of atmosphere which is so important in that of Bowen. The external setting of 'The Doll's House' is unimportant and is characterised only by a few brief phrases. We learn much more about the miniature doll's house than about its 'real' setting within the story, for the doll's house functions as a major image, figuring the bourgeois family home from which the little girl Kezia is emerging, which she is slowly preparing to indict, even perhaps to destroy. The material comfort and prosperity of bourgeois life is highlighted through the description of the doll's house:

> All the walls were papered. There were pictures on the walls, painted on the paper, with gold frames complete. Red carpet

covered all the floors except the kitchen; red plush chairs in the drawing-room, green in the dining room; tables, beds with real bedclothes, a cradle, a stove.[13]

Additionally, images of the circle and square run through the story, re-enforcing the idea of the 'line which had to be drawn somewhere', to quote Kezia's mother, between the haves and the have-nots. The focal image of 'The Doll's House', however, is that of the lamp, which figures grace, or an illumination beyond one's own petty desires. There is also of course a Biblical reference to 'the light of the world'.

What remains with us from 'The Doll's House' is a final, emblematic image. Two outcast children sit on a grass verge, expelled from the backyard of Kezia's home. However one of them, at least, has felt with Kezia the promise held out by the lamp:

> Presently our Else nudged up close to her sister. But now she had forgotten the cross lady. She put out a finger and stroked her sister's quill; she smiled her rare smile.
>
> 'I seen the little lamp,' she said softly.
>
> Then both were silent once more.

It could be argued that the 'long short' fiction is the form in which Elizabeth Bowen found a 'unique release' of her talents and faculties. In this type of fiction a number of characters may drift against each other, revealing personality and feeling only to an extent (we remember that Elizabeth Bowen's first book of stories had the tentative title *Encounters*); they may also be grouped together according to no apparent pattern or order. This sense of a lack of order and cohesion in modern life was something which she was particularly anxious to convey, and which she associated very largely with the dislocations caused by the Second World War.

In 'Summer Night' (1941), form and content are as one: the author's sense of the shifting and unsatisfactory nature of human contact is mirrored in the dislocations of the narrative. As one of the characters in the fiction aptly remarks:

> I was saying we should have to find a new form. . . . A new form for thinking and feeling . . .
>
> I say, this war's an awful illumination; it's destroyed our dark; we have to see where we are. Immobilised, God help us, and each so far apart that we can't even try to signal each other.

One of the most striking aspects of 'Summer Night' is the author's handling in it of cinematic and metonymic cutting devices. Bowen moves in an abrupt and apparently casual fashion among the lives of her characters, who are often linked simply by a contiguity of setting or time of day. So an estranged husband and wife share little but the 'lovely night' which just sustains their conventional conversation on the telephone. Ironically, the only person who feels that she can communicate with others is deaf, and her deafness, rather than giving her an intuitive understanding of others, merely protects her from the knowledge of failure in communication.

Characterisation is unusually open-ended in 'Summer Night'. In the case of each character we are left with a sense of the possibility of change, of a gathering together of latent forces. Meanwhile we, like the other characters, learn more about other people from their environment than from their action or speech. Elizabeth Bowen's extraordinary talent for the creation of atmosphere is most effectively released for this purpose. The description of Aunt Fran's room quoted below is an example. Aunt Fran is the elderly, unmarried sister of the pompous 'Major' whose wife has left him to spend the night with another man. The marginal nature of Aunt Fran's existence in his house is beautifully intimated:

> Round the room, on ledges and brackets, stood the fetishes she travelled through life with. They were mementoes – photos in little warped frames, musty, round straw boxes, china kittens, palm crosses, the three Japanese monkeys, *bambini*, a Lincoln Imp, a merry-thought pen-wiper, an ivory spinning-wheel from Cologne. From these objects the original virtue had by now almost evaporated. These gifts' givers, known on her lonely journey, were by now faint as their photographs: she no longer knew, now, where anyone was. All the more, her nature clung to these objects that moved with her slowly towards the dark.
>
> Her room, the room of a person tolerated, by now gave off the familiar smell of herself – the smell of the old. A little book wedged the mirror at the angle she liked. When she was into her ripplecloth dressing-gown she brushed and plaited her hair and took out her teeth.

'Summer Night' is concerned with the interlocking rather than with the meeting of lives, yet it is remarkable for the intimate sense of life which it conveys, a sense of vibrations caught and then missed in the steady air. A majestic landscape presides over all:

> As the sun set its light slowly melted the landscape, till everything was made of fire and glass. Released from the glare of noon, the haycocks now seemed to float on the aftergrass: their freshness penetrated the air. In the not far distance hills with woods up their flanks lay in light like hills in another world – it would be a pleasure of heaven to stand up there, where no foot ever seemed to have trodden, on the spaces between the woods soft as powder dusted over with gold.

'Mysterious Kôr' is more directly concerned than 'Summer Night' with the effects of the war. The title comes from a poem written in another age, when, as one of the characters puts it: 'they thought they had got everything taped, because the whole world had been explored, even the middle of Africa'. The two protagonists, Pepita and Arthur, feel the effects of the war in their personal life. They have been separated for a long while, and on Arthur's short leave can find nowhere to go where they can be alone. They loiter outside the gates of Regent's Park, reluctant to return to the flat which Pepita shares with the well-meaning but dense Callie who does not realise that on this particular occasion she might be *de trop* in the small flat.

As they stand at the entrance to the park, Pepita and Arthur watch the moon transforming the London cityscape:

> Full moonlight drenched the city and searched it; there was not a niche left to stand in. The effect was remorseless: London looked like the moon's capital – shallow, cratered, extinct. It was late, but not yet midnight; now the buses had stopped the polished roads and streets in this region sent for minutes together a ghostly unbroken reflection up. The soaring new flats and the crouching old shops and houses looked equally brittle under the moon, which blazed in windows that looked its way. The futility of the black-out became laughable: from the sky, presumably, you could see every slate in the roofs, every whited kerb, every contour of the naked winter flowerbeds in the park; and the lake, with its shining twists and tree-darkened islands would be a landmark for miles, yes, miles, overhead.

After they have stood for some minutes, Pepita draws away from Arthur murmuring 'Mysterious Kôr'. 'Mysterious Kôr' is something which Pepita in particular has built out of such dislocated moments as this – it has become an image which speaks to and reveals her subconscious desires. In this sense it is Surrealist, expressing desire through the kind of dislocated images which occur in dreams. For Pepita it is a dehumanised landscape which is desired and imagined. It is as though the ties of love and affection have become too much to bear in the uncertain world of the war: as though she seeks relief even from Arthur. A dream which extends the image of 'Mysterious Kôr' closes the story:

> She still lay, as she had lain, in an avid dream, of which Arthur had been the source, of which Arthur was not the end. With him she looked this way, that way, down the wide, void, pure streets, between statues, pillars and shadows, through archways and colonnades. With him she went up the stairs down which nothing but moon came; with him trod the ermine dust of the endless halls, stood on terraces, mounted the extreme tower, looked down on the statued squares, the wide, void, pure streets. He was the password, but not the answer: it was to Kôr's finality that she turned.

'Mysterious Kôr' works on a high level of emotion through the use of hallucinatory landscapes invested with all the anxiety of dream. It is an 'inward' story of the war, concerned with dislocations of private life and with the emotional rather than the physical effects of the war. As Arthur puts it to Callie in a rare moment of confidence:

> It makes me feel cruel the way I unsettle her: I don't know how much it's me myself or how much it's something the matter that I can't help. . . . They forget war's not just only war; it's years out of people's lives that they've never had before and won't have again.

'Mysterious Kôr' is a *tour de force*, catching the atmosphere of the forced conjunction of three people whose nerves have been frayed by the war. It is a short fiction which illustrates almost perfectly what Elizabeth Bowen meant when she wrote that for her 'the short story is a matter of vision, rather than of feeling'.[14]

V. S. Pritchett has been writing short stories for fifty years: his most recent collection was published in 1980.[15] In 1982 he was able to write that the short story 'is the glancing form of fiction that seems to be right for the nervousness and restlessness of contemporary life'.[16] He has explained and defended the form of the free story for over fifty years: it is fitting that his own work should provide such rich justification for the claims he has made for the medium.

Characterisation is Pritchett's forte in the short fiction form. In his fictions, as in those of Elizabeth Bowen, attention is paid to the uniqueness and idiosyncrasies of each character – in Pritchett's case to the extent that he has been charged with depicting only eccentrics and outsiders (rather as in Frank O'Connor's 'lonely voice' argument about the short story). Yet Pritchett has vigorously defended himself against such charges, saying that his characters seem to him to be not eccentric but simply 'very native English' in the way that they live out their fantasies in imagination while leading fairly humdrum lives. The idea of the double life runs through Pritchett's work. In 1948, for example, he wrote: 'I see that we may have two voices: the voice of the person we are and the voice of the person we fear or wish to become.'[17] Doubleness often enters his fiction through the use of characters who complement each other, each, to a certain extent, living out the desires of the other. However, such dualism does not imply a true breakdown or disintegration of the self, as it does in much Gothic and fantastic literature. Pritchett maintains an essentially monistic view of human character, merely wishing to stress that each of us has at least two and probably many more complementary 'modes of being' within us.

Like Elizabeth Bowen, Pritchett has an ample sense of the apparent futility of human life. Like her, he feels that it is important to 'objectify' this sense of futility, and draws inspiration from the special courage with which many people live out a life which may in objective terms be futile. This note from a review of Chekhov's letters applies equally well to the characters of his own fiction:

So, in the saddest as in the most sardonic of Chekhov's tales, we are conscious of the simple persistence of a person's power to live out his life; in this there is nothing futile. What one is most aware of is the glint of courage.[18]

In Pritchett's work character is always closely bound up with environment and to this extent his work is very English. He remains fascinated by the inexorable way in which a given social environment invades and shapes the individual consciousness. So in 'The Cage

Birds' he depicts a South London landscape which slowly diminishes the hopes and aspirations of those who live there:

> On some windows the blinds of a night worker were drawn and the milk bottle stood untouched at the door; at the Tube, papers and cigarette litter blowing, in the churchyards women pushing prams. The place was a fate, a blunder of small hopes and admired defeats. By the river one or two tall new buildings stuck up, prison towers watching in the midst of it. The bus crossed the river and then gradually made north to the park and the richer quarters.[19]

However, this sharp eye for social nuance does not mean that Pritchett's work is directed by any formal social commitment. Indeed, he has taken pains to define his position on this question. In *Why Do I Write?*, he suggested that a writer would necessarily respond to social pressures and to social change, but that this response would be indirect. If any 'social passion' entered a story, it would be of a 'diffused and personal kind'.

The idea of vision or revelation is central to the work of Pritchett as it is to that of Elizabeth Bowen. In a recent television interview, he characterised the novelist as a 'ruminant' grazing steadily through life's pastures. He preferred, he said, the 'side glance' at life afforded by the shorter forms of fiction. His use of a visual metaphor points to the Impressionist and painterly quality of his work, and also to his neo-Freudian interest in the lapsus, the gesture which betrays, the moment when the 'inner life exposes itself unguardedly'.

> He was lifting his knees high and putting his hand up when I first saw him, as if, crossing the road through that stinging rain, he were breaking through the bead curtain of a Pernambuco bar. I knew he was going to stop me. This part of the Euston Road is a beat of the men who want a cup of tea or their fare to a job in Luton or some outlying town.

So begins 'The Sailor', one of Pritchett's earlier stories (1945). Someone is introduced who is clearly going to be the subject of the story – the deictic 'He' establishes that. He is characterised to type at this first 'glance', but as the narrator-figure gradually becomes involved with him more complex questions about his identity begin to surface.

An adventitious encounter sets the story in motion, and similar encounters propel the narrative forward. The metonymic rather than metaphoric structure of the story is highlighted if we compare Pritchett's work with that of Joyce or Katherine Mansfield. In the work of the latter two writers, almost every detail of a given fiction will have a metaphoric as well as a narrative dimension, and will find its place in a composed and harmonious whole. Pritchett, however, like many novelists, prefers to stress the random, fluid nature of human existence, with its casual, arbitrary encounters and transitions. Life is almost viewed as continuous transition.

The kinetic structure of 'The Sailor' also mirrors the subject's personality. The key word for the sailor is 'lost'. He is first picked up by the narrator having wandered twenty miles over London in search of his nirvana – Whitechapel. The narrator gives him a job as a kind of orderly in his house in the country. This introduces some routine into the sailor's day-to-day life, but does not prevent him from suffering ever more frightening feelings of helplessness when he is forced to leave the house and negotiate the country lanes. His physical wanderings reflect his mental and emotional confusion. He is unable to choose a course of action, always needing external backing for any choice which he has made. The reverse side of this coin is that once embarked on a course of action he is unable to set limits to it. He moves endlessly between the poles of order and disorder or 'temptation', temptation meaning almost any kind of free activity: 'Orders at the one extreme, temptation at the other, were the good and evil of Thompson's life.' Thompson, the sailor, inhabits a 'moral wilderness' which he believes to be the creation of those around him:

> His memories were mainly of people who hadn't 'behaved right', a dejecting moral wilderness with Thompson mooching about in it, disappointed with human nature.

In reality the moral wilderness lies within. Thompson simply transfers his own inability to do 'right' to others.

Hence his bitter struggle with 'Temptation incarnate', the colonel's daughter who is the narrator's nearest neighbour. The colonel's daughter attempts to seduce Thompson, and we enjoy his comic dismay when he is found lingering in the lane outside with his arms around her. But this incident is less important for our view of Thompson than for the insight which it gives into the mind of the un-named first-person narrator. He, it is indicated, is a literary man who prides himself on his keen powers of observation. One of the first shocks which he receives lies in the discovery that while he has been watching Thompson, Thompson has been watching him. Moreover, the narrator has been confident in his analysis of the colonel's daughter, accepting her account of her background unquestioningly and trusting to her appearance as an indication of her age and status. In fact he has misread his neighbour completely – just as we have misread him. As we realise the extent of his gullibility, Pritchett uses inappropriate perspective as a metaphor for his easy, wish-fulfilling view of the world:

> 'Here,' she said. 'I was damn pretty when I was twenty-five, I'm thirty-nine. I've still got a good figure.'
> 'I would have put you at twenty-seven at the most,' I said truthfully.
> She walked towards me. I was sitting on the armchair and she stood very close. She had never been as close to me before. I had thought her eyes were dark blue, but now I saw they were green and grey, with a moist lascivious haze in them and yet dead and clock-like, like a cat's on a sunless day. And the skin, which had seemed fresh to me, I saw in its truth for the first time. It was clouded and flushed, clouded with that thickened pimpled ruddiness which the skin of heavy drinkers has and which in middle age becomes bloated and mottled.

The narrator makes his greatest error in his analysis of the sailor. Once he has established to his own satisfaction that the sailor is unstable and socially maladjusted, he casts him in the role of fool and foil, and ceases really to look at him any more closely. Then, in an extraordinary paragraph, Pritchett brings together the narrator and the sailor at a point when the latter is fighting another 'temptation' – an invitation to an evening at the British Legion. Pritchett foregrounds the word 'type', for typecasting is the vice of the narrator:

> When I returned, Thompson was fighting Temptation hard. If he went to the Legion how would he get back? No, best not. He took the Legion on in its strength. (She is a type, I thought.) At four he was still at it. At five he asked me for his money. (Well, we are all types, I was thinking.) . . . Yet, just when I thought he had lost, he had won. There was the familiar sound of the Wild West monologue in the kitchen. It was half past eight. The Legion was defeated.

The sailor triumphs over the narrator by defeating his expectations, and in so doing triumphs over the narrative which bears his name. The sailor remains irreducible, 'real' in the sense that he cannot finally be netted by words. He finally escapes from his own narrative, literally and figuratively:

> We stood on the kerb and I watched him walk off into the yellow rain and the clogged, grunting, and mewing traffic. He stepped right into it without looking. Taxis braked to avoid him. He was going to walk to Whitechapel. He reckoned it was safer.

Among Pritchett's fictions which deal more fully with relations of dependence, 'Handsome Is as Handsome Does' (1938) and 'Blind Love' (1969) stand out. The title of 'Handsome Is as Handsome Does' is ironic. The sense of the phrase – don't be deceived by appearances – is undercut by the actions of the male characters and the speech of a central female character. The fiction is structured around a beach accident, where it is indeed a handsome and heroic-looking young man who shows great courage in rescuing an elderly man from the sea. Appearance in this case is not deceptive. Later, however, Mrs Coram, the wife of a rather nondescript-looking man who was afraid to plunge into the sea, retells the story, casting her husband as the conquering hero. She seems to endorse the meaning of the title phrase by the sense of her words – but all the time she is denying this, deceiving by an appearance constructed by language.

Words are important in 'Handsome Is as Handsome Does', for one of the ways in which the Corams have become dependent on each other is through the matching of the wife's articulacy with her husband's continual struggles with language. Words deceive, but they also relieve, assuring us that we are in command of a situation or an experience – even though we may in fact distort or misrepresent it. This comfort and assurance is denied to Coram:

> He had thoughts but he could not get them out. They were tied up in knots like snakes, squeezing and suffocating him. Whenever he made a suggestion or offered an opinion, his short brow became contorted with thick frowns, like a bull's forehead, and he coloured. He lowered his forehead, not as if he were going to charge with fury, but as if he were faced with the job of pushing some impossible rock uphill. He was helpless.
>
> She would see this and, cunningly, tactfully, she would make

things easy for him. They had no children and, because of the guilt she felt about this and because of the difficulties he saw everywhere, they had become completely dependent on each other.

Frustration is indeed the keynote for this fiction. Coram is utterly frustrated by his inability to gain control over language while Mrs Coram is frustrated by her inability to have children. An analogy is suggested between the merging of the self with the other (the object) in language, and the merging of the self with the other in love. In both spheres the Corams show some kind of lack or deficiency – or this is how it appears to them. Lack unites and divides them: 'She had sown her disappointment in him, he had sown his frustration in her. Why? And why did they live in a circle they could not break?'

'Handsome Is as Handsome Does' is one of Pritchett's most painterly stories, in a slightly self-conscious way. In fact, the self-consciousness mirrors that of the characters, who are essentially cut off from their surroundings as from so many other things:

> The car topped the hill and she turned her head to look back upon the town. She was surprised. Two belfries stood above the roofs. She had never seen them before. The clay-coloured houses were closely packed together by the hills, and those that were in the sun stood out white and tall. The roofs went up in tiers, and over each roof a pair of windows stared like foreign eyes. The houses were a phalanx of white and alien witnesses. She was startled to think that she had brought her life to a place so strange to her.

Pritchett finally defines the inert and sterile life of the Corams through the image of a postcard:

> From the landing window as she went up she saw the familiar picture. The military rows of the vines in the red soil. The shadow-pocked mountains, the pines. It was like a postcard view taken in the sun, the sun not of today but of other days, a sun that was not warm but the indifferent, hard, dead brilliance of the past itself, surrounding her life.

Pritchett's tact and skill in scene-shifting are amply demonstrated in this fiction. He has written 'I love the intricacy of the short form, the speed with which it can change from scene to scene', and he is particularly deft in his matching of the speed of change to the demands of the narrative context. His episodes are not 'significantly' juxtaposed or orchestrated as in modernist fiction: the structure of this and many other of his stories embodies his sense of the random and haphazard course of most human lives.

'Blind Love' is another study of dependence. The title itself has sufficient resonance, summoning up the figure of Cupid and the old adage that love is blind – and again suggesting hazard and chance possibilities. The relationship of dependence in the story is that between a blind lawyer and his housekeeper. As in 'Handsome Is as Handsome Does' the theme of dependence is focused first of all through a question of language. (An inbuilt feeling for the inadequacy of language has always been one of the most tantalising aspects of Pritchett's talent.) The housekeeper must translate all visual experiences into words for her employer. But words are not enough: they cannot convey the fullness of visual experience, as Mrs Johnson realises:

> She was used to the view. It was a view of the real world; that, after all, was her world, not his. She saw that gradually in three years she had drifted out of it and had taken to living in Armitage's filed memory.

Yet Armitage has only lost his sense of sight: he still has a body. When Mrs Johnson first sees him groping, lost, but living in his body instead of moving along the metalled rails of his daily routine, she is shocked by the realisation that having lost the sense which is linked most closely to language and perception, Armitage has allowed his emotions to be driven from his mind into his body: 'Half naked to the waist, hairy on the chest and arms, he shocked because the rage seemed to be not in his mind but in his body like an animal's.' Armitage's attraction for Mrs Johnson lies in this strange sensuality: eventually the two become lovers. Superficially this might seem an ideal union, she interpreting the visual world to him, he interpreting the world of the senses to her. However, Pritchett carries his analysis of the situation a stage further. Clearly, having become blind, Armitage must feel maimed, stigmatised, in some way not 'whole'. Mrs Johnson too is maimed, though her fatal flaw can more easily be concealed for the purposes of everyday life. She has an ugly liver-coloured birthmark over one breast: she has concealed this until she married but it then cost her her husband.

Mrs Johnson understands that 'injury had led her to injury' and that this has much to do with her bond with Armitage. But she refuses to tell him about her birthmark, until a casual observer, seeing her half-naked beside a swimming pool, forces confession. This puts her on a more equal footing with Armitage and it subsequently transpires that he is as ready to accept her 'injury' as she had been to accept his.

This offers the two some kind of basis for living together, but theirs is still a life dominated by a need for secrets. Armitage, who has spent much of his life baffling people by his ability to lead a 'normal life', shares Mrs Johnson's secretive bent:

> Armitage and Mrs Johnson are in Italy now; for how long it is hard to say. They themselves don't know. Some people call her Mrs Armitage, some call her Mrs Johnson: this uncertainty pleases her. She has always had a secret and she is too old, she says, to give up the habit now. It still pleases Armitage to baffle people.

The biggest secret of all remains, quite simply, their life together. At the close of the story we are given some hints about this – Mrs Johnson loves Armitage's dependence on her, Armitage likes to frighten her with the idea that the blind can see straight into the minds of others. But then the author slips away, leaving us with a final sense of something invisible and inviolate in his characters, unsusceptible to the investigation of author or reader. Some secrets may be laid bare, but not the ultimate secrets of character or personality.

William Sansom began his career in an advertising agency, writing 'formula stories' in his spare time. What he saw during the blitz in London changed his idea of what a story should be and altered the course of his life and career. The fictions which he wrote in the war period won great acclaim, and still form the basis of his reputation, though he subsequently published novels and travel books as well as further collections of stories. It has been suggested earlier that the short fiction form was well suited to convey the disorientation of life in the war period, and the excellence of the work produced by Sansom and Bowen in particular indicates that the form was certainly favoured at this time for reasons other than the mundane one of paper shortages.[20]

Like Bowen, Sansom focuses on the effects of war on the civilian population, but his fictions are unlike hers in being more overtly disruptive. His work has frequently been compared with that of Kafka, and he has also been labelled a Surrealist. But these are not, ultimately, valid comparisons, for both Kafka and the Surrealists started from the premise that the 'barrier of the real' had already been broken. Sansom moves from the real to the dreamlike and horrific, but uses distorted images which still bear some relation to a commonly perceived, everyday reality: he does not attempt to cross into a no-man's land beyond the real. His war fictions contain hallucinatory and distorted images, but this is to make the point that war in its modern form is the ultimate distortion, a violation of almost all the normal impulses of life. Sansom's treatment of the London blitz may in this respect be compared with that of Thomas Pynchon in *Gravity's Rainbow* (1973).

'Fireman Flower' is the title-story from Sansom's first collection (1944), and the fiction reflects and creates a state of mind as we, with Fireman Flower, attempt to construct a private order out of the monstrous disorder of a large urban fire. The fire is an uncontained image for the war, and as Fireman Flower journeys through it Sansom uses various techniques to indicate his increasing dismay and disorientation. The narrative opens with a carefully specific description of a London night scene which might almost have come from Elizabeth Bowen:

> At the time he was riding to a most important fire. Looking out from the back of the van he could see how clean the streets had been washed by the night. . . . Sometimes, on an acute camber, a silver thread of petrol fountained from a pin-hole in the petrol tank cap. There was little other movement. The vehicle raced evenly forward. The fireman saw only the dark linoleum road slipping backwards: or, if he raised his eyes, the departing rows of houses, the terraces, the crescents, regular, eyeless, washed grey by the moonlight.[21]

As the fireman draws nearer to the fire and his nervousness increases we see one way in which he attempts to control his fear, using the apparent rationale of official orders to combat the situation:

> My task is succinctly – to discover the kernel of the fire. I must disregard the fire's offshoots, I must pass over the fire's deceptive encroachment . . .
> . . . we are all engaged upon this job of the fire, and we are all equipped similarly with both the incentive to complete the job and the weapons with which to work.

The absurdity of such an attempt to impose a rational structure on an irrational situation is conveyed through Flower's stilted diction, which does not have the stamp of truth or belief. His alienation and inability to come to grips with the situation are further indicated through his distorted perception of scenes which are swiftly cut down to size by the narrator:

> Yet here was this immense edifice standing quite alone! And Flower's pump was now racing up a broad highway that led straight towards the great central door, a road that dramatized the building's tremendous isolation, the aloof building that reared so hugely against the nightblue sky, alone on its firelit plain, unencumbered by the city, a black castle flecked with orange flames that crashed from its windows and among its high turrets like the flames in a fairy tale.
>
> But it was neither castle nor cathedral. It was a black-bricked warehouse of hideous design.

When Flower finally arrives at the fire, we move with him through a montage of phantasmagoric scenes, in each of which he seeks the cause or meaning of the fire. At first he sees the movement of men around the fire as part of a rational exercise with a rational goal. A fellow fireman endorses this view:

> We cannot think to control what is beyond our sphere of command. However, up to that point they have worked out for us an excellent routine, with which we have always been satisfied, which has in the past proved its worth, and which for these reasons is beyond question.

Flower is at first seduced by this account, but then begins to question the motives and goals of the 'they' who are in overall control. What had at first seemed rational now seems to have no solid basis in fact or reason, and Flower has to reject this as a 'story-book' view of the fire. He next experiences the fire as imaging the triumph of the senses over the intellect. Floating in a warm, scented bath (the fire hoses are playing over crates of broken perfume bottles) he is almost able to approve this development:

> Can sensuality, after all, be no forlorn dead-end, but instead a highway from which great things can be obtained? They say – 'Food, a roof and a mate – only with these provided can one be free to start

thinking on aware planes.' In that case, possibly the finer the roof, the sweeter the food, the subtler the mate – possibly these refinements may stimulate rather than divert?

But, again, he is swiftly disillusioned, and, panicking, runs backwards, literally and metaphorically, to scenes from his former life. Their cosy familiarity first attracts and then repels him, as he begins to form the idea that hope for mankind must lie in change and in the future. He turns from the past to thoughts of his fiancée:

> Pink patchouli and the odious whalebone – how could I love these when there are Joan's fresh cheeks, Joan's clean sunbed? That is the struggle, though . . . the wrestling of security with hope, of the womb with the bright dirigible, of safety with the will to create!

The logical consequence is that Flower is moved to reject the past and accept all that the future may bring, particularly in terms of the development of machinery and technology. He thus begins to see the war as a necessarily destructive period out of which will come new possibilities for mankind:

> Life as he had known it had been broken down. From the elements a new world had been moulded. Iron, fire, brick, smoke, and water from the huge hydrants were patterned into a new choreography that enlivened fiercely the blood and the spirit.

But almost immediately after Flower has expressed his Nietzschean feelings of joy-in-destruction, he is distracted by a new scene, and once again a visual phenomenon changes the direction of his thought. A wall behind him crumbles and brings a new transformation through the humble agent of flour (there is surely a pun here – Flower's imagination has a similar power to transform mundane reality):

> Like milky lava it had spread down from ceiling height, fanning majestically to either side and far out across the floor. Now it had set in a sheer wall of oiled ice, lucently marvellous, smooth, polished, yet intimating from within that it would be soft and wet to touch. The high white walls, the white-crusted girders, the duning and the silting of those soft flourbeds, and now finally the flow of the great pellucid glacier merged into a harmony of massed shape and tactile wonder that radiated some limitless composure of beauty unaffected by dramas and associations, pure.

And again Flower turns his back on an understanding he has won, and changes his mind about the true meaning of the fire. This new scene has a beauty which stirs him to a deeper, more mystical 'explanation' of the fire:

> Here the harmony soothes, yet elates. Here is a limitless spiritual ideal . . . here must be the real kernel of the fire, where joy and melancholy become one sensation, where one can trace the web of this great fire to the finely balanced pattern at its very centre.

Then the text continues, characteristically, 'But just as he was thinking this, Flower glanced over his shoulder', and we are offered yet another change of perspective. Flower suddenly tires of all his attempts to understand the fire, and in reaction to the strain climbs up to the top of the building, where he can breathe the night air. By chance, he finds the true 'source' of the fire lying at his feet: a 'random, reasonless rocket'. All Flower's attempts to divine the causes of the fire come to this, and as he accepts, as he must, the random nature of this particular drama, his sympathies extend into a simple love of all things that exist, however random or arbitrary their existence may seem to be:

> Then he turned towards the numberless roofs that stretched far away into the distance, and with a great quiet love he let himself grow aware of them, of the sleeping chimneys that told of armchairs beneath, of windvanes that knew all weathers, of curved cherubs upon the mansards of palaces, of low leaking roofs where the garret washing still dripped.

The fiction ends with a celebration of the random and fortuitous nature of human perception and experience. It is this which links Sansom so closely to Bowen and to Pritchett.

'The Wall', also from the collection *Fireman Flower*, works in a rather similar way. In this short fiction Sansom makes specific reference to the photographic and cinematic techniques which had helped to free his fiction from conventional narrative appearances. The unnamed narrator, for example, 'photographs' the first terrifying sight of a wall on fire, about to fall towards him: the whole scene is depicted as in a freeze frame. As the wall actually begins to crumble, the narrator, mesmerised, still sees the scene in photographic or cinematic terms:

Although at this time the entire hemispherical scene appeared static, an imminence of movement could be sensed throughout – presumably because the scene was actually moving. Even the speed of the shutter which closed the photograph on my mind was powerless to exclude this motion from a deeper consciousness.[22]

'The Wall', like 'Fireman Flower', is concerned with the relationships between illusion and reality, chance and design. Sansom's later fictions have less urgency than those dealing with the war, and have less immediate impact, but deal sensitively with the less exotic crises of life under normal civilian circumstances. 'Nevermore Without End' (1950), for example, documents an inevitable and expected change in feeling between two lovers who meet again after three years' separation. They strive in vain to re-create old feelings:

> Close as they walked – they walked like brother and sister. They walked abreast, he remembering vaguely that to take an arm is not to cling to an arm, and that lovers who cling walk always in some way turned a little in towards each other. He tried this.[23]

Their love is linked closely to climate and scene: it has blossomed in the cold beauty of a Copenhagen winter, but seems impossible to recover in the easy diffuseness of summer.

'Gliding Gulls and Going People' (also from 1950) is still more relaxed in form than 'Nevermore Without End'. It is structured around a boat trip amongst the wild scenery of Northern Scotland. In a wide-angled shot, as it were, we first see a solid mass of human beings waiting to embark on their excursion; then ten characters are singled out in close-up. Completely unconnected with each other, they none the less form an intriguing cross-section of the boat's clientèle.

The boat trip is fairly overtly a metaphor for life itself: a round trip which the passengers are continually struggling to enjoy. They try to seize certain moments from time, to arrest and possess them, but fail precisely because of their acquisitively grasping attitude. They find it difficult to be open to the landscape, to really see it for themselves – preferring to see 'what on a hundred calendars had been dreamed and painted for them'. One man even passes the journey reading his Boswell,[24] in preference to actually looking at the Hebrides as they pass before him.

If the journey is a metaphor for life, there is also a fairly direct comparison between the human beings on the boat and the gulls over and above it. The gulls move in an apparently purposeless fashion, bumping against each other, then flying off for no apparent reason; concerted in their activity only in the struggle for food. Similarly on board the ship people move around aimlessly, making no real contact in their chance encounters, united only in their need for food. At one point Sansom rudely juxtaposes the beauty of the landscape and the indifference to it exhibited by the passengers as much as by the voracious gulls:

> as everybody turned from their places to the companion-way and the blind bowels of the dining saloon, so Eigg and Rum came magnificently at last into full view.
>
> And the ship, naked of sightseers, ploughed past them. . . . All around, mountains and misted horizon and metal-green sea would have lain as empty in those days as now. . . . Gigantic mountainous Rum came to port – and at last the Cuillins topped in vertiginous cloud towered terribly to starboard.
>
> Yet no-one saw. Even the gulls, questing open-eyed round, had swooped to the sea and were pecking the first plate-emptyings thrown out in the ship's wake.[25]

The comparison of gulls and people suggests a distaste for humanity which emerges more distinctly elsewhere in this fiction. So Sansom describes a young man trying to decide which girl to pick up in the following predatory terms: 'And those eyes under their short lids, bitter and ambitious, lustful, swivelled warily between the two grouped and the one sitting. Where was the better chance?' Human beings are presented as selfish, inward-looking and avaricious – but within their limitations they are still searching for happiness. The landscape, in this particular fiction, offers a beauty beyond the self which the passengers have at least the wit to lament as it passes beyond their grasp:

> Islands reaching out towards some place irrevocable, a place that only might have been, and now in a visionary moment at end of day shown somehow as a real possibility. Perhaps for the first time many of those people began to look at what was passing with moved hearts, with curious regret . . .
>
> . . . For the first time the journey is seen as it is, for the first time it is felt to be sliding away forever from grasp. Never again, nevermore. Evanescent as the water at the ship's keel, the white ephemeral wake, water that marks the passage, white and wide, that melts and vanishes in personless flat green.

'Gliding Gulls and Going People' is in many ways an exemplary free story – episodic, Impressionist, founded, in Elizabeth Bowen's key phrase, on vision rather than feeling. And the more we examine the free story the more apparent it becomes that vision, in both senses of the word, is central to this form of short fiction. In discussing technique, Bowen, Pritchett and Sansom refer in turn to 'vision', 'the glance', 'the eye of the painter'; they also make frequent comparisons with photographic and cinematic art. It is as though their fictions are predicated on the idea of the eye/I as a camera: thus these fictions not only have a very strong visual impact, but depend philosophically on the notion of reflection rather than (self) reflexion. The fundamental assumption is that fiction can reflect and illuminate objective reality: subjective bias can emerge only to a limited extent through choice of shading or camera angle.

The 'free story' has never had a programme and its exponents have, by definition perhaps, rejected the impulse to aesthetic prescription. None the less, the free story has established itself as a very definite, and very popular, form of short fiction: one might even argue that it has been *the* dominant short form in this century. When we examine most contemporary 'short story' anthologies, we find that free stories tend to form the backbone of the collection. In particular, as has been indicated, the form has proved attractive to writers who are also novelists, for example Angus Wilson and Susan Hill. It is surely time for the free story to emerge from the critical shadows, to be recognised as a form distinct from modernist and postmodernist short fiction on the one hand, and the short story or tale on the other.

6 Postmodernist and Other Fictions

'Postmodernist' is a label which has been applied to widely differing kinds of art. Like all movements, postmodernism is extremely difficult to define. The hermeneutic value of the central concept has tended to diminish the more widely the term has been used and the more frequently its values have been canvassed. We must look to the statements of the original practitioners of postmodernism if we are to gain an authentic sense of the movement. In particular we must look to these writers if we wish to pick up the sense of a shared animating purpose which is at the heart of this, as of any other, artistic movement. It is this which is so inadequately conveyed through the terms of conventional critical summary.

John Barth was the first to characterise postmodernist literature as the 'literature of exhaustion'.[1] In the preface to 'Seven Exemplary Fictions' (1969) Robert Coover took up Barth's term and added to it his own sense of a new apocalypse. Here he addresses Cervantes, the creator of the novel:

> But, *don* Miguel, the optimism, the innocence, the aura of possibility you experienced have been largely drained away, and the universe is closing in on us again. Like you, we, too, seem to be standing at the end of one age and on the threshold of another. We, too, suffer from a 'literature of exhaustion', . . . But these probes (in contemporary fiction) are above all – like your Knight's sallies – challenges to the assumptions of a dying age, exemplary adventures of the Poetic Imagination, high-minded journeys towards the New World and never mind that the nag's a pile of bones.[2]

But perhaps the nag/the novel form may be transformed, as Coover goes on to suggest:

> The novelist uses familiar mythic or historical forms to combat the

content of those forms and to conduct the reader (*lector amantísimo*!) to the real, away from mystification to clarification, away from magic to maturity, away from mystery to revelation. And it is above all to the need for new modes of perception and fictional forms able to encompass them that I, barber's basin on my head, address these stories.[3]

The 'new fictional forms' to which he refers have tended to be forms of short fiction. Like the modernists, postmodernist writers seem to have found short fiction a peculiarly appropriate form, suiting their experiential and philosophical concerns. Postmodernism as a movement also resembles modernism in being an international phenomenon. The exemplary figures are Beckett, an Irishman writing in French, and Borges, an Argentinian who is most widely known through English translations of his work. Postmodernism must first be considered in its international context, before we begin to focus more precisely on contemporary short fiction in English.

As we have seen, modernist writers questioned the concept of story and concentrated on the Impressionist or Symbolist moment of experience. Postmodernist writers have worked further in this direction, breaking experience down into smaller and smaller units. There has been a general movement away from conventional social and behavioural codes, the sense of a common grammar of experience, and a new concern with the individual units of language. Hence the 'difficulty' of much postmodernist writing. The characteristic fragmentation of postmodernist discourse is the direct result of a confrontation with language as itself problematic. The primary question is that of the ability of language to express. In asking – or expressing – this question, postmodernist writers have involved themselves in the kind of paradox we might legitimately expect from a 'literature of exhaustion'.

Plot in postmodernist fiction tends to be either minimal or wildly excessive. In those fictions in which plot is minimal we might sense an affinity with some contemporary painting and sculpture. The 'landscapes' of the minimalist Sol LeWitt, for example, might fruitfully be compared with the residual landscapes of Beckett's late fictions. Sometimes the link may be more tangible, as, for example, in the 'collaboration' between Beckett and Jasper Johns which produced the illustrated edition of Beckett's *Fizzles/Foirades* (1976).

In those fictions in which plot is excessive, the excess tends to have a self-cancelling effect. When writers such as Borges play with double or multiple plot, we are not required to assent to any one of the 'stories' offered in the same sense in which we must assent to a curve of events in the fiction of such writers as Sean O'Faolain or Elizabeth Bowen. In postmodernist fiction there is no obligation for us to believe any story, on any level: we are not necessarily required, even, to construct a sense of metaphysical coherence in a story in which physical coherence is lacking. Postmodernism presents us with a sense of infinite possibility, the other aspect of which is a sense of limitless futility: where we can choose anything, choice and shape may cease to have meaning and value. Borges presents an extreme version of the case in the famous fiction 'The Garden of Forking Paths':

> In all fictional works, each time a man is confronted with several alternatives, he chooses one and eliminates the others; in the fiction of Ts'ui Pen, he chooses – simultaneously – all of them. *He creates*, in this way, diverse futures, diverse times which themselves also proliferate and fork.[4]

Like story, the idea of personality is eroded in postmodernist fiction. Narrator-figures exist, but there is radical uncertainty about their status. This uncertainty is expressed in two main ways: through shifts in narrative voice from first to third person (as in the work of Beckett) or through an unexpected use of tense (as in the work of Ian McEwan, whose use of the imperfect tense has a blurring effect, effectively separating the narrator from his material). The characters of post-modernist fiction are still less coherent than the narrators. Repeated patterns of behaviour are recognised, but the concept of the 'whole' character or personality is radically questioned. Small forays are made into the realms of human personality, but for the most part the artist stands back, circumspect as the neurophysiologist confronted with the complexity of the human nervous system. It may be significant in this context that postmodernist writers have felt the need to draw on models of human behaviour developed in the experimental sciences, for example in psychology.

'Fragments are the only forms I trust', the postmodernist writer Donald Barthelme has written. An increasing sense of the fragmenta-tion of human experience will necessarily put pressure on conventional notions of the temporal and causal ordering of this experience. As Borges has suggested in the fiction 'Tlön, Uqbar, Orbis Tertius', the idea of cause and effect is almost inseparable from our idea of time. He has tried to drive a wedge between the two concepts, and suggests that ideally – in the philosophical sense – we might entirely transcend the notion of time. In the new world of Tlön:

> One of the schools of Tlön goes so far as to negate time: it reasons that the present is indefinite, that the future has no reality other than as a present hope, that the past has no reality other than as a present memory.[5]

This questioning of one of the fundamental ways in which we order experience marks a crucial point of departure. Modernist writers had started to question language as a means of coding experience: postmodernists have extended their concern to other systematised languages, for example that of mathematics, which is frequently referred to in the fiction of Beckett and Borges. Postmodernist writers have also investigated other, perhaps more fundamental ways in which we code experience. Temporal ordering is one such example, spatial organisation another. The latter is called into question in Ian McEwan's fiction 'Solid Geometry', which plays with the idea that, as the narrator laconically remarks, 'dimensionality is a function of consciousness'.

The work of Beckett provides a link between modernism and postmodernism. His first book of short pieces, *More Pricks than Kicks*, was published in 1934 and shows strong signs of the influence of Joyce. Faced with the example of his compatriot, Beckett adopted the time-honoured strategy of the apprentice, alternately emulating and parodying the stance and style of the master. *More Pricks than Kicks* is shaped as a story cycle, after the manner of *Dubliners*, and Beckett succeeds in extending the parallel with *Dubliners* and *Ulysses* to a point of comic excess, offering exaggeratedly detailed descriptions of the monuments and buildings, parks and street intersections of Dublin. The protagonist of *More Pricks than Kicks* has a name as anomalous as that of Stephen Dedalus, and rather as the name of Dedalus points us to the world of Greek myth, so the name Belacqua points to the *Divine Comedy* as a literary point of reference. The difference lies in the way Beckett can play, ironically, with the whole idea of literary reference in the context already created by *Ulysses*.

This is illustrated most clearly in the first piece in *More Pricks than Kicks*, 'Dantë and the Lobster'. In the opening paragraph the *Paradiso* and the mundane world of Belacqua become hopelessly confused. However, the syntactical muddle creates an effect which is almost wholly comic:

> It was the morning and Belacqua was stuck in the first of the canti in the moon. He was so bogged that he could move neither backward nor forward. Blissful Beatrice was there, Dante also, and she explained the spots on the moon to him. She showed him in the first place where he was at fault, then she put up her own explanation. She had it from God, therefore he could rely on its being accurate in every particular. All he had to do was follow her step by step.[6]

Again the effect is dependent partly on an element of excess. Beckett produces parallels between the world of the *Divine Comedy* and the world of Belacqua which far exceed the number required to make a mock-heroic point. The process of the perception of analogy becomes enjoyable for its own sake – as in the witty parallels drawn between 'real' and metaphorical bogs and steps.

'Dantë and the Lobster' further resembles the short fictions of *Dubliners* in that it is a piece strongly marked by the use of Symbolist patterning and leitmotif. The torments of hell, for example, are not only directly referred to by Belacqua in a discussion of Dantë, but are figured through his incendiary attack on his lunchtime toast, and through his aunt's equally energetic assault on the lobster which is to be boiled alive. The fate of the lobster is further paralleled with that of the 'handsome assassin' McCabe, whose last hours on earth are linked in Belacqua's mind with the last few seconds the lobster has to live. This kind of patterning is almost like that of Joyce – but again Beckett is playing with a technique rather than taking it completely seriously. There is something subtly discordant in the kind of patterning described above: Beckett is parodying one of Joyce's favourite techniques in order to free himself from the elder writer's dominance.

The closing section of 'Dantë and the Lobster' repays closer attention. Much of the text is cast in indirect free form, but in the final section a narrator begins to emerge who can be distinguished clearly from Belacqua. The appearance of such a narrator has the effect of foregrounding the fictionality of the text, as in a sentence such as 'Let us call it Winter, that dusk may fall now and a moon rise.' But the narrator also has the crucial last three words of the text. The emergence at this point of a voice speaking against the authority of Belacqua is important. It is as though a 'voice' has been submerged throughout the fiction, but as it finally achieves utterance we realise that it is crystallising, summarising, what the text has been saying all along through its particular forms and articulations:

> Belacqua looked at the old parchment of her face, grey in the dim kitchen.
> 'You make a fuss' she said angrily 'and upset me and then lash into it for your dinner.'
> She lifted the lobster clear of the table. It had about thirty seconds to live.
> Well, thought Belacqua, it's a quick death, God help us all.
> It is not.[7]

In his later work Beckett has been increasingly preoccupied with strategies which will enable this kind of 'voice' to achieve itself, to achieve utterance.

In *More Pricks than Kicks* Beckett begins to dissolve the organic wholeness of the world and of story. This dissolution extends through all his later work, but the notion of story comes under greatest pressure in the short prose pieces as opposed to the novels and plays. With short fictional works reader-expectations are perhaps more definite than they are with the novel. The reader expects to find if not a tightly knitted plot, clear symbolic or metaphorical patterning: when neither of these is present he is left with very few clues as to how to read the fiction. In longer prose works, and indeed in drama, various alternative strategies of organisation tend to emerge – for example long-term repetition and accumulation.

Beckett's short prose pieces thus present a considerable challenge to the reader. They are among his most innovatory works and test our conceptions of what a short fiction might be. The *Fizzles* and *Residua* are at the outermost reaches of our notions of short fiction. They lack conventional characterisation and action, and frequently lack temporal ordering and causal consistency. However in them Beckett effects a change which is crucial for the short fiction form: he shifts the major unit of expression from the 'story' or overall structure to the sentence. We read these short texts very much on the level of the sentence, and in this context it is perhaps worth stressing again the point that Beckett usually writes initially in French. One major difference between French and English sentence structure lies in the frequently wide separation between subject and verb in French, with adjectival clauses intervening. Beckett carries this reflexive style over into his English works. This use of a 'foreign' syntax makes the reader work much harder with the text, actively participating in the creation of the relationships which constitute it.

We can see the beginnings of this kind of use of syntax in the opening paragraph of the early novella, 'First Love':

> I associate, rightly or wrongly, my marriage with the death of my father, in time. That other links exist, on other levels, between these two affairs, is not impossible. I have enough trouble as it is in trying to say what I think I know.[8]

The opportunities afforded by a disjointed syntax are exploited more fully in Beckett's later work: for example in the opening lines of 'From an Abandoned Work' (1958):

> Up bright and early that day, I was young then, feeling awful, and out, mother hanging out of the window in her nightdress weeping and waving. Nice fresh morning, bright too early as so often. Feeling really awful, very violent.[9]

The nearest equivalent for a text such as 'From an Abandoned Work' probably lies in nineteenth-century Symbolist prose. In their density and lapidary quality Beckett's later prose texts may be compared with the *poëmes en prose* of Mallarmé. This link with the early prose poem is an important one, suggesting a line of continuity and development from the Symbolists' interest in prose style, through to the modernist concern for prose, to the experimental short pieces of English and American postmodernists. There is a strong tradition of experiment in the short prose form, among writers who have felt that, as Katherine Mansfield put it, the 'lovely medium of prose' is, by comparison with the older art of poetry, an 'undiscovered country still'.

In 1954 Beckett published *Nouvelles et textes pour rien*. The *nouvelles* or novellas are relatively straightforward in style and overall structure, though they are dominated by images of dislocation and dismay which have a Surrealist reach and power. In 'The Calmative', for example, Beckett evokes a landscape like that in a painting by de Chirico:

> The further I went into the city the more I was struck by its deserted air. It was lit as usual, brighter than usual, although the shops were shut. But the lights were on in their windows with the object no doubt of attracting customers and prompting them to say, I say, I like

that, not dear either, I'll come back tomorrow, if I'm still alive. . . .
The trams were running, the buses too, but few, slow, empty,
noiseless, as if under water.[10]

In general, the novellas tend to describe problems which are actively
worked out in the *Textes pour rien* and other later works. The notion of
antimony, for example, which will be crucial in Beckett's late prose
fiction, is first addressed in 'The Calmative':

But it might have been three or four in the morning just as it might
have been ten or eleven in the evening, depending no doubt on
whether one wondered at the scarcity of passers-by or at the
extraordinary radiance shed by the street-lamps and traffic-lights.
For at one or other of these no one could fail to wonder, unless he
was out of his mind. Not a single private car, but admittedly from
time to time a public vehicle, slow sweep of light silent and empty. It
is not my wish to labour these antimonies, for we are needless to say
in a skull.[11]

The idea of the voice ('the murmur') as in some way analogous to the
helpless heartbeat is developed in 'The End':

To know I had a being, however faint and false, outside of me, had
once had the power to stir my heart. You become unsociable, it's
inevitable. It's enough to make you wonder sometimes if you are on
the right planet. Even the words desert you, it's as bad as that.
Perhaps it's the moment when the vessels stop communicating, you
know, the vessels. There you are still between the two murmurs, it
must be the same old song as ever, but Christ you wouldn't think
so.[12]

The concept of 'voice' is central to the *Texts for Nothing*, replacing
any conventional idea of character. For Beckett at this point the self
may be constituted through the many voices which represent its
internal contradictions and dichotomies:

How can I go on, I shouldn't have begun, no, I had to begin.
Someone said, perhaps the same, What possessed you to come? I
could have stayed in my den, snug and dry, I couldn't. My den, I'll
describe it, no, I can't. It's simple, I can do nothing any more, that's
what you think. I say to the body, Up with you now, and I can feel it

struggling, like an old hack foundered in the street, struggling no more, struggling again, till it gives up. I say to the head, Leave it alone, stay quiet, it stops breathing, then pants on worse than ever.[13]

If the self is equated with a voice or voices it might be considered to be structured like language.[14] For Beckett it seems that everything is structured through language: we can only know and be through its terms, and our knowledge and being will suffer from concomitant limitations. In particular Beckett is interested in the limitation implied by the inherently antithetical nature of language. He asks whether 'no's knife' must always be turned in 'yes's wound' and frequently expresses a desire to achieve a presence beyond the antithetical relations of the word/the world.

In the *Texts for Nothing* Beckett uses two main strategies to evoke or to gesture towards such a presence, to 'name my unnamable words' (Text 6). First, he manipulates the literal space surrounding a text, using its blankness to suggest that which lies beyond words. The space, the silence which follows the ending of Text 7, for example, is crucial to its meaning:

And to search for me elsewhere, where life persists, and me there, whence all life has withdrawn, except mine, if I'm alive, no, it would be a loss of time. And personally, I hear it said, personally I have no more time to lose, and that will be all for this evening, that night is at hand and the time come for me too to begin.

Secondly, he uses paradox and contradiction as the structures closest to the 'third term', to that which exists outside language. At the end of Text 8 he writes of 'another aim, that of being or of ceasing, better still, before having been'. Text 9 then opens with an account of the limitations of language:

And the yeses and the noes mean nothing in this mouth, no more than sighs it sighs in its toil, or answers to a question not understood, a question unspoken, in the eyes of a mute, an idiot, who doesn't understand, never understood, who stares at himself in a glass, stares before him in the desert, sighing yes, sighing no, on and off.

What the speaker(s) of the texts desire is a 'new no', a 'cancellation' which will be beyond cancellation:

No, something better must be found, a better reason, for this to stop, another word, a better idea, to put in the negative, a new no, to cancel all the others, all the old noes that buried me down here, deep in this place which is not one, which is merely a moment for the time being eternal, which is called here, and in this being which is called me and is not one, and in this impossible voice, all the old noes dangling in the dark and swaying like a ladder of smoke, yes, a new no, that none says twice, whose drop will fall and let me down, shadow and bubble, to an absence less vain than inexistence.

The last text, Text 13, ends on a final note of paradox or antimony, as the speaker speaks of that which cannot be spoken:

And were there one day to be here, where there are no days, which is no place, born of the impossible voice the unmakable being, and a gleam of light, still all would be silent and empty and dark, as now, as soon now, when all will be ended, all said, it says, it murmurs.

The *Texts for Nothing* do not stand as independent works, but evolve together as a series. Each of the *Six Residua* and the *Fizzles*, however, can stand as an independent work. Moreover the brevity of these late pieces is not a function of the fact that they are in some sense 'unfinished': it is rather that part of what Beckett has to say is involved in their brevity, their uncompromising starkness. Each piece constitutes an encounter with a reality (or unreality) which human kind cannot bear for very long.

'Imagination Dead Imagine' (1966) is probably the best-known of Beckett's short prose pieces. To some extent it is concerned with issues previously raised in the *Texts for Nothing*. In the opening lines Beckett confronts man's inability to transcend the limitations of human consciousness. The paradox of the title suggests that the difficulty is one which lies primarily in language, in what Derrida would call its *differance*.[15] However, in this text Beckett then goes on to 'dramatise' the unimaginable. In making this effort, in 'Imagination Dead Imagine', 'Ping' and 'Lessness' – as opposed to merely stating the raw fact of human limitation – Beckett creates powerful metaphors which defamiliarise the fundamental elements of human consciousness and existence. 'Imagination Dead Imagine' is an exercise in negation, as Beckett conjures first the absence of the empirical world, and then the absence of the imagination itself. The 'little fabric' of the rotunda (itself an imagined world), which had seemed to present a 'world still proof against enduring tumult', has by the close of this text been lost apparently beyond all hope of recovery:

> Leave them there, sweating and icy, there is better elsewhere. No, life ends and no, there is nothing elsewhere, and no question now of ever finding again that white speck lost in whiteness, to see if they still lie still in the stress of that storm, or of a worse storm, or in the black dark for good, or the great whiteness unchanging, and if not what they are doing.[16]

The spare imagery of 'Imagination Dead Imagine' accords with the abstract nature of the subject matter. Beckett creates a sense of the abstract or noumenal by stripping his text bare of all but the most fundamental phenomenal attributes. Colour is reduced to the two basic terms of black and white; space to the most economical combinations of the circle and semi-circle.

A similarly reduced landscape exists in 'Ping', in which a solitary human figure is 'fixed' in a cube composed of shining white planes. White is, we are told, the 'last colour': it is broken (and thus made visible) only because the human figure produces the 'trace' of its white body on the whiter background; also an open eye interrupts the white prospect. 'Eyes alone unover given blue light blue almost white.'[17] The eye is naturally associated with perception and memory, and its appearance leads into a specific memory. A blue sky is retrieved from the past: 'Ping perhaps a nature one second with image same time a little less blue and white in the wind.'[18]

'Ping' opens with the words 'All known' but these are immediately countermanded by the following words 'all white' – 'all' white cannot by definition be known. The confident tone of the opening is subverted for 'Ping' is concerned only with the movement towards knowledge through memory. The word 'ping'[19] which recurs at irregular intervals throughout the text often precedes a particular flash of memory. The sound itself is mechanical and its insistent but random nature may suggest something rather like the working of man's mechanical or voluntary memory. In 'Ping' the operations of voluntary memory seem to be successful only to a certain degree: the text closes at the point when such memory seems to have achieved all it can: 'Head haught eyes white fixed front old ping last murmur one second perhaps not alone eye unlustrous black and white half closed long lashes imploring ping silence ping over.'[20] Yet there is a sense in which even this much memory can be said to exceed the requirements of the text. The lyrical force of the passage somehow detaches it from its logical context: an overplus of feeling almost threatens the stability of the prose. The tension which results is characteristic of Beckett's later prose works. These give a continuing sense of the pressure of feeling on form: emotion is heightened the nearer the text seems to come to a point of stylistic breakdown.

In two of Beckett's late texts, however, it seems that all traces of tension have been subsumed by the processes of the prose. In 'Still' (1973) and 'Old Earth' (1974)[21] the questioning of language which had prevented earlier texts from self-fulfilment has largely ceased. There is a movement towards acceptance of the contingencies of language and experience, and with this comes a readiness to exploit and explore familiar cadences and images. So 'Still' opens with an evocation of sunset which depends for its effect partly on the fact that Beckett here adopts the 'poetic' syntax which he had avoided for so long: the effect is achieved also through the pre-existing associations of the 'twilight of such day/As after sunset fadeth in the west':

> Bright at last close of a dark day the sun shines out at last and goes down. Sitting quite still at valley window normally turn head now and see it the sun low in the southwest sinking. Even get up certain moods and go stand by western window quite still watching it sink and then the afterglow.

At an early point in 'Still' a new confidence in the value of the human imagination is indicated as Beckett momentarily privileges a much-needed imaginative truth over empirical evidence:

> Quite still again then at open window facing south over the valley in this wicker chair though actually close inspection not still at all but trembling all over. Close inspection namely detail by detail all over to add up finally to this whole not still at all but trembling all over. But casually in this fading light impression dead still even the hands clearly trembling and the breast faint rise and fall.

The manifold implications of the word 'still' give the clue to Beckett's adoption of English for the first version of this text. As this figure sits, apparently motionless, in time, still (in spite of all) the 'little body' of man is able to make some peace with itself:

> The right hand slowly opening leaves the armrest taking with it the

whole forearm complete with elbow and slowly rises opening further as it goes and turning a little deasil till midway to the head it hesitates and hangs half open trembling in mid air. Hangs there as if half inclined to return that is sink back slowly closing as it goes and turning the other way till as and where it began clenched tightly on end of rest. Here because of what comes now not midway to the head but almost there before it hesitates and hangs there trembling as if half inclined etc. Half no but on the verge when in its turn the head moves from its place forward and down among the ready fingers where no sooner received and held it weighs on down till elbow meeting armrest brings this last movement to an end and all still once more.

All in the text leads up to the moment when the head finally rests in the hand, and considerable tension is generated as we move towards this point. Beckett creates this tension partly through a Steinian 'insistence', or repetition with variation; also in the passage quoted above he uses slow-motion to retard the narrative at the critical juncture.

'Old Earth' is more static, more prose poem-like: it is composed of only fifteen sentences. In this text too Beckett exploits familiar associations. The earth (clay) reminds us of mortality as it lies cold in the twilight, and with the cockchafers whirring into the shadows Beckett provides us with a characteristically mordant equivalent for the butterfly as an emblem of the transience of life: 'Three years in the earth, those the moles don't get, then guzzle guzzle, ten days long, a fortnight, and always the flight at nightfall.' 'The sky, the different skies' are truly celestial, offering an image, elusive and delusive though it may be, of a freedom which is heavenly.

In 'Old Earth' Beckett exploits the opportunities of the short prose form to the full. The prose itself is spare but supple, adroitly elliptical:

Not long now, how I gaze on you, and what refusal, how you refuse me, you so refused.

Moments of life, of mine too, among others, no denying, all said and done. Happiness, what happiness, but what deaths, what loves, I knew at the time, it was too late then.

The text is shaped much like a lyric poem and mimes the truth that we can never 'end', only 'end again', endlessly, while we live. The tranquillity which the speaker imagines he has found towards the close of the text ('now, simply stay still') is illusory: he has hardly articulated his sense that he has reached a vantage point appropriate for a 'long gaze' when his peace is broken by the irrepressible activity of memory:

> No but now, now, simply stay still, standing before a window, one hand on the wall, the other clutching your shirt, and see the sky, a long gaze, but no, gasps and spasms, a childhood sea, other skies, another body.

Jorge Luis Borges is an exemplary, heuristic figure. His writing has affected the development of short fiction in Europe and the United States as well as Latin America, and because his work has been so influential in translation it is to an extent valid to treat it in a European context. Borges has himself said that he regards Argentinian civilisation as essentially European. In his essay 'The Argentine Writer and Tradition' he also suggests that a writer need not necessarily work closely within a national tradition. A writer may benefit from a more tangential relationship with the culture which he chooses to make his own:

> What is our Argentine tradition? I believe we can answer this question easily and that there is no problem here. I believe our tradition is all of Western culture, and I also believe we have a right to this tradition, greater than that which the inhabitants of one or another Western nation might have. I recall here an essay of Thortstein Veblen, the North American sociologist, on the pre-eminence of Jews in Western culture ... he says that they are outstanding in Western culture because they act within that culture and, at the same time, do not feel tied to it by any special devotion; 'for that reason,' he says, 'a Jew will always find it easier than a non-Jew to make innovations in Western culture'; and we can say the same of the Irish in English culture. ... I believe that we Argentines, we South Americans in general, are in an analogous situation; we can handle all European themes, handle them without superstition, with an irreverence which can have, and already does have, fortunate consequences.[22]

Borges, like Beckett, questions language as a means of coding experience. He does not, as many critics have suggested, use language as a self-referential, closed system. Borges would not deny that literature should express truth: he would, however, deny that truth is always available through expression. Taking this point of view, he prefers to approach truth indirectly, through suggestion, following Symbolist tradition (*'Suggérer, voilà le rêve'*). His own word to describe his technique is 'allusion'.

Reality for Borges, as for the Symbolists, is an experience, a moment of apprehension without specific content or specific linguistic terminology. Reality is intuited, but remains strictly speaking inexpressible. And as if to emphasise further the limitations of language, Borges, like Beckett, frequently refers in his fiction to other systems of coding, other epistemologies, that of mathematics for example. Moreover in *The Book of Imaginary Beings* (1967) he mounts a direct attack on language in the form of the categories so far realised within it. He does not merely question the validity of any given invention, but proposes the unimpeded opportunity for creating new ones:

[*Fauna of China*]
The *Ping-feng*, which lives in the country of Magical Water, resembles a black pig with a head at each end.

In the region of the Queer Arm, people have a single arm and three eyes. They are exceptionally skilful and build flying chariots in which they travel on the winds.

The *Ti-chiang* is a supernatural bird dwelling in the Mountains of the Sky. Its colour is bright red, it has six feet and four wings, but has neither face nor eyes.[23]

Borges is not preoccupied only with language: he goes further to question the concept of time which is at the heart of a materialist world view. This concern with time has, of course, important consequences for his medium. Because Borges questions time and a materialist world view he distrusts the novel form which is unavoidably involved with these concepts. So he turns to short fiction, which is less closely involved, structurally and thematically, with the processes of time and with relations of cause and effect. Within the form of the short fiction Borges attempts to create circular themes and structures and becomes involved with his famous games with plot. Specifically, he plays with the dimensions of time through the use of double or multiple plots. In 'Death and the Compass', for example, one story is subverted by another. The detective Lönnrot seeks to unfold a murder mystery. In the great tradition of literary detectives (including Borges's loved Father Brown) he is credited not only with powers of reason, but also with a kind of insight above the level of mere ratiocination: 'Lönnrot believed himself a pure reasoner, an Auguste Dupin, but there was something of the adventurer in him, and even a little of the gambler.'[24] As in Poe's Dupin stories we see everything through the eyes of a detective-narrator. But at the very point where he seems to have 'solved' the mystery, Borges takes the opportunity to point out Lönnrot's limitations. Lönnrot has not in practice allowed chance or inspiration to deflect him from his reasonable path; in following his own chain of logic, however, he falls victim to the superior or encompassing logic of his enemy, Red Scharlach. Two plots thus converge: we move from one plot/time scheme (Lönnrot's) to another (that of Red Scharlach). The final effect is curious: the two plots seem to cancel each other out, creating a temporal vanishing point coinciding exactly with the moment of Lönnrot's death.

In the still more famous 'The Garden of Forking Paths' Borges explores the possibility of multiple plot, and the idea that time itself may be infinite. As in 'Death and the Compass', the basic unit of the fiction is that of the detective tale, here multiplied endlessly. The fiction opens with a frame story concerning a historian of the First World War (narrator 1). He comes across the signed confession of a military spy of the period (narrator 2). In turn this spy takes us to the 'garden of forking paths' which is at the centre of the narrative, but which provides no resolution for it. For the garden of forking paths is a maze in the form of a book. It has taken years for its interpreter to understand it as fiction: it cannot easily be read for it flouts all conventions of genre. A key is needed to unlock its form:

I lingered, naturally, on the sentence: *I leave to the various futures (not to all) my garden of forking paths.* Almost instantly, I understood: 'the garden of forking paths' was the chaotic novel; the phrase 'the various futures (not to all)' suggested to me the forking in time, not in space. A broad rereading of the work confirmed the theory. In all fictional works, each time a man is confronted with several alternatives, he chooses one and eliminates the others; in the fiction of Ts'ui Pen, he chooses – simultaneously – all of them. *He creates*, in this way, diverse futures, diverse times which themselves also proliferate and fork.[25]

We thus come upon a book which is 'unfinished' by definition: it is potentially infinite. The apprehension of this potentiality induces a vertiginous feeling, almost a feeling of terror. Borges describes the feelings of the book's interpreter in terms which indicate this: 'He [the author] believed in an infinite series of times, in a growing, dizzying net of divergent, convergent and parallel times.'[26] The vertiginous feeling is increased for the 'real' reader because Borges does not close off his frame stories satisfactorily. We become involved in the adventures of narrator 2, the spy Yu Tsun, but in the event are told nothing of his fate. Borges in turn declines to take us back to the world of the original frame story. He achieves this by the simple expedient of omitting the final punctuation mark which should close off Yu Tsun's story.[27] Without closing speech marks this narrative cannot be inserted back into the world of the original historian-narrator.

On the one hand the narrator in Borges's fiction fears chaos and the 'crassly infinite', and frequently takes refuge in human (and humane) images of order and calm:

> The record on the phonograph revolved next to a bronze phoenix. I also recall a *famille rose* vase and another, many centuries older, of that shade of blue which our craftsmen copied from the potters of Persia. ('The Garden of Forking Paths')[28]

On the other hand the narrator is oppressed by a sense of the finite quality of the human mind. In 'Tlön, Uqbar, Orbis Tertius' Borges uses an unusually romantic image forcibly to remind us of the limited structures which we impose on reality:

> The contact and the habit of Tlön have disintegrated this world. Enchanted by its rigour, humanity forgets over and over again that it is a rigour of chess masters, *not of angels*. [my italics][29]

In a sense however the finite and the infinite are two sides of the same coin, or, to put it another way, the infinite is itself a finite concept. It is Borges's achievement to embody this paradox in fictions which continually slip away from the reader, refusing to come to rest at a stable point of narrative closure.

It has often been suggested that Borges's investigations into the nature of time lead him to an a-historical conception of the universe. Thus it has been argued that history for Borges consists of a handful of key metaphors: like the medieval poets and philosophers, it has been suggested, he feels no obligation to produce the individual, original image but places value on *auctorité*, on all things which have previously been recorded in books. While this hypothesis 'explains' Borges's delight in his collections of 'imaginary beings' and 'extraordinary tales', it rather rides roughshod over the delicacy and subtlety of his imaginative powers. Were it not in itself a paradox we might say that Borges is *the* uncommitted writer. Thus while in many of his fictions he strives to create a-temporal images, in others he grapples with the problem of temporality in narrative or deftly refutes his 'refutation' of time:

> Time is the substance I am made of. Time is a river which sweeps me along, but I am the river; it is a tiger which destroys me, but I am the tiger; it is a fire which consumes me, but I am the fire. The world unfortunately, is real; I, unfortunately, am Borges.[30]

A similar vigilance underlies his treatment of 'character' in fiction. He has written of his distrust of the notion of character (a distrust shared of course by many short story/short fiction writers). He does not, he says, wish to add the 'metaphysical notion of self to a succession of mental states'. He 'denies the successive':

> Each moment is autonomous. Neither vengeance nor pardon nor prisons nor even oblivion can modify the invulnerable past. To me, hope and fear seem no less vain, for they always refer to future events: that is, to events that will not happen to us, who are the minutely detailed present.[31]

In the fiction 'Funes the Memorious' he takes to its logical conclusion the premise, fundamental to the traditional novel, that a character is compounded of his past. Ireneo Funes, after a riding accident, undergoes a profound change in consciousness:

> For nineteen years he had lived as one in a dream: he looked without seeing, listened without hearing, forgetting everything, almost everything. When he fell, he became unconscious; when he came to, the present was almost intolerable in its richness and sharpness, as were his most distant and trivial memories.[32]

Because he can remember everything, Funes can 'remember' nothing in the usual sense of the world. For as Borges points out elsewhere, memory abstracts from reality:

I cannot walk through the suburbs in the solitude of the night without thinking that the night pleases us because it suppresses idle details, just as our memory does.   ('A New Refutation of Time')[33]

Funes cannot subordinate detail to general categories so that language itself becomes too generalised a medium for his perceptions:

> Locke, in the seventeenth century, postulated (and rejected) an impossible language in which each individual thing, each stone, each bird and each branch, would have its own name; Funes once projected an analogous language, but discarded it because it seemed too general to him, too ambiguous. In fact, Funes remembered not only every leaf of every tree of every wood, but also every one of the times he had perceived or imagined it.[34]

Borges here suggests that no one can be compounded of the past. Memory confuses and elides what has actually existed: it should not therefore be the basis for one's present sense of self. However, in 'The Shape of the Sword' Borges takes the alternative view. Here he suggests that a man is made, irrevocably, by the experiences which enter most deeply into his imagination. Whether these are real or illusory, they will vitally affect him through life. So in this fiction one Vincent Moon is shown as unable to free himself from an experience which happened years ago and 'in another country'. The persistence of a remembered experience colouring his mind and sensibility is figured by a 'half moon' (half Moon) scar which never fades. At the close of the fiction we see Moon able to define himself only with reference to this past experience: 'I denounced the man who protected me: I am Vincent Moon.'

Having explored the relationship between time and individual identity, Borges in some of his more recent fictions embarks on an examination of the nature of space and matter. In two influential short pieces, 'The Book of Sand' and 'The Disk' he addresses, as he says in the Afterword of *The Book of Sand* 'two opposite and inconceivable concepts'. In 'The Book of Sand' Borges dreams or imagines something which has infinite materiality. In 'The Garden of Forking Paths' he had already toyed with the notion of an infinite book:

> I could think of nothing other than a cyclic volume, a circular one. A book whose last page was identical with the first, a book which had the possibility of continuing indefinitely.[35]

However, the earlier image does not strictly suggest infinity, since it presupposes an element of repetition and recognition. The Book of Sand itself is a more breathtaking concept:

> The stranger asked me to find the first page.
> I laid my left hand on the cover and, trying to put my thumb on the flyleaf, I opened the book. It was useless. Every time I tried, a number of pages came between the cover and my thumb. It was as if they kept growing from the book.
> 'Now find the last page.'
> Again I failed. In a voice that was not mine, I barely managed to stammer, 'This can't be.'[36]

The image of endless materiality, endless growth, has its counterpart in the fiction 'The Disk', which is, as Borges explained, 'about the Euclidean circle, which has only one side'. In this fiction Borges lifts a geometrical reality into a three-dimensional reality/unreality:

> With a certain misgiving, I touched my fingertips to his palm. I felt something cold, and saw a glitter. The hand closed abruptly. I said nothing. The man went on patiently, as if speaking to a child.
> 'It is Odin's disk,' he said, 'It has only one side. In all the world there is nothing else with only one side.'[37]

Borges's dissolution of the terms of space and matter may have had as great an influence on younger writers as his manipulation of the theme of time. The 'laws' of the three dimensions are subverted to disquieting effect in the work of younger postmodernist writers.

In England during the last few years the 'short story' has staged something of a comeback. After a period during the fifties and sixties when publishers were reluctant to take collections of short fiction, and there were few magazine outlets, there has been a resurgence of interest and confidence. Publishers are now accepting more short fiction, and wider magazine outlets have become available. There is a feeling that the short form is *the* form for innovation, and many of the best young writers are turning first to short fiction, rather as in the early modernist period. Beckett and Borges are, of course, the great, dominating figures: their cultivation of the short form during the lean years has had enormous influence.

Ian McEwan is the best known of such younger writers: his first collection of short fictions, *First Love, Last Rites* (1976) was hailed by critics and each of his subsequent books has added to his reputation. McEwan has so far published two collections of short fiction, some plays for television, and two novels, which might better be termed novellas. They have been characterised by critics as 'long stories':[38] it is clear that their form is closely dependent on the form of the preceding short pieces. McEwan's fictions are polyvalent in content and form. Aspects of human nature which seem at once bizarre and familiar are explored in fictions with deliberately, extravagantly unbelievable plots. Space and time, personal and sexual identity are set free: tension is then engendered by the contrast between the subject matter and the modestly controlled narrative tone.

'Solid Geometry' is a short fiction which has become notorious because of the banning of the television play McEwan adapted from it in 1979. He has given an account of the origins of the piece which suggests the importance of Borges, not as a direct influence, but as one who pointed to certain themes which are particularly apt for short fiction:

> A mathematician friend from Chile had recently told me of a 'proof' for a plane without a surface and had outlined for me the consequences of such a proof being valid. Independently of this I had been reading Bertrand Russell's diaries and I wanted to write a story which would somehow illustrate the way diary writing, in its selectivity, closely resembles fiction writing. Thirdly, I wanted to write about the collision of two intellectual worlds.[39]

The fiction is extremely neat, as McEwan himself has said. It works on three time levels which correspond to the three 'themes' mentioned above. Levels 1 and 2 and 2 and 3 intersect by means of a repeated 'conjuror's trick'. This trick, a vanishing act, appears to defy the laws of space and time:

> I came into the possession of certain documents which not only invalidate everything fundamental to our science of solid geometry but also undermine the whole canon of our physical laws and force one to redefine one's place in Nature's scheme. These papers outweigh in importance the combined work of Marx and Darwin.[40]

Ian McEwan has said that 'Solid Geometry' is concerned with some of the issues which had faced him in writing fiction:

When I returned to England, determined to carry on writing . . . I found the cautious, analytical voices of a literary education vying with the intuitive and carefree. Albert and Maisie became the exaggerated representatives of each – the highly rational and destructive against the loving but self-deluded. The intended irony was that Albert uses the very system ('the mathematics of the Absolute') to dispose of her, that Maisie endorses and he has repudiated.[41]

In a very real sense 'Solid Geometry' is about the process of making fictions: at one point in the text the narrator even says 'Perhaps we *are* in a fiction seminar.' In the text one way of looking at life, the rational and discursive, is opposed to another, the mystical and lyrical. The first overwhelms the second. The rational Albert survives as Maisie does not, and he manages this because he approaches the unknown in a completely different manner. Instead of 'filling [her] mind with other people's mystic banalities and giving [herself] nightmares' Albert, like the other males in the story, seeks to subdue the unknown to rational, logical codes. A new area of experience is hardly intuited before a 'new' language of mathematics is evolved to express it: 'The pages are covered with scribbles, diagrams and symbols. It seems that Hunter had to devise a new set of symbols, virtually a whole new language, to express his ideas.'[42] But in coding experience we limit it, on the level of language and also in wider semiotic/behavioural terms. McEwan thus seems to suggest that the 'selectivity', the degree of coding involved in fictionality itself is in a sense invidious.

Sometimes, however, reality seems to lie not 'outside' a code but within it. McEwan focuses on the ways in which different codes intersect and mirror each other, and moves towards the idea of an all-embracing code or structure. His play *The Imitation Game* (1980), which is about code breaking on a literal, military level, and also about codes of sexual behaviour, illustrates this concern. And in many of his short fictions McEwan focuses on codes of sexual behaviour. He stresses the disjunction between sex and gender identity, and through the games played by his 'characters' we perceive ways in which an enlightened understanding of the codes of sexual behaviour can lead to some kind of rapprochement between the sexes. 'Disguises', an early piece, is an example. Dressing-up games figure largely in McEwan's fiction and dressing for dinner is, as the narrator remarks, 'the motif of this story'. Through the changes of dress and role undertaken by the characters we are shown how the outward, social signs of sexual identity have become more important than actual sexual difference in the way we construct sexuality. So the little boy Henry who is required to dress for dinner in girls' clothes reacts far more strongly to the set of girls' clothes than he does to a real girl, Linda:

> One afternoon retiring after tea, opening the door of his room Henry found a girl lying face down across his bed; stepping a little closer, it was not a girl it was a kind of party frock and a wig of long blonde hair, white tights, black leather slippers. Catching his breath he touched the dress, cold, ominously silky, it rustled when he picked it up, all flounces and frills, layer on layer with white satin and lace edged with pink, a cute bow falling at the back. He let it fall back on the bed, *the most girlish thing he ever saw*, wiped his hand on his trousers, not daring to touch the wig which seemed alive. [my italics][43]

When he actually has to put the clothes on he controls his panic by projecting his 'feminine' feelings onto his mental image of Linda:

> He removed the wig, it was clownish, his short black hair with the party frock, it made him laugh. He put the wig back on, did a short dance across the room, Henry and Linda at once, closer than in the car, inside her now and she was in him. It was no longer an oppression, he was free of Mina's anger, invisible inside this girl. He began to brush out the wig, the way he saw Linda do it when she came home from school.[44]

Henry is offered other opportunities to swop gender. When he visits Linda her mother Claire (who is, confusingly, 'young and old at the same time') encourages him to abandon his new suit and change into some of Linda's clothes – 'we must find you some clothes to play in'. At this point Henry is, despite his innocence, still essentially in control. Although he is not sufficiently on his guard against Claire and her possible motives for dressing him up, he is still able to manage the situation in the light of the normal codes of sexual behaviour, learnt, presumably from his dead mother whose 'image six months on was elusive like a faint star'. When he goes up to see Linda in her room, he quickly abandons the borrowed clothes and joins her in a curiously innocent idyll:

> She rolled over to face him, in the pink gloom she smelled animal

and milky, this was the beginning and end of his Sunday when he came to recall it to himself, his heart thumping from the pillow to his ear, lifting his head once to let her free her hair, and talking, mostly about school, her first week there, the friends they knew and the teachers.[45]

Gradually, however, images of sexual conflict multiply so that Henry loses his manly confidence. His collapse comes at a party held by his aunt/guardian Mina. 'Come disguised' she has told her guests, and Henry assumes therefore that this is to be a fancy-dress party. He finds a 'monster' outfit for himself, but when the party finally takes place it seems to him that he is the only one in disguise. He is unable to read the signs, unable to see that this is a gathering of Mina's transvestite friends. And because he is unable to read the signs the 'system' is operating him rather than the other way round. So Henry has no option but to regress to little boyhood, giving up the attempt to understand and thus control the situation:

> They were none of them baffled by each other, these talkers and drinkers, assuming they were in some disguise they knew who they were, found it easy to talk. . . . More wine more wine, something nervous made him bring the glass to his mouth every ten seconds, for not being noticed, for being no one at a grownups' party, some small boy who held the door open when they came in.[46]

'Reflections of a Kept Ape' (1978) is also about codes of behaviour. In this particular fiction the human species is observed from the vantage point of an ape: McEwan adopts simian rather than Martian tactics of defamiliarisation (and of course his fictions precede much 'Martian' poetry). The ape-narrator is a 'lover-turned-spy', observing the baffling rituals which make up the life of Sally Klee:

> From where I sit I hear her thread into her typewriter a single sheet of paper, off-white, A4, 61 mg per square metre, the very same paper on which she effortlessly composed her first novel. She will ensure the machine is set at double space. Only letters to her friends, agent and publisher go single space. Decisively she punches the red key which will provide, when there are words to surround it, a neat, off-white emptiness to precede her first sentence. An awesome silence settles over the house.[47]

The kept ape protests that he is not equal to the task of understanding the human race, particularly in the case of Sally Klee the writer:

> Now everything was as it had been and as Sally Klee would expect it to be – typewriter, pens, blotting paper, a single withering daffodil – and still I knew what I knew and understood nothing at all. Simply, I was unworthy.[48]

But his claims are undercut to comic but also slightly sinister effect by the elegantly 'literary' surface of his narrative. The 'ape' effortlessly compares himself to Sterne's Uncle Toby, muses on a possible misquotation from Yeats, echoes lines from 'My Last Duchess' ('and the smiles in my direction ceased'). Moreover, he opens his narrative with a sentence which turns up again in an 'extract' from Sally Klee's novel – is the ape therefore the true keeper of Sally Klee the feminist muse?

Like 'Solid Geometry', 'Reflections of a Kept Ape' is largely 'about' fiction making. The central image offers a bizarre representation of writer's block and addresses the notion that the artist always writes the same book:

> Was art then nothing more than a wish to appear busy? Was it nothing more than a fear of silence, of boredom, which the merely reiterative rattle of the typewriter's keys was enough to allay? In short, having crafted one novel, would it suffice to write it again, type it out with care, page by page? (Gloomily I recycled nits from torso to mouth.) Deep in my heart I knew it would suffice.[49]

This self-referential quality is kept up to the end. The text closes with a passage which is both funny and moving, and which, interestingly, relates to Nabokov's account of the image which inspired *Lolita*:

> As far as I can recall, the initial shiver of inspiration was somehow prompted by a newspaper story about an ape in the Jardin des Plantes who, after months of coaxing by a scientist, produced the first drawing ever charcoaled by an animal: this sketch showed the bars of the poor creature's cage.[50]

McEwan, too, is concerned with the codes, the bars and barriers of fiction and existence:

Standing here directly behind Sally Klee I am struck by a vivid memory from my earliest infancy. I am staring at my mother who squats with her back to me and then, for the first time in my life, I see past her shoulder as through a mist pale, spectral figures beyond the plate glass, pointing and mouthing silently. I advance noiselessly into the room and squat down a few feet behind Sally Klee's chair. Now I am here, it seems an impossible idea she will ever turn in her chair and notice me.[51]

Both McEwan's novels or novellas are organised around a central, compelling image: both deal with bizarre personal and sexual relations in a context far removed from everyday life. The children in *The Cement Garden* (1978) cut free from social relations when their parents die; Colin and Mary in *The Comfort of Strangers* (1981) inhabit a vacuum, holidaying abroad in a hostile city which deceives with its appearances of familiarity. McEwan has made some comments which seem relevant to these issues in an introduction to *The Imitation Game*:

The English class system, its pervasiveness, its endless subtleties, had once been a rich source for the English novel. The system whose laws, customs, religion and culture consistently sanction the economic ascendancy of one sex over another could be a still richer source; men and women have to do with each other in ways that economic classes do not. Patriarchy corrupts our most intimate relationships with comic and tragic consequences, and as a system it can be described in microcosm through its smallest and most potent unit, the family.[52]

'Intimacy' is the key word here. It could be argued that McEwan's adoption of the short fiction and novella forms is bound up with this focus on our most private and usually well-guarded feelings. While short fiction does not deal exclusively with private emotion – inevitably the sense of privacy and exclusion depends on an implied social context – it can shed the weight of social commentary which seems inherent in the novel form. Such commentary will involve certain *a priori* assumptions about social relations. In this context it is intriguing to note the parallel between McEwan's adoption of short fiction for 'feminist' purposes and its popularity as a form among feminist writers of a century ago. They too wanted to open up new areas of experience without having any *a priori* commitment to a particular type of social analysis.

Clive Sinclair's short fictions, like those of McEwan, are stylistically sophisticated and self-referential. The most striking feature of his work is the sense he conveys of the magic of fiction, the joys of invention, parody and play. Like John Barth, he has underscored the analogy between sexual and artistic creativity: the influence of Barth may also lie behind his positive attitude to fiction making. This passage from John Barth, for example, might serve as a gloss on Sinclair's work:

> Inasmuch as concepts, including the concepts *Fiction* and *Necessity*, are more or less necessary fictions, fiction is more or less necessary. *Butterflies* exist in our imaginations, along with *Existence*, *Imagination*, and the rest. Archimedeses, we lever reality by concealing ourselves apart from its other things, them from one another, the whole from unreality. Thus Art is as natural an artifice as Nature; the truth of fiction is that Fact is fantasy; the made-up story is a model of the world.[53]

In the collections *Hearts of Gold* (1979) and *Bedbugs* (1982), the reality principle gives way to the possibility principle. What is possible is actual – though what is actual may be unreal, or redundant. What really matters is the narrator's capacity for invention – and it is at this point that postmodernist fiction may seem to join hands with the older 'story-telling' tradition. But there is a crucial difference, implied in the comments of John Barth. For if the terms 'fiction' and 'reality' are interchangeable, it is clear that we are inhabiting a world where the relations of language are more important than its terms. With no absolute, empirical points of reference, language itself and its structures will tend to dominate in the creation of meaning.

If Barth is one influence, Borges is another. Like Borges, Sinclair challenges our sense of chronicity and cause and effect through the use of excessive plot. In the title-fiction of *Hearts of Gold*, for example, the detective Smolinsky plays with explanation, unravelling a B-movie plot with a variety of interpretations all of which and none of which are true. An ending is imposed on the text in a quite arbitrary fashion, as if to emphasise the fact that it is Smolinsky's imagination which is the author's prime concern. Smolinsky is a private eye/I – a secret agent, but an agent of the text, of a narrative which has the appearance of being self-generating.

'A Moment of Happiness', also from *Hearts of Gold*, is set in Prague: the narrator is an inhabitant of the city who lives, as he says, in a perpetual state of fear – 'That's a state of mind, not my address' –

though in a sense it is his address. He is morbidly preoccupied with the motions of his own body: he likens them to the processes of the body politic, which, too, must be constantly on the alert against 'infection'. Accordingly he prepares to give information to the secret police, betraying a couple of tourist 'friends'. He seems to treat personal relations in as cavalier a fashion as he treats abstract notions of truth. He is a tremendous liar and much of the text is taken up with his tall stories about his origins. He is compelled continually to re-invent himself, organising his past as the state organises history, and for some of the same reasons:

> The State does its best to ensure control of the future, but there is no guarantee. The best it can do is rearrange the past to suit itself, and to stabilise the present in such a way that it becomes, simultaneously, a reflection of both past and future, thus liable to strict checks.[54]

The narrator also wants to control the past, the present and the future: his 'only desire in this life' is to wrest a moment from the flux of time, to conjure an image of himself (an image of his perception of himself) which will be outside time and process. The analogy, of course, is with the artist, also seeking an artificial permanence:

> Robert opens his camera case. He fiddles with the exposure meter, sets the speed and the correct aperture. He places the camera to his eye and twists the lens till he has me in sharp focus. I smile. The shutter clicks. And so on a small piece of celluloid is a picture of me. Preserving me for that single 1/60th of a second in my life when I am not afraid.[55]

In 'Genesis' (from *Bedbugs*), Sinclair again plays with the boundaries between fiction and reality. He takes for his subject the Absolute Fiction, in both senses of the term: this fiction is an image for the absolute and at the same time is absolutely fictional. The 'narrator', an angel, takes us through different levels of reality, from a smog-filled contemporary Los Angeles (where else, as he quips) to Los Angeles as it was in the 'primeval slime'; from the minds of his Los Angeles 'students' to the mind of God. The barriers between different worlds are elided through language: the narrative medium is expertly exploited to this end. Favourite tactics are punning and the revival of dead metaphors: in this way apparently different worlds merge and are shown to be aspects of each other:

Shod in Chinese slippers I shuffle from the Museum into a trio of demons sent to chastise me. They look like death, their transparent black flesh revealing all their muscles and bones.[56]

What is Heaven like? Like nothing on earth.[57]

Mankind is 'grounded by the gravity of the grave', the artist Artie may be 'artful enough to persuade an angel into bed with his wife'.

There is a likeness between God and the fiction maker – again one is reminded of John Barth ('God wasn't too bad a novelist, except he was a Realist'). Sinclair's version of this is more elaborate:

Like creators everywhere, God felt that His critics misunderstood His intentions. He agreed that humanity's misfortunes were upsetting, but insisted that this was a deliberate effect of His art. PERHAPS MY TALENT FOR VERISIMILITUDE IS A LITTLE DISTURBING? BUT YOU MUST REMEMBER THAT WHAT YOU SEE IS NOT REAL. IT IS A FICTION. HEAVEN CAN BE DULL. THAT'S WHY I CREATED THE WORLD.[58]

We are further entertained by the now familiar analogy between sexual and artistic creativity: the angel 'breathes life into the sterile womb' of a 'real' woman and inspires her husband's artistic imagination. Coincidentally the angel's son is born and Artie publishes a best-seller. He writes, says the *New York Review of Books*, 'like an angel'.

Adam Mars-Jones's first collection, *Lantern Lecture*, was published in 1981: 'Lantern Lecture' itself was first published in *Quarto* in 1980. Part of the distinctive quality of his fiction comes from the way in which he disposes factual material, available to us all, in patterns of elegant asymmetry (and achronicity). By this means hidden structures of behaviour or perception are focused and highlighted. His work is also marked by a tension between the factual subject matter and the highly abstract prose style – very far from the sensuous particularity of Ian McEwan.

All three texts in *Lantern Lecture* take their point of departure in factual material, but develop in diverse ways. 'Lantern Lecture' is a lantern lecture-like rendering of the life of Philip Yorke, a (non-Welsh-speaking) Welsh eccentric. The text is divided into fragments of unequal length: their irregular arrangement tends to give an impres-

sion of the 'disorder' of Yorke's mind. Mild-mannered Philip Yorke
experiences life as an endless continuum. Past, present and future
inhabit the 'same' time, a fact reflected in the continuous present tense
of his narrative.

Yet in taking life in this way and refusing to conform to certain
norms – for example he will not behave as a middle-aged man 'should'
behave; he will not act the part of the squire-turned-responsible-
trustee of his former home – Philip Yorke is merely acting on a
perception of life which we all to some extent share. On one level we all
experience life as a seamless present: the moments which have
impinged most deeply on our consciousness merge together to create
our inmost sense of self. Such moments glow like lantern slides in the
memory: they can be recalled at will, reshuffled and arranged in what
order we please, and they will almost certainly be heavily 'touched up'
by the selective process of memory. So in 'Lantern Lecture' Philip
Yorke's handling of a particular medium, the lantern lecture, becomes
an image for the way in which we all create reality, drawing on a
'combination of showmanship and absence of mind'. The idea that we
are all in this sense artists is of course one with which we are familiar
through the work of the early modernists. Virginia Woolf, notably, was
occupied by this theme in *Between the Acts* (1941), a text to which
'Lantern Lecture' seems close. There may be an acknowledgement of
Woolf's presence in a passage which briefly reminds us of the use of the
mirror-device in *Between the Acts*. Mars-Jones writes:

> Mr Yorke delights his tenants and their families with a Christmas
> magic-lantern show. A small oil-lamp flickering in the dense warmth
> is enough to project the photographic images and the abstract
> designs of coloured glass. *Little Philip loses all sense of time.* The
> lights go up again; but it is some moments before the spectators
> realise that thanks to the heavy deposits of soot on their faces, they
> look less like an audience than a troop of nigger-minstrels,
> performers in their own right. [my italics][59]

'Hoosh-mi' is dated 1977, the year of the Silver Jubilee, and it is a
text dedicated to the defamiliarisation of the royal family. Mars-Jones
identifies certain media codes and examines the ways in which they
affect our sense of personality. He sees the members of the royal family
as sacrificial victims whose alienation from their true 'selves' provides
an extreme instance of a modern malaise:

> It is only on the surface that the Royal Family is at all

backward-looking or conservative; in reality, its members are faced with such a flood of bogus information from the world and from its media that their attempts to make sense of their lives could hardly be more contemporary. Perhaps in fact their predicament looks forward to the future, to a time when the advertised global village turns out to be a single overlit hall of mirrors.

'Hoosh-mi' starts from fact in the sense that its picture of royal life derives from published sources. It soon develops, however, into a 'farrago of scurrilous untruths', as the sub-title has it. The term farrago is interesting, suggesting as it does a mixing of genres. In 'Hoosh-mi' a number of styles are employed: that of a scientific paper, of an official report, of a paper from a learned journal. The 'untruth' then lies in the element of speculation and in the improbable development of the plot. Mars-Jones devises apparently impossible situations which are in fact no more impossible than those the members of the royal family customarily have to face. What is missing ordinarily is our understanding of the complex pressures on them. On the one hand, each member of the family must exhibit some sign of 'personality': on the other, as soon as they do so the gesture or attribute is taken off and relayed back to them by the public media. The members of the royal family are thus caught between the pre-fabricated images which people form of and for them and the images which they themselves 'create'. And the visual techniques, in particular, employed by the media are so slick that the images become as it were immediately devoid of content, of any sense of an originating principle. Hence Mars-Jones's frequent use of the mirror image in this text: multiple mirrors, in particular, suggest exactly that quality of infinite regress, and infinite dilution of the personality, which he associates with the royal family.

'Bathpool Park' extends many of the concerns of 'Hoosh-mi'. Based on the Black Panther murder case it is a text founded on the premise that the truth is so preposterous that it must be fictionalised. Also, however, it is suggested that this particular truth is in some way the product of previous fictions. Neilson, the Black Panther, is rather like the queen of 'Hoosh-mi': he is unable to grasp the reality behind the misleading codes of life and treats the codes as if they were 'true' instead of in the spirit of 'as if'. Once again Mars-Jones fastens on the importance of social and linguistic codes, using structuralist tools of analysis to penetrate Neilson's behaviour. Thus he links Neilson's criminal activities with a crucial spell in the army. Because of the army's place in the social superstructure, many kinds of behaviour are allowed within it which are not permissible elsewhere. Neilson has learnt the *code* of military behaviour, too well, but has failed to grasp its context. He is unable to recognise that what is acceptable within the army is not acceptable outside it, and after his period of service tenaciously clings to the forms of military life:

> Lights go out 11 p.m. Dog barks at No. 4. Escape route this way. If boxed in here, no way out.
>
> The attention to details of logistics, as also the vestigial use of *we* in a solitary context, derives from his time in the Army. The phobia about dogs, which he had seen used as trackers while on a tour of duty in Kenya, dates from the same period. Neilson's crimes were an extension of his military service.

Much of Neilson's behaviour is described in linguistic or rhetorical terms: after his arrest, for example, he is described as constructing for himself a 'grammar of innocence'. His use of a gun as a symbolic weapon is described thus: 'The times the gun went off, it had been misunderstood. The postmasters were killed by a rogue element of criminal language.' Such structuralist flourishes culminate in a Martian conceit at one point, when the behaviour of the police is compared with that of literary critics before a difficult text:

> The police therefore approached the ransom messages with scepticism, and extracted some satisfying contradictions from them. Like textual scholars establishing the spuriousness of a manuscript, they made much of divergences of tone and detail, form and content. Why was neither hostage nor messenger specified? Why was Dymo-tape chosen as the medium . . . etc.

This description also functions as an intra-textual note on the 'actual' author's proceedings.

In 'Bathpool Park' there is no sense of an objective reality: the extended analysis of court-room procedure makes it plain that in opting for one version of events we are doing no more than choosing among fictions. The chief witness himself finally comes to depend on the media for 'information' about the 'true' sequence of events:

> The newspapers then, which had supplied so much information, true and untrue, timely and untimely, in the course of the case, at last

supplied him with details of Lesley's death, and then reported them all over again, when he reproduced them in his testimony in court.

As in 'Hoosh-mi' we are left with a sense of an attenuation of reality through media overkill. There is also a feeling of helplessness before the numerous opportunities which we now have to perceive ourselves as (exteriorised) images. We have become 'shades of shadows', in Clive Sinclair's phrase, through the many mirrors made available through modern technology.

The work of Mars-Jones, Sinclair and McEwan contains elements borrowed from other disciplines: their work exists in an intellectual space defined to a considerable extent by the terms of linguistics and sociology. The way in which these writers borrow concepts from other disciplines in order to comment critically on their own work distinguishes them from Beckett and Borges: their work is more mannered in this respect.

All the writers considered in this chapter, however, have been committed to an exploration of the fundamental ways in which we encode reality. They have been very much aware of the processes of perception and representation, and these processes have tended to occupy the foreground of their work. As in the early modernist period, the short form seems to be highly appropriate for these contemporary concerns. If the novel is the most obviously mimetic of literary forms, especially *vis à-vis* the concept of time, the short form may be seen as its necessary foil, questioning by its very nature and structure novelistic assumptions about extensive time and material reality.

The contemporary interest in the short form is thus very much part of the postmodernist tendency. As in the modernist period, the short form is in the vanguard of experimental writing: developments which we can now see in it may radically affect the evolution of the novel as well as the short form.

Notes

Notes to the Introduction

1. D. H. Lawrence, *Studies in Classic American Literature*, Phoenix Edition of the works of D. H. Lawrence (1964) p. 2.
2. There is a discussion of the provenance of this term in Seymour Chatman, *Story and Discourse: Narrative Structure in Fiction and Film* (New York, 1978) p. 201.
3. *How Writing is Written*, vol. 2 of the previously uncollected writings of Gertrude Stein, ed. Robert Bartlett Haas (Los Angeles, 1974) p. 30.
4. Virginia Woolf, 'Mr Bennett and Mrs Brown', *Collected Essays 1* (1966) p. 320.
5. This change has been discussed most memorably in Graham Hough, *The Last Romantics* (1947) and in Frank Kermode, *Romantic Image* (1957).
6. Jack D. Flam, *Matisse on Art* (Oxford, 1973) p. 37 (from 'Notes of a Painter', 1908).
7. Ezra Pound, *Literary Essays*, ed. with an Introduction by T. S. Eliot (1960) p. 4.
8. Virginia Woolf, 'Modern Fiction', *Collected Essays II* (1966) p. 107.
9. Edgar Allan Poe, *Selected Writings*, Penguin edn (Harmondsworth, 1967) p. 499. (Poe is restating Coleridge's dictum, 'A poem of any length neither can be, or ought to be, all poetry' – S. T. Coleridge, *Biographia Literaria*, ed. J. Shawcross (Oxford, 1907) vol. 2, p. 11.)
10. Poe, *Selected Writings*, p. 500.
11. *Ibid.*, p. 444.
12. *Ibid.*, p. 446.
13. *Ibid.*, p. 446.
14. *Ibid.*, p. 139.
15. *Ibid.*, p. 141.
16. *Ibid.*, p. 395.
17. Though they may be deployed to reinforce the idea of community in a situation where community or communal ideals are threatened – for example in a colonial situation.
18. Goethe's definition of the subject of a story.
19. James Joyce, *Stephen Hero* (1944) p. 188.
20. Katherine Mansfield, *Novels and Novelists*, ed. J. M. Murry (New York, 1930) p. 32.
21. Nadine Gordimer, in 'The International Symposium on the Short Story', *Kenyon Review*, vol. 30 (1968) p. 459.
22. *Selected Stories of Thomas Hardy*, chosen and introduced by John Wain (1966) Introduction, p. xiv.

23. Jorge Luis Borges, *The Aleph and Other Stories 1933–1969* (1971) pp. 237–8.

Notes to Chapter 1: Impressionists and Imperialists

1. W. Somerset Maugham, *Points of View* (1958) p. 150.
2. Cynthia L. White, *Women's Magazines 1693–1968* (1970) p. 59.
3. Malcolm Elwin, *Victorian Wallflowers*, Academy Books edn (1937) pp. 254–5.
4. Arthur Symons, *The Symbolist Movement in Literature* (1899) p. 6.
5. Walter Pater, *The Renaissance: Studies in Art and Poetry* (1900) pp. 248–9.
6. Richard Le Gallienne, *Prose Fancies*, second series (1896) p. 102.
7. *Ibid.*, pp. 103–4.
8. *Ibid.*, p. 107.
9. George Egerton, 'A Lost Masterpiece: A City Mood, Aug. '93', *The Yellow Book: An Illustrated Quarterly*, vol. I (April 1894) p. 194.
10. *Ibid.*, p. 196.
11. *Ibid.*, p. 190.
12. *Ibid.*, p. 194.
13. *Ibid.*, p. 196.
14. *Ibid.*, p. 190.
15. *Ibid.*, p. 191.
16. Frances E. Huntley, 'A Pen-and-Ink Effect', *The Yellow Book*, vol. VI (July 1895) p. 288.
17. Hubert Crackanthorpe, 'The Haseltons', *The Yellow Book: An Anthology*, ed. Fraser Harrison (1974) p. 165.
18. Arthur Morrison, *Short Stories*, in the Harrap series 'Short Stories of To-day and Yesterday' (1929) p. 151.
19. Quoted in Derek Stanford (ed.), *Stories of the 90's* (1968) Introduction, pp. 13–14.
20. Robert Louis Stevenson, *New Arabian Nights*, Tusitala Edition of the works of Robert Louis Stevenson (New York, 1882) p. 252.
21. *Henry James and Robert Louis Stevenson: A Record of Friendship and Criticism*, ed. with an Introduction by Janet Adam Smith (1948) p. 91.
22. Henry James, *Hawthorne*, with an Introduction and notes by Tony Tanner (1967) p. 42.
23. *Henry James and Robert Louis Stevenson*, p. 104.
24. Vladimir Propp, *Morphology of the Folk Tale*, trans. Laurence Scott (Austin, Texas, 1968) p. 92.
25. Stevenson, *New Arabian Nights*, p. 243.
26. *Ibid.*, p. 244.
27. *Ibid.*, pp. 246–7.
28. *Ibid.*, p. 263.
29. Robert Louis Stevenson, *Dr Jekyll and Mr Hyde and Other Stories*, ed. with an Introduction by Jenni Calder, Penguin edn (Harmondsworth, 1979) p. 29.
30. *Ibid.*, p. 82.

31. *Ibid.*, pp. 83–4.
32. *Ibid.*, p. 31.
33. *Henry James and Robert Louis Stevenson*, p. 91.
34. Stevenson, *Dr Jekyll and Mr Hyde and Other Stories* p. 101.
35. *Ibid.*, p. 106.
36. *Ibid.*, p. 153.
37. *Ibid.*, p. 109.
38. *Ibid.*, p. 169.
39. Thomas Hardy, *Selected Stories*, chosen and introduced by John Wain (1966) p. xiv.
40. T. S. Eliot, *After Strange Gods* (1934) pp. 57–8.
41. *Henry James and Robert Louis Stevenson*, p. 195.
42. Rudyard Kipling, *Kim* (1927) pp. 403–4.
43. Rudyard Kipling, *Life's Handicap: Being Stories of Mine Own People* (1918) p. 372.
44. *Ibid.*, p. 206.
45. *Ibid.*, p. 209.
46. *Ibid.*, p. 403.
47. Quoted in Stanford (ed.), *Stories of the 90's*, Introduction, pp. 13–14.

Notes to Chapter 2: The Tale-Tellers: I

1. Rudyard Kipling, *Something of Myself* (1937) p. 207.
2. See Roman Jakobson, 'Two Aspects of Language and Two Types of Aphasic Disturbances', in *Fundamentals of Language*, ed. R. Jakobson and M. Halle (The Hague, 1956) pp. 52–82.
3. For example by Walter Allen in *The Short Story in English* (Oxford, 1981) p. 72.
4. Rudyard Kipling, *Life's Handicap: Being Stories of Mine Own People* (1918) p. 181.
5. Rudyard Kipling, *Short Stories*, vol. 2, Penguin edn (Harmondsworth, 1971) p. 29.
6. *Ibid.*, p. 41.
7. Rudyard Kipling, *Short Stories*, vol. 1, Penguin edn (Harmondsworth, 1971) p. 93.
8. *Ibid.*, p. 94.
9. *Ibid.*, p. 107.
10. Kipling, *Short Stories*, vol. 2, p. 172.
11. *Ibid.*, p. 175.
12. *Ibid.*, p. 175.
13. *Ibid.*, p. 163.
14. *Ibid.*, p. 167.
15. *Ibid.*, pp. 177–8.
16. *Ibid.*, p. 176.
17. *Ibid.*, p. 167.
18. *Ibid.*, p. 221.
19. *The Short Stories of Saki (H. H. Munro)*, complete with an Introduction by Christopher Morley (1930) p. 540.

20. *Ibid.*, p. 155.
21. *Ibid.*, p. 182.
22. *Ibid.*, p. 185.
23. *Ibid.*, p. 625.
24. *Ibid.*, p. 123.
25. *Ibid.*, p. 396 ('The Achievement of the Cat').
26. The Standard Edition of the *Complete Psychological Works of Sigmund Freud*, vol. 8: *Jokes and their Relation to the Unconscious* (1960) p. 167.
27. Ian Reid, *The Short Story* (1977) p. 61.
28. In *Somerset Maugham and his World*, the book under review.
29. William Trevor, *Spectator*, 26 February 1977, pp. 18–19.
30. Mary Doyle Springer, *Forms of the Modern Novella* (Chicago, 1975).
31. W. Somerset Maugham, *Points of View* (1958) p. 153.
32. Roland Barthes, *Image–Music–Text*, essays selected and translated by Stephen Heath (1977) pp. 92–3.
33. W. Somerset Maugham, *A Writer's Notebook*, Penguin edn (Harmondsworth, 1967) pp. 104–5.
34. W. Somerset Maugham, *Collected Short Stories*, vol. 4, Penguin edn (Harmondsworth, 1963) p. 337.
35. *Ibid.*, p. 147.
36. Jorge Luis Borges, *The Aleph and Other Stories 1933–1969* (1971) p. 278.

Notes to Chapter 3: Modernist Short Fiction

1. Nadine Gordimer, in 'The International Symposium on the Short Story', *Kenyon Review*, vol. 30 (1968) p. 459.
2. James Joyce, *Stephen Hero* (1944) p. 188.
3. James Joyce, *Dubliners*, Penguin edn (Harmondsworth, 1963) pp. 35–6.
4. *The Critical Writings of James Joyce*, ed. Ellsworth Mason and Richard Ellmann (1959) p. 116.
5. Joyce, *Dubliners*, p. 68.
6. *Ibid.*, p. 83.
7. *Ibid.*, pp. 7–8.
8. *Ibid.*, p. 15.
9. *Ibid.*, p. 16.
10. *Ibid.*, p. 173.
11. *Ibid.*, pp. 194–5.
12. *Ibid.*, pp. 189–90.
13. *Ibid.*, p. 220.
14. The Hogarth Press had published Katherine Mansfield's long story *Prelude* in 1918. There are several interesting references to Katherine Mansfield's work in Virginia Woolf's diary for the years 1917–22.
15. Virginia Woolf, *A Haunted House and Other Stories*, Penguin edn (Harmondsworth, 1973) pp. 9–10.
16. *Ibid.*, p. 11.
17. *Ibid.*, p. 12.
18. *Ibid.*, p. 13.

19. Virginia Woolf, *A Room of One's Own* (1929) p. 140.

20. Woolf and Stein's contemporary, Dorothy Richardson, discussed this issue in her preface to the first full edition of *Pilgrimage* (1938).

21. *The Diary of Virginia Woolf*, vol. 2: *1920–24*, ed. Anne Olivier Bell (1978) p. 13.

22. *A Change of Perspective: The Letters of Virginia Woolf*, vol. 3: *1923–28*, ed. Nigel Nicolson and Joanne Trautmann (1977) p. 385 (letter to Roger Fry, 27 May 1927).

23. Quoted in the Introduction to *Mrs Dalloway's Party: A Short Story Sequence by Virginia Woolf*, ed. Stella McNichol (1973) p. 15.

24. *The Diary of Virginia Woolf*, vol. 2, p. 325 (21 December 1924).

25. Virginia Woolf, 'The Art of Fiction', *The Moment and Other Essays* (1947) p. 92.

26. *How Writing is Written*, vol. 2 of the previously uncollected writings of Gertrude Stein, ed. Robert Bartlett Haas (Los Angeles, 1974) p. 155.

27. *Ibid.*, p. 30.

28. *Gertrude Stein: Writings and Lectures 1911–1945*, ed. Patricia Meyerowitz (1967) pp. 124–5.

29. *Selected Writings of Gertrude Stein*, ed. Carl Van Vechten, with an essay by F. W. Dupee (New York, 1972) p. 329.

30. See Ferdinand de Saussure, *Course in General Linguistics*, trans. Wade Buskin (1964) pp. 117–18, for a discussion of linguistic 'difference'.

31. *How Writing is Written*, p. 39. All subsequent quoted passages are from this edition.

32. Paul Hernadi, *Beyond Genre: New Directions in Literary Classification* (New York, 1972) p. 182.

33. From *Death in the Afternoon*, quoted in Charles A. Fenton, *The Apprenticeship of Ernest Hemingway: The Early Years*, Mentor edn (New York, 1961) pp. 182–3.

34. Ernest Hemingway, *Green Hills of Africa* (1936) p. 33.

35. Ernest Hemingway, *Winner Take Nothing*, Triad/Panther edn (1977) p. 62 (all subsequent references are to this edition).

36. *The Collected Stories of Katherine Mansfield* (1945) p. 197. All subsequent references are to this edition.

Notes to Chapter 4: The Tale-Tellers: II

1. Frank O'Connor, *The Mirror in the Roadway* (New York, 1956) p. 305.

2. Quoted in Richard Ellmann, *James Joyce* (New York, 1959) p. 169.

3. Sean O'Faolain, 'The Cruelty and Beauty of Words', *Virginia Quarterly Review*, vol. 4 (1928) p. 221.

4. Lionel Trilling, *Sincerity and Authenticity* (1972) p. 136.

5. Quoted in Richard Ellmann, *James Joyce*, p. 107.

6. *The Stories of Frank O'Connor* (New York, 1952) pp. 196–7. All subsequent quotations are from this edition.

7. Herbert Marcuse, *Eros and Civilisation: A Philosophical Enquiry into Freud* (Boston, Mass., 1966) p. 75.

8. O'Connor has described his Lawrentian attachment to his mother and dislike of his drunken father in the autobiography *An Only Child* (1961).
9. Sean O'Faolain, *Vive Moi!: An Autobiography* (1965) p. 242.
10. Sean O'Faolain, *The Heat of the Sun* (1966) pp. 7–8.
11. From the foreword to *The Finest Stories of Sean O'Faolain* (New York, 1965).
12. *The Collected Poems of W. B. Yeats* (1971) p. 288 ('Remorse for Intemperate Speech', ll. 11–13).
13. O'Faolain, *Vive Moi!*, p. 190.
14. Sean O'Faolain, *Midsummer Night Madness: Collected Short Stories*, vol. 1, Penguin edn (Harmondsworth, 1982) p. 43.
15. *Ibid.*, p. 22.
16. *Ibid.*, p. 17.
17. *Ibid.*, p. 11.
18. *Ibid.*, p. 13.
19. Sean O'Faolain, *I Remember! I Remember!* (1962) p. 169.
20. *Ibid.*, p. 177.
21. *Ibid.*, p. 182.
22. *The Collected Poems of W. B. Yeats* (1971) p. 217 ('Sailing to Byzantium', ll. 7–8).
23. *Midsummer Night Madness*, p. 367.
24. *Ibid.*, p. 358.
25. *Ibid.*, pp. 364–5.
26. *Ibid.*, p. 372.
27. *Ibid.*, p. 375.
28. O'Faolain, *I Remember! I Remember!*, p. 120.
29. *Ibid.*, p. 121.
30. T. F. Powys, *God's Eyes A-Twinkle* (an anthology of his stories) (1947) p. 175. All subsequent quotations are from this edition.
31. Walter Benjamin, *Illuminations*, Fontana edn (1977) pp. 86–7.

Notes to Chapter 5: The Free Story

1. *The Faber Book of Modern Stories*, ed. with an Introduction by Elizabeth Bowen (1937) p. 7.
2. V. S. Pritchett, *The Tale Bearers: Essays on English, American and Other Writers* (1980) p. 38.
3. *Why Do I Write?: An Exchange of Views between Elizabeth Bowen, Graham Greene and V. S. Pritchett* (1948).
4. Victoria Glendinning, *Elizabeth Bowen: Portrait of a Writer* (1977).
5. *Faber Book of Modern Stories*, Introduction, p. 15.
6. V. S. Pritchett, *The Myth Makers: Essays on European, Russian and South American Novelists* (1979) p. 48.
7. *The Collected Stories of Elizabeth Bowen* (1980) pp. 378–9 ('The Disinherited'). All subsequent quotations are from this edition.
8. *Faber Book of Modern Stories*, Introduction, p. 8.
9. *Ibid.*, p. 16.
10. V. S. Pritchett, *Collected Stories* (1982) Preface, p. x.

11. *Faber Book of Modern Stories*, Introduction, pp. 18–19.
12. *Why Do I Write?*, p. 25.
13. *The Collected Stories of Katherine Mansfield* (1945) p. 394.
14. Elizabeth Bowen, *A Day in the Dark and Other Stories* (1965) Preface, p. 7.
15. V. S. Pritchett, *On the Edge of the Cliff* (1980).
16. Pritchett, *Collected Stories*, Preface, p. xi.
17. *Why Do I write?*, p. 19.
18. Pritchett, *The Myth Makers*, p. 47.
19. Pritchett, *Collected Stories*, p. 276. All subsequent references are to this edition.
20. Adduced as a reason for the flourishing of the short story in this period by Robert Hewison in *Under Siege: Literary Life in London 1939–45* (1977) p. 80.
21. William Sansom, *Fireman Flower and Other Stories* (1944) p. 126. Subsequent references to this story are from this edition.
22. *Ibid.*, p. 111.
23. William Sansom, *The Passionate North* (1950) pp. 89–90.
24. James Boswell, *Journal of a Tour to the Hebrides* (1785).
25. Sansom, *The Passionate North*, pp. 198–9. Subsequent references to this story are from this edition.

Notes to Chapter 6: Postmodernist and Other Fictions

1. In an article published in *Atlantic*, vol. 220, no. 20 (Aug. 1967) p. 29.
2. Robert Coover, *Pricksongs and Descants*, Picador edn (1973) pp. 61–2.
3. *Ibid.*, p. 62.
4. Jorge Luis Borges, *Labyrinths*, Penguin edn (Harmondsworth, 1970) p. 51.
5. *Ibid.*, p. 34.
6. Samuel Beckett, *More Pricks than Kicks*, Picador edn (1974) p. 9.
7. *Ibid.*, p. 19.
8. Samuel Beckett, *The Expelled and Other Novellas*, Penguin edn (Harmondsworth, 1982) p. 9.
9. Samuel Beckett, *Six Residua* (1978) p. 11.
10. Beckett, *The Expelled and Other Novellas*, p. 54.
11. *Ibid.*, p. 61.
12. *Ibid.*, p. 91.
13. Samuel Beckett, *Stories and Texts for Nothing* (New York, 1967) p. 75. All subsequent references to the *Texts* are to this edition.
14. Just as Jacques Lacan suggests that the unconscious is structured like language (*Ecrits*, Paris, 1966).
15. In the double sense of to differ (or oppose) and to defer.
16. Beckett, *Six Residua*, p. 38.
17. *Ibid.*, p. 41.
18. *Ibid.*, p. 42.
19. 'Bing' in the French original.
20. Beckett, *Six Residua*, p. 44.

21. Both from *For to End Yet Again and Other Fizzles* (1976). All subsequent references are to this edition.
22. Borges, *Labyrinths*, p. 218.
23. Jorge Luis Borges, *The Book of Imaginary Beings*, Penguin edn (Harmondsworth, 1974) p. 67.
24. Borges, *Labyrinths*, p. 106.
25. *Ibid.*, p. 51.
26. *Ibid.*, p. 53.
27. This is true too in the original Spanish – see Jorge Luis Borges, 'El jardín de senderos que se bifurcan', *Ficciones* (Buenos Aires, 1967) p. 111.
28. Borges, *Labyrinths*, p. 49.
29. *Ibid.*, p. 42.
30. *Ibid.*, 269.
31. *Ibid.*, p. 258.
32. *Ibid.*, p. 91.
33. *Ibid.*, p. 258.
34. *Ibid.*, p. 93.
35. *Ibid.*, p. 51.
36. Jorge Luis Borges, *The Book of Sand*, Penguin edn (Harmondsworth, 1981) p. 89.
37. *Ibid.*, pp. 85–6.
38. For example by J. R. Banks in the article 'A Gondola Named Desire', *Critical Quarterly*, vol. 24 (Summer 1982) p. 28.
39. Ian McEwan, *The Imitation Game*, Picador edn (1982) p. 11.
40. Ian McEwan, *First Love, Last Rites*, Picador edn (1976) pp. 31–2.
41. McEwan, *The Imitation Game*, p. 12.
42. McEwan, *First Love, Last Rites*, p. 36.
43. *Ibid.*, p. 104.
44. *Ibid.*, p. 114.
45. *Ibid.*, p. 121.
46. *Ibid.*, p. 124.
47. Ian McEwan, *In Between the Sheets*, Picador edn (1979) p. 30.
48. *Ibid.*, p. 39.
49. *Ibid.*, p. 38.
50. Vladimir Nabokov, *Lolita*, Corgi edn (1974) p. 328.
51. McEwan, *In Between the Sheets*, p. 41.
52. McEwan, *The Imitation Game*, pp. 14–15.
53. John Barth, *Letters*, Granada edn (1981) pp. 32–3.
54. Clive Sinclair, *Hearts of Gold*, Penguin edn (Harmondsworth, 1982) p. 38.
55. *Ibid.*, p. 39.
56. Clive Sinclair, *Bedbugs* (1982) p. 15.
57. *Ibid.*, p. 14.
58. *Ibid.*, p. 15.
59. Adam Mars-Jones, *Lantern Lecture*, Picador edn (1982) p. 25. All subsequent references are to this edition.

Select Bibliography

(Place of publication is London, unless otherwise stated.)

ORIGINAL WORKS

Barth, John, *Chimera*, Quartet edn (1977).

Barth, John, *Lost in the Funhouse*, Bantam edn (New York, 1981).

Barth, John, *Letters*, Granada edn (1981).

Beckett, Samuel, *Stories and Texts for Nothing* (New York, 1967).

Beckett, Samuel, *More Pricks than Kicks*, Picador edn (1974).

Beckett, Samuel, *For to End Yet Again and Other Fizzles* (1976).

Beckett, Samuel, *Six Residua* (1978).

Beckett, Samuel, *The Expelled and Other Novellas*, Penguin edn (Harmondsworth, 1982).

Borges, Jorge Luis, *Ficciones* (Buenos Aires, 1967).

Borges, Jorge Luis, *Labyrinths*, Penguin edn (Harmondsworth, 1970).

Borges, Jorge Luis, *The Aleph and Other Stories 1933–1969* (1971).

Borges, Jorge Luis, *The Book of Imaginary Beings*, Penguin edn (Harmondsworth, 1974).

Borges, Jorge Luis, *The Book of Sand*, Penguin edn (Harmondsworth, 1981).

Bowen, Elizabeth, *A Day in the Dark and Other Stories* (1965).

Bowen, Elizabeth, *Collected Stories* (1980).

Coover, Robert, *Pricksongs and Descants*, Picador edn (1973).

D'Arcy, Ella, *Monochromes* (1895).

Egerton, George, *Keynotes* (1893).

Hardy, Thomas, *Selected Stories of Thomas Hardy*, chosen and introduced by John Wain (1966).

Hemingway, Ernest, *Green Hills of Africa* (1936).

Hemingway, Ernest, *Winner Take Nothing*, Triad/Panther edn (1977).

Joyce, James, *Stephen Hero* (1944).

Joyce, James, *Dubliners*, Penguin edn (Harmondsworth, 1963).

Joyce, James, *Ulysses*, Penguin edn (Harmondsworth, 1969).

Kipling, Rudyard, *Life's Handicap: Being Stories of Mine Own People* (1918).

Kipling, Rudyard, *Kim* (1927).

Kipling, Rudyard, *Short Stories*: vols 1 and 2, Penguin edn (Harmondsworth, 1971).

Le Gallienne, Richard, *Prose Fancies*, second series (1896).

Mansfield, Katherine, *Collected Stories* (1945).

Mars-Jones, Adam, *Lantern Lecture*, Picador edn (1982).

Maugham, W. Somerset, *Collected Short Stories*, 4 vols, Penguin edn (Harmondsworth, 1963).

McEwan, Ian, *First Love, Last Rites*, Picador edn (1976).

McEwan, Ian, *In Between the Sheets*, Picador edn (1979).

McEwan, Ian, *The Imitation Game*, Picador edn (1982).

Morrison, Arthur, *Short Stories*, in the Harrap series 'Short Stories of To-day and Yesterday' (1929).

Munro, H. H. ('Saki'), *The Short Stories of Saki (H. H. Munro)*, complete with an Introduction by Christopher Morley (1930).

Nabokov, Vladimir, *Lolita*, Corgi edn (1974).

O'Connor, Frank, *The Stories of Frank O'Connor* (New York, 1952).

O'Faolain, Sean, *I Remember! I Remember!* (1962).

O'Faolain, Sean, *The Heat of the Sun* (1966).

O'Faolain, Sean, *Midsummer Night Madness: Collected Short Stories*, vol. 1, Penguin edn (Harmondsworth, 1982).

Poe, Edgar Allan, *Selected Writings*, Penguin edn (Harmondsworth, 1967).

Powys, T. F., *God's Eyes A-Twinkle* (1947).

Pritchett, V. S., *Collected Stories* (1982).

Richardson, Dorothy, *Pilgrimage*, 4 vols (1938).

Sansom, William, *Fireman Flower and Other Stories* (1944).

Sansom, William, *The Passionate North* (1950).

Sinclair, Clive, *Hearts of Gold*, Penguin edn (Harmondsworth, 1982).

Sinclair, Clive, *Bedbugs*, 1982.

Stanford, Derek (ed.), *Stories of the 90's* (1968).

Stein, Gertrude, *Gertrude Stein: Writings and Lectures 1911–1945*, ed. Patricia Meyerowitz (1967).

Stein, Gertrude, *Selected Writings of Gertrude Stein*, ed. Carl Van Vechten, with an essay by F. W. Dupee (New York, 1972).

Stein, Gertrude, *Reflection on the Atomic Bomb*, vol. 1 of the previously uncollected writings of Gertrude Stein, ed. Robert Bartlett Haas (Los Angeles, 1974).

Stein, Gertrude, *How Writing is Written*, vol. 2 of the previously uncollected writings of Gertrude Stein, ed. Robert Bartlett Haas (Los Angeles, 1974).

Stevenson, Robert Louis, *New Arabian Nights*, Tusitala Edition of the works of Robert Louis Stevenson (New York, 1882).

Stevenson, Robert Louis, *Dr Jekyll and Mr Hyde and Other Stories*, ed. with an Introduction by Jenni Calder, Penguin edn (Harmondsworth, 1979).

Woolf, Virginia, *A Mark on the Wall* (1917).

Woolf, Virginia, *Kew Gardens* (1919).

Woolf, Virginia, *Mrs Dalloway* (1925).

Woolf, Virginia, *Between the Acts* (1941).

Woolf, Virginia, *Mrs Dalloway's Party: A Short Story Sequence by Virginia Woolf*, ed. with an Introduction by Stella McNichol (1973).

Woolf, Virginia, *A Haunted House & Other Stories*, Penguin edn (Harmondsworth, 1973).

BIOGRAPHY AND AUTOBIOGRAPHY

Adam Smith, Janet (ed.), *Henry James and Robert Louis Stevenson: A Record of Friendship and Criticism* (1948).

Ellmann, Richard, *James Joyce* (New York, 1959).

Fenton, Charles A., *The Apprenticeship of Ernest Hemingway: The Early Years*, Mentor edn (New York, 1961).

Glendinning, Victoria, *Elizabeth Bowen: Portrait of a Writer* (1977).

Kipling, Rudyard, *Something of Myself* (1937).

Mansfield, Katherine, *The Letters of Katherine Mansfield*, 2 vols, ed. J. M. Murry (1928).

Mansfield, Katherine, *Katherine Mansfield's Letters to John Middleton Murry, 1913–22*, ed. J. M. Murry (1951).

Maugham, W. Somerset, *A Writer's Notebook*, Penguin edn (Harmondsworth, 1967).

O'Faolain, Sean, *Vive Moi! An Autobiography* (1965).

Woolf, Virginia, *A Change of Perspective: The Letters of Virginia Woolf*, vol. 3: *1923–28*, ed. Nigel Nicolson and Joanne Trautmann (1977).

Woolf, Virginia, *The Diary of Virginia Woolf*, vol. 2: *1920–24*, ed. Anne Olivier Bell (1978).

CRITICISM

Allen, Walter, *The Short Story in English* (Oxford, 1981).

Banks, J. R., 'A Gondola Named Desire', *Critical Quarterly*, vol. 24 (Summer 1982) pp. 27–31.

Barthes, Roland, *S/Z*, trans. Richard Miller (1975).

Barthes, Roland, 'Introduction to the Structural Analysis of Narratives', in *Image–Music–Text*, essays selected and translated by Stephen Heath (1977) pp. 79–124.

Bates, H. E., *The Modern Short Story* (1941).

Beachcroft, T. O., *The Modest Art: A Survey of the Short-Story in English* (1968).

Benjamin, Walter, *Illuminations*, Fontana edn (1977).

Bergonzi, Bernard, 'Appendix on the Short Story', in *The Situation of the Novel* (1970).

Bowen, Elizabeth (ed.), *The Faber Book of Modern Stories* (1937).

Bowen, Elizabeth, *Why Do I Write?: An Exchange of Views between Elizabeth Bowen, Graham Greene and V. S. Pritchett* (1948).

Bowen, Elizabeth, *Afterthought: Pieces about Writing* (1962).

Chatman, Seymour, *Story and Discourse: Narrative Structure in Fiction and Film* (New York, 1978).

Eliot, T. S., *After Strange Gods* (1934).

Elwin, Malcolm, *Victorian Wallflowers*, Academy Books edn (1937).

Fergusson, Suzanne C., 'Defining the Short Story: Impressionism and Form', *Modern Fiction Studies*, vol. 28 (Spring 1982) pp. 13–24.

Flam, Jack D., *Matisse on Art* (Oxford, 1973).

Frank, Joseph, 'Spatial Form in Modern Literature', *Sewanee Review*, vol. 53 (1945) pp. 221–40, pp. 433–56, pp. 643–53.

Freud, Sigmund, The Standard Edition of the *Complete Psychological Works of Sigmund Freud*, vol. 8: *Jokes and their Relation to the Unconscious* (1960).

Friedman, Norman, 'What Makes a Short Story Short?', *Modern Fiction Studies*, vol. 4 (1958) pp. 103–17.

Genette, Gérard, *Narrative Discourse*, trans. Jane E. Lewin (Oxford, 1980).

Good, Graham, 'Notes on the Novella', *Novel*, vol. 10 (1976–7) pp. 197–211.

Hanson, Clare, 'Katherine Mansfield and Symbolism: the "artist's method" in *Prelude*', *Journal of Commonwealth Literature*, vol. 16 (August 1981) pp. 25–39.

Hanson, Clare and Andrew Gurr, *Katherine Mansfield* (1981).

Hernadi, Paul, *Beyond Genre: New Directions in Literary Classification* (New York, 1972).

Hewison, Robert, *Under Siege: Literary Life in London 1939–1945* (1977).

Hough, Graham, *The Last Romantics* (1947).

Hough, Graham, *Image and Experience: Studies in a Literary Revolution* (1960).

Ingram, Forrest, L., *Representative Short-Story Cycles of the Twentieth Century* (The Hague, 1971).

Issacharoff, Michael, *L'Espace et la Nouvelle* (Paris, 1976).

Jakobson, Roman and Morris Halle, 'Two Aspects of Language and Two Types of Linguistic Disturbances', in *Fundamentals of Language*, ed. R. Jakobson and M. Halle (The Hague, 1956).

James, Henry, *Hawthorne*, with an Introduction and notes by Tony Tanner (1967).

Joyce, James, *The Critical Writings of James Joyce*, ed. Ellsworth Mason and Richard Ellmann (1959).

Kermode, Frank, *Romantic Image* (1957).

Lacan, Jacques, *Ecrits* (Paris, 1966).

Lacan, Jacques, 'Seminar on "The Purloined Letter" ', *Yale French Studies*, vol. 48 (1972) pp. 38–72.

Lawrence, D. H., *Studies in Classic American Literature*, Phoenix Edition of the works of D. H. Lawrence (1964).

Lodge, David, 'Hemingway's Clean, Well-Lighted, Puzzling Place', *Essays in Criticism*, vol. 21 (Jan. 1971) pp. 33–56.

Lodge, David, *The Modes of Modern Writing: Metaphor, Metonymy and the Typology of Modern Literature* (1977).

Lukács, Georg, *The Theory of the Novel*, trans. Anna Bostock (1971).

Mansfield, Katherine, *Novels and Novelists*, ed. J. M. Murry (New York, 1930).

Marcuse, Herbert, *Eros and Civilisation: A Philosophical Enquiry into Freud* (Boston, Mass., 1966).

Maugham, W. Somerset, *Points of View* (1958).

Nabokov, Vladimir, 'Frank Kafka (1883–1924)', essay excerpted from *Lectures in Literature*, ed. Fredson Bowers; published in *Partisan Review*, vol. 47 (1980) pp. 341–71.

O'Connor, Frank, *The Mirror in the Roadway* (New York, 1956).

O'Connor, Frank, *The Lonely Voice: A Study of the Short Story* (1963).

O'Faolain, Sean, *The Short Story* (Cork, 1972).

Pater, Walter, *The Renaissance: Studies in Art and Poetry* (1900).

Peterson, Richard F., 'Frank O'Connor and the Modern Irish Short Story', *Modern Fiction Studies*, vol. 28 (Spring 1982) pp. 53–67.

Pound, Ezra, *Literary Essays*, ed. with an Introduction by T. S. Eliot (1960).

Pratt, Mary Louise, 'The Short Story: the Long and the Short of it', *Poetics: International Review for the Theory of Literature*, vol. 10 (1981) pp. 175–94.

Prince, Gerald, *A Grammar of Stories* (The Hague, 1973).

Pritchett, V. S., *The Myth Makers: Essays on European, Russian and South American Novelists* (1979).

Pritchett, V. S., *The Tale Bearers: Essays on English, American and Other Writers* (1980).

Propp, Vladimir, *Morphology of the Folk Tale*, trans. Laurence Scott (Austin, Texas, 1968).

Reid, Ian, *The Short Story* (1977).

Robey, David (ed.), *Structuralism: An Introduction* (Oxford, 1973).

Rohrberger, Mary and Dan E. Burns, 'Short Fiction and the Numinous Realm: Another Attempt at Definition', *Modern Fiction Studies*, vol. 28 (Spring 1982) pp. 5–12.

Roskies, D. M. E., 'Telling the Turth in Kipling and Freud', *English*, vol. 31 (Spring 1982) pp. 1–17.

Saussure, Ferdinand de, *Course in General Linguistics*, trans. Wade Buskin (1964).

Springer, Mary Doyle, *Forms of the Modern Novella* (Chicago, 1975).

Stark, John O., *The Literature of Exhaustion: Borges, Nabokov and Barth* (Durham, N.C., 1974).

Symons, Arthur, *The Symbolist Movement in Literature* (1899).

Symons, Arthur, *Studies in Prose and Verse* (1904).

Todorov, Tzvetan, *Poétique de la Prose* (Paris, 1971).

Todorov, Tzvetan, 'The Structuralist Analysis of Literature: the Tales of Henry James', in David Robey (ed.), *Structuralism: An Introduction* (Oxford, 1973) pp. 73–103.

Trilling, Lionel, *Sincerity and Authenticity* (1972).

Waldrop, Keith, 'Gertrude Stein's Tears', *Novel*, vol. 12 (Spring 1979) pp. 236–43.

White, Cynthia L., *Women's Magazines 1693–1968* (1970).

Woolf, Virginia, *A Room of One's Own* (1929).

Woolf, Virginia, *The Moment and Other Essays* (1947).

Woolf, Virginia, *Collected Essays* (1966).

Index

187